Moving from Training
to Performance

AMERICAN SOCIETY FOR TRAINING & DEVELOPMENT

Moving from Training to Performance

A Practical Guidebook

Dana Gaines Robinson and
James C. Robinson, Editors

Berrett-Koehler Publishers, Inc.
San Francisco

Moving from Training to Performance: A Practical Guidebook. Copublished in 1998 by the American Society for Training & Development (ASTD) and Berrett-Koehler Publishers, Inc.

Additional copies may be obtained by contacting either of the following copublishers. Quantity discounts are available.

American Society for Training & Development
1640 King Street, Box 1443
Alexandria, VA 22313-2043
800.628.2783 phone
703.683.1523 fax
www.astd.org

Berrett-Koehler Publishers, Inc.
450 Sansome Street, Suite 1200
San Francisco, CA 94111-3320
415.288.0260 phone
415.362.2512 fax
www.bkpub.com

Printed in the United States of America.

 Printed on acid-free and recycled paper that is composed of 50% recovered fiber, including 10% postconsumer waste.

Library of Congress Cataloging-in-Publication Data
Moving from training to performance: a practical guidebook/Dana Gaines
    Robinson and James C. Robinson, editors.
        p. cm.
Includes bibliographical references and index.
ISBN 1-57675-039-6 (alk. paper)
1. Employees—Training of. 2. Performance. I. Robinson, Dana
Gaines, 1944– . II. Robinson, James C., 1930– .
HF5549.5.T7T69   1998
658.3'124—dc21

                                                            98-21647
                                                                CIP

05 04 03 02 01 00 99 98   10 9 8 7 6 5 4 3 2 1

Table of Contents

Section Three: The Organization Level of Alignment

Section Four: The Performer Level of Alignment

Section Five: Putting It All Together

Preface

To cite a phrase made famous in one of Bob Dylan's songs . . ."The times—they are a changin'. "

There could not be a more poignant statement to acknowledge the transformations occurring within the profession of human resource development (HRD). This profession is generally acknowledged to be more than 50 years old. For most of those 50 years, people in the profession have focused on enhancing the skills and knowledge of employees, managers, and others with whom they work. The primary vehicle for achieving this output was the design and delivery of training curricula—mostly in a leader-led modality.

We do not need to look very far into the future to know that this will no longer be the focus of the work done within the HRD profession. Just consider the results from a recent survey of more than 300 senior and executive-level professionals, conducted by the American Society for Training & Development (ASTD). These industry leaders, all of whom work within organizations, identified the 10 most probable trends in the profession—both now and in three years' time. The trend labeled "shift from providing training to improving performance" was ranked as the third most probable trend to occur today, and the most probable trend of all within the next three years ("Trends in HRD," *National HRD Executive Survey*, ASTD, 1998). We are literally changing the mission of our profession—away from providing skills or knowledge and toward a focus on human performance improvement. This change has major implications for both individuals (the people who do this work and are referred to as performance consultants in this book) and for the functions in which they work (referred to as performance departments throughout the book). But just what are those implications? And how does one make the transition from operating as a training department to working as a performance improvement function? What actions are needed? How long will it take? What are the land mines to be avoided?

These are the questions this book has been developed to answer. Within its covers you will find the contributions of more than 20 people. Approximately half of these contributing authors are consultants who specialize in the field of human performance improvement. These individuals offer their perspectives based upon their observations of the best-in-class. The other half of the contributing authors are people who work in an organization, either as the leader of, or a contributor to, the performance department. These individuals can tell the story as no other—from the perspective of someone who is making it happen today, in a real organization with all of the challenges therein.

The intent of this book is to provide you, the reader, with a multitude of practical, proven, real-world tactics and strategies for performing as a performance consultant and for transforming a training department into a performance improvement function.

For Whom Is This Book Written?

This book is targeted primarily for people who work within an organization in roles such as the following:

—instructional designer
—manager of training and HRD functions
—OD consultant
—performance consultant
—performance technologist
—relationship manager.

In addition, the book will be a valuable resource to external consultants who specialize in the area of performance improvement; there are several chapters and case studies that relate directly to the practitioner, whether internal or external.

Overview of the Book's Organization and Contents

This book is a rich blend of concepts, practices, job aids, examples, and case studies. It is organized into five sections. Section One lays the conceptual framework for what is meant by a shift from training to performance. In the chapter by Geary Rummler, you will be introduced to the three levels of alignment, which are required when making any substantive change—such as the one being discussed in this book. These three levels of alignment are

—Process Level
—Organization Level
—Job/Performer Level.

Each of these levels forms the basis for the three subsequent sections.

Section Two focuses on the process of human performance improvement (HPI). The chapters discuss the four major phases associated with the HPI process: partnering (chapter 3), assessing (chapter 4), implementing performance change (chapter 5), and measuring (chapter 6). Each chapter is authored by a consultant with substantive expertise in that process area; a case study, authored by an internal practitioner, follows each chapter. It is these cases that will describe how each specific phase of the process comes to life in the real world of today's organizations.

Section Three focuses on the organization level of alignment. The chapters discuss how to organize and structure a performance department whether you are a large function (chapter 7) or a small one (chapter 8). Again, these chapters are authored by individuals who have already made the transition to performance. The authors describe what has worked for them and what they would do differently.

In Section Four the focus shifts to the job/performer level. This section describes what it is people in the job of performance consultant actually do (chapter 9) and the skills required to be successful (chapter 10). In addition, there are two case studies authored by internal practitioners who are performance consultants. These cases will provide a firsthand view of the results that are produced by these individuals as they fulfill the responsibilities of their jobs.

Finally, in Section Five we move to a more global view. Chapter 11 describes some of the important to dos when transitioning an entire department to a focus on performance. In chapter 12 we look ahead to answer the question, "Where do we go from here as we continue the journey, as a profession, into human performance improvement?"

Another element of this book that will prove useful to the reader is the glossary. Unfortunately, our profession lacks a shared and common language to describe its many principles and techniques. A review of the glossary prior to reading the book will familiarize the reader with the terms as they are used here. A list of the most current books that are available on the subject of human performance improvement is included in this book as a list of resources. If you want to read even more about this subject, here is a great list from which to select.

Acknowledgments

As with any book, this one could not have been produced without the work of multiple people. First and foremost, as editors we want to thank all of those who have contributed to the book by authoring either a chapter or a case study. In the truest sense of the word, these people are the book. Then there are the behind-the-scenes people who have brought their talents and energy to this project. Specifically we want to acknowledge and thank Lori Calhoun of Partners in Change, Inc. (Partners). She worked as the project manager from Partners' side, keeping everything moving and the communications among authors, editors, and ASTD humming. In addition, the ASTD staff has earned one large thank you.

Finally, we want to acknowledge and thank all of the people in the HRD field who have made a professional commitment to human performance improvement and who are advancing this work daily. While this has been written for the practitioner, it is also from the practitioner that we have learned many of the techniques presented here. In this regard we have come full circle, with the processes of learning and teaching having become one.

Dana Gaines Robinson
James C. Robinson
Pittsburgh, Pennsylvania
May 1998

Conceptual Framework

This section provides both the rationale for, and the conceptual framework used in, making a transition from a focus on training to a focus on performance improvement. In essence, the chapters in this section provide the architecture for making the transition; the remaining chapters in the book describe the how-tos for bringing this architecture to life.

In chapter 1, the Robinsons describe the four types of needs that performance departments work to define and align with their clients. This chapter provides clarity on what is produced by performance departments.

In chapter 2, Geary Rummler outlines the three levels of alignment that must be engineered to support a focus on performance. These three levels are referred to as organization, process, and job/performer. Each of these three levels serves as the focus for one of the following sections in the book. In this manner, the book illustrates how these three levels, as presented by Rummler, are aligned by people working within the human resource development (HRD) profession today as they transition from a focus on training to a focus on performance.

1

A Focus on Performance: What Is It?

by Dana Gaines Robinson and James C. Robinson

QUICK READ

● The training profession is undergoing major structural change in several areas, one of which is to transition away from a focus on learning as the output and toward a focus on performance improvement.

● To successfully focus on performance, the department must be redesigned so that its goal is to enhance human performance in support of business goals. This requires that the department work with clients to define and align four types of needs:

—Business needs

—Performance needs

—Learning needs

—Work environment needs.

● There must be people in the performance department, frequently referred to as performance consultants, who are responsible for partnering with clients in order to achieve the goal of performance improvement.

There is no doubt that the human resource development (HRD) profession is structurally transforming itself. Consider these facts:

● In *Rethinking Human Resources: A Research Report,* published in 1995 by the Conference Board, 58 percent of large U.S. corporations reported they had downsized their HRD departments. In many instances, the staff had decreased by 50 percent.

● Outsourcing of jobs, traditionally associated with training and human resource functions, continues to increase. The American Society for Training & Development's (ASTD) Benchmarking Forum, a consortium of 50 organizations, reports that contract workers make up 23 percent of the training design and development staff and 30 percent of their instructors. Sixty-six percent of people who responded to a 1996 fax forum in *Training & Development* magazine expect to be external providers in 10 years' time. There are now entire training departments that are outsourced to a provider. For example, DuPont's training function is staffed by Forum Corporation employees.

● Alternative delivery to leader-led training is growing. Currently, almost 31 percent of structured learning is delivered by means other than leader-led; most of this is through multimedia.

● While many traditional jobs, such as trainer and instructional designer, are leaving organizations, other jobs are increasingly in demand. Organizations are hiring performance technologists, performance consultants, and interactive learning specialists, for example.

It is safe to say that the training profession is undergoing the most dramatic changes since training was formally acknowledged to be a profession in the 1940s. Prior to that time, training was done in an ad hoc manner; during World War II, it became clear that there are a set of principles and skills required to do training effectively. And now, as we move into the next century, this profession is being restructured.

What is behind all of this restructuring? A combination of forces are converging and creating a new environment in which the training profession must operate. Some of these forces relate to acknowledgment that the results achieved from training, in its traditional sense, are unsatisfactory. Other forces focus on the opportunities that today's economic and business environments provide. These forces are summarized in table 1.

T A B L E 1   Converging Forces for Transformation of Training Profession

Opportunities Presented by New Business Realities	Growing Dissatisfaction with Traditional Training Processes and Results
1. The globalization of business and the intense competitive pressures it produces are resulting in a focus on people as the greatest competitive edge of an organization. While products and services can be replicated, the collective intelligence of employees is unique to an organization. Unleashing the potential of people is vital to business success.	1. Almost $60 billion is spent each year on developing America's workers. These are direct costs only; if the cost of the employees' time off the job (in order to attend training) is added to this investment, the figure rises to between $200 and $300 billion.
2. Skill needs of employees continue to escalate and are in continuous change. Learning is now a life-long requirement with organizations needing to provide the infrastructure to support continuous learning.	2. Typically, less than 30 percent of what people learn is ever actually used on the job.
3. Technology yields many opportunities. First, employees need to know how to effectively utilize the technology—a performance improvement opportunity! But technology is also being used as a	3. Many training functions continue to report on their activity (for example, number of participant days; results of reaction evaluations collected in classes) and not on their results. This raises questions as to the value of training.
	4. While not quantifiable, there is strong evidence of an ambivalent relationship (at best) between many training functions and the management they are to support.
(cont'd. on page 6)	*(cont'd. on page 6)*

THE ROOTS OF A PERFORMANCE FOCUS

The structural change to the training profession that is of greatest interest to us in this book is the shift to a focus on performance improvement. Many wonder, is this just another fad? Is this an entirely new direction? The answer is a resounding "No" to both questions.

The focus on performance, as currently demonstrated, is based on the discipline of human performance technology (HPT) and dates back to the 1950s. *Human performance technology* is defined as "the science of improving human performance in the workplace through analysis and the design, selection, and

T A B L E 1 Converging Forces for Transformation of Training Profession *(continued)*

Opportunities Presented by New Business Realities	Growing Dissatisfaction with Traditional Training Processes and Results
method for learning, providing options for just-in-time, just-enough learning. Not only does this enable learning experiences to be more timely but it also frees up staff members to complete tasks other than those associated with training delivery.	In many surveys, trainers note that their number one concern is lack of management support. In some instances, training professionals view management as their adversary and not their partner. As James Pepitone indicated, in his book *Future Training*, "In effect, management and its practices became the problem that training was determined to fix with a continuous list of social and developmental training programs."* When management is asked for their opinion of the training function, they often note that the department and their work are not integrated into the business of the business; in essence, training is viewed as peripheral to the real business of the organization.

*James Pepitone. *Future Training*. Dallas: AddVantage Learning Press, 1995, p. 62.

implementation of appropriate interventions." Table 2 provides a list of just a few of the noted individuals who have contributed significantly to the formation and continuing development of this discipline. A major concept or principle, attributed to the work and research of the individual, also is listed. Anyone who is serious about a focus on performance needs to be familiar with the writing and teaching of each of these contributors; many of their published works are listed in the resources section of this book.

Clearly, the focus on performance is not new. What is new are two elements that are receiving enhanced emphasis due to contemporary business requirements.

1. **Need to partner with management.** As noted in table 1, training functions have traditionally operated more in parallel to management than in partnership with them. In today's business world this cannot continue; so a function

T A B L E 2 Major Contributors to the Discipline of Human Performance Technology	
Individual	**Major Principle or Concept Attributed to This Individual**
B.F. Skinner	Behavior can be influenced by the responses that are given to that behavior (for example, operant conditioning).
Tom Gilbert	The absence of performance support in the work environment, and not the absence of knowledge or skill, is the single greatest block to exemplary performance.
Bob Mager	Learning objectives must be defined in performance terms. Therefore, each objective needs to define the following: • what the learner is to do • the conditions under which performance is to occur • the quality or level of performance considered acceptable.
Joe Harless	Effective performance solutions require analysis of the system in which the performer is working before proceeding with the interventions. Joe Harless invented the term *front-end assessment*.
Geary Rummler	Three levels of performance must be aligned in order to sustain exemplary human performance; change in just one level will be insufficient. The three levels are as follows: • process • organization • job/performer.

that focuses on performance improvement allocates significant resources (for example, people and time) to the formation and sustenance of partnerships with management. Typically the individuals with whom these partnerships are formed are referred to as clients. Therefore, the term *performance consultant* was developed to distinguish the role of the individual from the performance function, which is the other half of this partnership. Research completed by Partners in Change, Inc., regarding the job of performance consultant, determined that people in this job spend an average of 25 percent of their time forging and growing relationships with their clients. Partnerships are becoming a significant output to be produced by some members of the performance team. (Note: A function that focuses on performance will be referred to as a performance department throughout this book.)

2. **Linkage to business needs.** In today's business world, the identification of human performance requirements begins with clarification of the current and future business goals of an organization. Once the business goal is defined, a performance department works with its clients to answer the question, "What must people do more, better, or differently if this business goal is to be achieved?" In this manner, the performance requirements that are defined and addressed are certain to be linked to business and operational goals. The second benefit is that by focusing on business needs, the performance department is more assured of working in a strategic and proactive manner, rather than in a tactical, reactive manner. This is because entering at the business-needs level reduces the probability that solutions regarding how to enhance performance and skill have already been decided. The situation is solution-free with all of those decisions still to come.

Perhaps an example would be helpful. A retail organization made a business decision to double its revenue and the number of store units in the next five years; profits also were to increase in a comparable manner. Some stores were targeted to obtain superstore status, meaning their volume was to increase significantly. It was clear that these business goals would have tremendous implications for the performance requirements of some store managers. But what must a store manager do more, better, or differently to manage a store with a 60 percent to 80 percent increase in volume? And what must all store managers do more, better, or differently if the organization's total revenue and profit goals were to be realized? The answers to these questions were obtained through the work of people in the performance department. Some members of the department, working in a performance role, partnered with management of the organization to obtain the information needed to answer the questions noted. Working as performance partners, they then identified learning and nonlearning actions required to shape the required performance. This is a performance focus approach in action and certainly illustrates the critical need for partnerships with management.

CHARACTERISTICS OF A PERFORMANCE FOCUS

Table 3 summarizes the key differences between a traditional focus and a performance focus. As illustrated, these two approaches are not either-or in nature but instead operate on a continuum. Most departments are somewhere between the two endpoints on this continuum.

As noted in the list of characteristics, front-end assessment is mandatory when focusing on performance. In essence, there are four needs that must be defined and aligned, prior to embarking on initiatives to change performance. Figure 1 illustrates the four types of needs.

Business needs are the goals for a unit, department, or organization. They are virtually always expressed in operational or numeric terms. Examples of

T A B L E 3 Characteristics of a Traditional and Performance Focus	
Traditional Focus	**Performance Focus**
←	→
Focuses on what people need to learn; acquisition of skill and knowledge is the end.	Focuses on what people need to do; acquisition of skill and knowledge is a means to an end.
Event oriented.	Process oriented.
Primarily enters the work process reactively (for example, someone calls).	Enters the work process both proactively (through own initiation) and reactively.
Biased in favor of a single solution; this is usually some type of structured learning experience.	Unbiased toward solutions; relies on multiple solutions of which training is only one.
Can, and does, work independently of client partnerships.	Must be partnered to a client with ownership for success jointly shared.
Front-end assessment is optional; work environment barriers to desired performance are rarely identified.	Front-end assessment is mandatory; work environment barriers to desired performance are identified.
Success is measured in terms of the quality of the solution or event (for example, quality of training program, selection system, appraisal system).	Success is measured in terms of contribution to performance change and operational impact.

business needs include a goal to grow market share (as measured in percentage of total market), increased customer satisfaction (as measured in percentage of customers who express satisfaction with service in a survey or the percent of business that occurs with repeat customers), and increased safety performance (as measured in a reduction of preventable accidents).

Performance needs are the on-the-job requirements describing what people must do if the business needs are to be achieved. These are expressed and measured in behavioral terms. Performance needs are typically identified for specific jobs and clarify what people in a job must actually do to achieve desired results.

Learning needs define the skill or knowledge that people must have in order to perform successfully. *Work environment needs* identify the systems and processes that surround performers in their job environment; it is vital that these systems and processes encourage, not discourage, desired performance. In essence, learning and work environment needs are enablers of performance; the actions required to improve performance are derived from these two sets of needs.

Figure 2 provides an example of four needs that are defined and aligned. In this example, the business need was to increase customer satisfaction. The organization was experiencing escalating customer complaints and a loss of customers. The primary causes for this situation were determined; they included the fact that customers were dissatisfied with how their problems were being addressed by the customer service representatives (CSRs).

F I G U R E 1   Hierarchy of Needs

When phoning the CSRs for assistance, customers felt they received the runaround, with no one willing to take accountability for ensuring that their problem was addressed. The responsibility was being placed on the customer to determine how the system worked and to take actions needed to get to the appropriate people. A decision was made to hold CSRs accountable for stewarding a customer's problem through to resolution. This would mean that the CSRs would take the initiative to locate the appropriate department and person with whom the customer should speak, for example. This was a new job performance requirement and answered the question, "What must CSRs do more, better, or differently if we are to improve the level of satisfaction our customers have with our service?"

In order to perform as needed, however, CSRs had both learning and work environment needs. They required knowledge of whom to call for any specific situation or problem. This did not require a training course; instead, a job aid was developed to assist CSRs in making that determination. Of greater concern was the CSRs' reward system. CSRs were measured on their call rate (for example, number of calls managed per day) and call span (average length of call). This reward system was nonsupportive of the new

---

F I G U R E   2   Example: Aligning and Defining Four Types of Needs

Business Needs
Increase customer satisfaction.

Performance Needs
Customer service representatives (CSRs) assume ownership for resolving problems brought to their attention by customers.

**Learning and
Work Environment
Needs**
*CSRs know who in the organization
can resolve various problems.
CSRs are rewarded for taking time
to resolve customer problems.*

---

performance requirement. If CSRs were to assume responsibility for resolving customer problems brought to their attention, they needed to remove themselves from the phone to investigate the situation and locate the best option. This would reduce their call rate and increase their call span— CSRs would be performing in opposition to their own reward system. So this system needed to be adjusted to reflect the new performance requirement. By defining and aligning all four needs before taking action, the probability increased that the outcome would be successful. In fact the CSRs did perform as required, and the customer satisfaction ratings did improve.

Of course, no individual working from a training or performance department could accomplish these results alone. In this instance, the person in the role of performance consultant was partnered with the owner of the business need, who was the director of the Customer Service Department. It was through the partnership of internal consultant and client that these results were obtained. This is the work of a performance department: to partner with clients for purposes of defining and aligning business, performance, learning, and work environment needs.

TRANSITIONING TO A FOCUS ON PERFORMANCE

Clearly there has never been a greater opportunity or need for training departments to transform into departments that partner with clients for purposes of achieving exceptional performance and business results. There is, however, a great deal of work associated with successfully transforming into performance departments; it will not occur just because the departments rename themselves. Research at Partners in Change, Inc., has indicated that the transition process requires between two and four years to successfully complete.

What is required? How do you successfully make this transition? And what are the land mines to anticipate and, if possible, to avoid? In the following chapters, you will read from those who either are in the process of making this transition or have successfully completed the transition. In essence, this is straight talk from practitioner to practitioner. The stories are organized around the three levels of alignment, which Geary Rummler and Alan Brache have clearly shown to be required for success when embarking upon a change such as the one described in this book. So we will begin with Geary himself describing what is meant by each level and how it supports an initiative such as the one required when transitioning from a training to a performance focus.

2

The Three Levels of Alignment

by Geary Rummler

QUICK READ

● Building a performance department is a complex and challenging task that will take three to five years to accomplish. In order to create such a department, three levels must be aligned. They are as follows:

—Organization level

—Process level

—Job/performer level.

● Each of these three levels requires that work be completed in support of goals, design, and measurement of that level.

● Actions will also need to be taken in each of the following areas:

—Leadership

—Performance infrastructure

—Credibility

—Formal charter.

The objective of this chapter is to provide a framework and road map for transforming a training department into a performance department, which partners with clients for purposes of achieving exceptional performance and business results. It is assumed that the reader of this chapter

- is an experienced trainer or training manager;

- has been frustrated over the years with managers who try to solve every manner of performance problem with training;

- recognizes that in order to influence the performance of individuals and organizations, other interventions than training need to be employed (sometimes in concert with training and sometimes instead of training);

- has embraced the notion of performance consultant as an extension of the traditional role of the professional trainer and feels that by playing this extended role he or she can bring more value to the organization;

- wishes to develop the capability to carry out performance consulting for the benefit of the host organization (the company or institution that employs the reader and his or her performance improvement colleagues), and that this capability will necessitate either (1) the **modification** of the current training department or function to become more performance oriented; or (2) the **formation** of a performance consulting department;

- is embarking on a journey to transform a traditional training department (providing only training products) into a more performance-oriented department that solves performance problems and employs solutions other than training.

In summary, the assumption is that the reader is ready to take this journey but would like some assistance. There are three sections to this chapter that should help with the journey. The first presents the alignment model to which the Robinsons refer in chapter 1. The second proposes a road map for using the alignment model to build a performance department and discusses its application. The third section presents some thoughts on planning the journey.

PART I. THREE LEVELS OF PERFORMANCE AND ALIGNMENT

The task of building or modifying a department is a formidable one. To assist with that challenge, this chapter will provide some insight into the components, or building blocks, which must be in place in order to modify or build a performance department. This insight comes in the form of a framework called a performance matrix (see figure 4 on page 21). There are two dimensions that make up this matrix: (1) the three levels of performance; and (2) the performance needs.

Three Levels of Performance

Research and experience have identified three levels of performance in a function or department that must be recognized, aligned, and managed in order for that department to perform effectively and efficiently. These three levels are the organization, process, and job/performer levels. Each level will be described in turn.

Level 1: Organization Level

Figure 1 depicts the organization level. Any organization, or department, is a system, taking in various inputs and producing valued products and services for its customers and, in the private sector, providing an economic return for its stockholders. This system exists in a larger system, a supersystem consisting of the following elements:

● its markets (the consumer market, to whom it delivers its products and services, and various stakeholder groups, which in the private sector are the stockholders or sources of capital)

● its competition

● the resources it needs to produce the necessary outputs (capital, technology, human resources, and material)

● its geopolitical environment, consisting of the general economy, legislation, and prevailing cultural mores.

An organization is an adaptive system, adapting to changes in its supersystem and internal workings. An organization must continuously and successfully adapt to feedback from the environment, most notably the market (sales, customer complaints, market trends) and changes in resource availability and public sentiment, or it will fail to exist. The fundamental truth is that this entity must adapt or die.

An organization can be any size; it can be the total corporation, a division of the corporation, or a department or function within a division. It is rela-

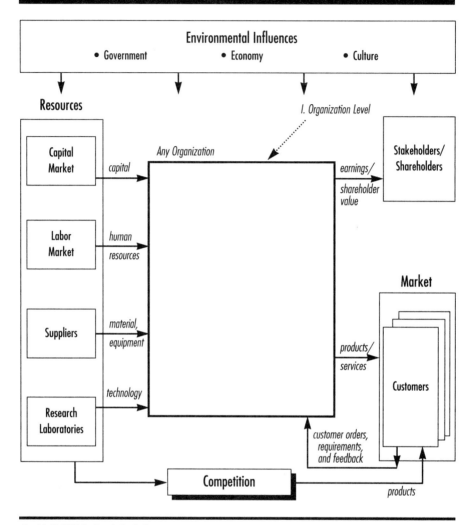

F I G U R E 1   Three Levels of Performance — I

Environmental Influences
• Government   • Economy   • Culture

Resources

I. Organization Level

Capital Market — *capital* → Any Organization → *earnings/ shareholder value* → Stakeholders/ Shareholders

Labor Market — *human resources*

Market

Suppliers — *material, equipment*

products/ services → Customers

Research Laboratories — *technology*

customer orders, requirements, and feedback

Competition — *products*

tive. Every level of an organization shares the same characteristics: It exists in a supersystem consisting of markets or customers, competition, critical resources, and general environmental factors; it converts inputs into outputs; it must adapt to change or fail to exist; and it consists of processes and jobs. At the organization level, the key performance variables are the following:

● Strategy and goals. (What markets does it intend to serve, with which products and services, at what levels of price and quality?)

● Structure. (Is the organization structured to effectively and efficiently provide and support those products and services for that market, at that price, with that quality? Are the processes in place to produce these products and services at the desired price and quality?)

● Measurement. (Is the organizational performance being measured in a way that supports the strategy?)

● Management. (How is performance being tracked and corrective action being taken?)

Level 2: Process Level

The diagram in figure 2 illustrates another level of performance—the process level. As we look inside an organization, we see myriad cross-functional processes by which work gets done and managed. Furthermore, organizations produce their outputs through these processes. (Examples of such cross-functional processes include the product development process, the merchandising process, the order fulfillment process, the production process, the sales process, the billing process, and the recruiting process.) Figure 2 shows both the structure on the organizational level and the cross-functional processes. It is important to understand what it is about processes that makes them an integral part of performance.

A *process* is defined as "a series of steps or activities that convert specified inputs into required outputs." For example, a customer order is converted into a shipped product; customer needs and organization needs are converted into a new product; or business environment data and corporate goals are converted into a corporate strategy. All work gets done through processes. All organization outputs are produced through processes. Everything that touches a customer is the result of a process.

Therefore, an organization is only as good as its internal processes, and these processes *must* support the organization's strategy. Processes are the link between individual performance and organizational performance. In those organizations that tend to "manage by function" (the engineering function, the production function, the sales function), effective cross-functional process flow (such as the process required to bring out new products) is seriously inhibited.

The performance variables that determine the effectiveness at the process level parallel those at the organizational level and include the following:

● Process existence. (Do the necessary processes exist to achieve the organization's strategy?)

● Process goals. (Are the process goals and requirements aligned with the organization goals?)

● Process design or structure. (Are the processes designed or structured to meet the process goals and requirements?)

FIGURE 2 Three Levels of Performance — II

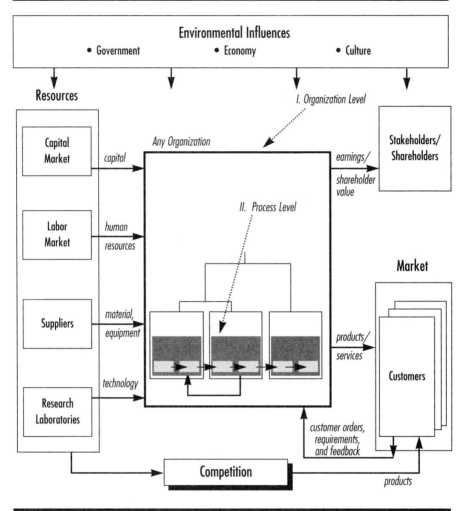

● Process measurement. (Are appropriate process performance measures in place?)

● Process management. (Is process performance being monitored, deviations analyzed, and corrective action taken?)

It is absolutely essential that the process level be aligned with the organization level.

Level 3: Job/Performer Level

As stated earlier, organizational outputs are produced through processes. Processes in turn are performed and managed by individuals and teams doing various jobs, from the customer service representative to the chief executive officer (CEO). Functions and jobs at all levels of the hierarchy exist to support processes. Figure 3 shows the job/performer level with respect to the organization and process levels.

The performance variables that determine effectiveness at the job/performer level are as follows:

● Job existence. (Do the necessary jobs exist to perform the processes?)

● Job/performer goals. (Are the job goals appropriate for meeting the process goals?)

F I G U R E   3   Three Levels of Performance — III

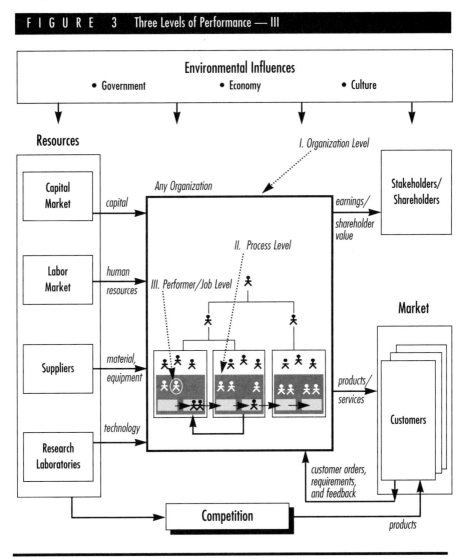

● Job design or structure. (Are the jobs designed to allow their effective and efficient performance?)

● Job measures. (Are appropriate job performance measures in place?)

● Job management. (Is job performance monitored, cause of deviation diagnosed, and corrective action taken?)

And once again, it is absolutely essential that the job/performer level be aligned with the process and organization levels.

Performance Needs

The three levels of performance constitute one dimension of the framework. The second dimension comprises three factors—performance needs—that determine effectiveness at each level (and the effectiveness of any system).

1. **Goals.** The organization, process, and job/performer levels each need specific standards that reflect customers' expectations for product and service quality, quantity, timeliness, and cost.

2. **Design.** The structure of the organization, process, and job/performer levels needs to include the necessary components, configured in a way that enables the goals to be efficiently met.

3. **Management** (and **measurement**). Each of the three levels requires a management system and practices that ensure that goals are current and are being achieved.

Combining the three levels with the performance needs results in the performance matrix, consisting of nine performance variables. The performance matrix, which appears in figure 4, represents a comprehensive set of performance variables that can be used by managers at any level (corporate, division, department) to both design and manage an organization. They also constitute the fundamental building blocks for any organization.

Alignment: the Key

Now we have a framework that depicts the three critical **interdependent** levels of performance. The overall performance of an organization or department (how well it meets the expectations of its customers) is the result of goals, structure, and management actions at all three levels.

The performance matrix clearly has implications for organization design. **Jobs** cannot be designed and goals established without an understanding of the processes to be performed by the people in the job and the requirements placed on these processes by customers and upper management. In turn,

FIGURE 4 The Performance Matrix

Performance Levels	Performance Needs: Goals	Performance Needs: Design	Performance Needs: Management
Organization	Have we developed and communicated a viable strategy and appropriate organization-wide goals?	Have we established an organization structure that enables the Organization and Process Goals to be met?	Are we planning, allocating resources, monitoring, and troubleshooting the organization as a system of integrated processes?
Process	Have we established a manageable number of end-of-process and upstream goals that link to the Organization Goals and reflect customer and financial needs?	Have we designed processes that enable the Process Goals to be met?	Have we installed an Infrastructure for continuously monitoring and improving our core processes?
Job/Performer	Have we established Individual/team goals that are linked to Process Goals?	Have we designed jobs that will enable the Job Goals to be met?	Have we selected the people, provided the training, and provided the resources, feedback, and rewards which will enable the Job Goals to be met?

processes cannot be specified and requirements set in a vacuum. They have to be tied to and driven by the organization's strategy and goals and customer expectations. The organization designer, like the architect and building contractor, must start with the foundation of the organization level (strategy, goals, structure, and measures), move to the building blocks of the process level (process goals, structure, and measures), and do the detailed finishing work with the job/performer level (job goals, structure, and measures). Since the primary focus of this chapter and book is the **design** of a performance department, let's look at how this can be done.

PART II. DESIGNING A PERFORMANCE DEPARTMENT

In Part I we presented a general framework (the performance matrix) for understanding the components or building blocks of performance and organization effectiveness. The fundamental message of Part I is the need for alignment of the three levels of performance. In Part II we will present a road map for application of these three levels to the design of a performance department.

Figure 5 shows a version of the performance matrix that contains a recommended sequence for building or modifying a department.

F I G U R E 5 Steps in Designing a Performance Department			
	Goals	Design	Management
Organization	1	2	3
Process	4	5	6
Job/Performer	7	8	9

Note that the recommended sequence starts in the organization-goals cell and snakes across and down the three levels. Also recognize that this is a high-level road map showing the general sequence, and that there will be considerable interaction and iteration between the cells and steps. (Like any map, this shows the ultimate destination but does not capture all the side trips and stops for gas that will actually be taken on a given journey.) This chapter will follow the road map to embark on an organization design trip—a high-level overview, highlighting the special issues for the performance consultant and the design of the performance department.

Organization Level

Although processes are the key to getting the work done, there are some fundamental decisions that must take place at the organization level before all else. (See figure 6.) These decisions can be revisited and refined, but they must be addressed before going beyond the organization level. These decisions form the foundation for the department being designed.

F I G U R E 6			
	Goals	Design	Management
Organization	1	2	3
Process	4	5	6
Job/Performer	7	8	9

Step One—Organization Goals
There are a number of decisions to make in this cell. They all have to do with the *direction* of the organization system. The starting point is to understand the supersystem. The supersystem is the context for everything that is

done in the performance department and must be taken into consideration in the design of the organization and in the day-to-day operation of the organization. There are in fact two levels of the supersystem—that of the host organization and that of the performance department.

Supersystem of the host organization. Anyone in the performance improvement business must have a thorough, and continual, understanding of the host organization's supersystem—both the current state and trends. This includes the marketplace and trends in customer expectations; the products and services (current and planned); the competition (now and emerging); the resource requirements and potential constraints on availability; and all the factors in the general business environment (pending legislation, economic conditions, public sentiment) that may influence the performance of the host organization and clients.

Supersystem of the performance department. The host organization makes up the major part of the performance department supersystem. Elements in the performance department supersystem include the following:

● Market—all the potential clients and individuals in the larger organization that the performance department will serve.

● Products and services—all the policies, interventions, and services the performance department will make available to its clients.

● Competition—plenty of competition, within and without the host organization. Within, there is competition from other functions and services such as industrial engineering, information systems, human resources, organization development, quality, reengineering, and any individual who professes expertise in some subject matter. Without, there are a large number of consultants whom the clients can call upon.

● Resources—funding, technology (performance, training, information), suppliers, and staff.

● General environment—the environment both inside the host organization and without. Without, there are all the factors in the business environment that the host organization must adapt to in order to survive and prosper—economic conditions, legislation, competitive initiatives, critical resources. Within, there are the organization's policies, culture, and budgets.

The fundamental truth is that the performance department must be knowledgeable about all these forces in the supersystem and adapt as necessary in order to achieve its strategic goals. Once the performance consultant has an understanding of the supersystem context for designing the performance department, then he or she has the following work to do in Step One:

1. **Determine vision and mission.** This should represent a clear departure from the past. A traditional training organization is usually committed to

providing training, or trained employees. The performance department should be committed to delivering improved employee and organization performance—a big and critical difference.

2. Define success for the department in terms of quantifiable goals. This is where meat is put on the mission bones. Does success mean an impact of a defined dollar amount on the host organization's bottom line? Does it mean "80 percent of our requests for assistance from line managers will be to 'improve performance' (in contrast to requests for training)"; or perhaps, "70 percent of the solutions delivered by the department will be 'nontraining' solutions"?

3. Determine the markets that will be served. Will the markets be business units (the first choice), functions (the second choice), or populations, such as first-line managers, second-line managers, and so forth (avoid at all costs)? Part of the criteria for market segmentation is to identify entities within the host organization that have measurable performance goals. Business units always do. Functions usually do. There is another decision regarding markets: Will the department serve every part of the host organization, or will it go only where there is an expressed need, and support, for its services?

4. Determine the products and services that will be delivered—and by whom. What interventions, other than training, will the department deliver directly? Think of the three levels of performance. Presumably, it will provide services to improve job performance. Will this include changes in job design, technology support, and compensation? Will the department provide process redesign services to improve process performance? Measurement systems? Organization restructuring and strategy clarification to improve organization-level performance? Perhaps the performance department strategy is to provide job/performer-level interventions immediately, process-level interventions in a year, and organization-level interventions in three years.

Once the services that the department will provide have been determined, consider those services that will be brokered (1) to other departments in the organization and (2) to suppliers who are external to the organization. Each of these options requires that some people in the performance department remain conversant with these options and the quality with which they are performing. Finally, determine which services and interventions, if needed, will *not* be supported in any manner by the department. This is a difficult but necessary decision, as no department can be all things to all people.

5. Determine the customer/market requirements. What do the clients expect from a performance department?

6. Determine the performance goals for all relevant dimensions of organization performance. "Relevant dimensions" will no doubt include quality of products and services offered, budget performance, innovation in product and service offerings, and staff development. These measures and goals will constitute the macro-level measures that will become the cornerstone for the total organization measurement system designed in Step Three.

The decisions made in this step set the direction for the performance department organization. Now build a foundation to support that direction.

Step Two—Organization Design

This step requires making decisions that have to do with establishing a structure to achieve the direction set forth in Step One. Components of this structure include processes, functions, information technology, and policy. To make the proper decisions, do the following:

1. Determine what processes are required to produce and deliver the products and services. Processes make up the infrastructure of an organization and need to be identified first. Identify the processes necessary to achieve the strategy (direction) of the performance department. If it has been operating as a traditional training department, it already has one set of processes (for example, "training needs analysis process," "training design/development process," or "trainee registration process"). Now the department is going to require additional or different processes (for example, "performance analysis process," "performance design process," or "client management process").

2. Design the system of processes required to produce and deliver the products and services. This work has to do with determining how the processes will fit together to provide an efficient system for delivering improved performance to clients. Will the processes be organized by client group, by product and service, or some combination?

3. Determine how information technology will support the system and processes. These may be preliminary decisions or assumptions, based on the vision established in Step One. Specifically, make assumptions about how technology will be used in the following areas:

● The solution delivery process? (Is "Web training" a possibility? Electronic Performance Support Systems?)

● Performance analysis? (Is the department building economic models?)

● Design and production? (Will it automate measurement systems using an intranet and Web sites?)

● Trainee registration process? (Will it establish registration over the intranet? Automated trainee recordkeeping?)

These decisions or assumptions will need to be revisited continually, as the organization design evolves and the department confronts the reality of budgets.

4. **Determine the functions and departments required to support the processes and organization of the performance department.** Now that the processes and their relationship have been determined, it is possible to see what functions (for example, instructional design) need to be established in order to develop and manage the various areas of expertise.

5. **Develop any required policies to support the system.** For example, what will be the funding policy for the performance department? Will the performance department function on a "charge back" basis or have an annual expense budget? Or some combination?

6. **Determine the resources necessary to support the system.** Establish the budget necessary to achieve the performance goals and identify the human resources that will be required.

Once these design decisions are made, the organization is beginning to take shape.

Step Three—Organization Management
With the direction established and the structure determined, it is now time to put the first pieces of the critical management system in place by accomplishing the following tasks:

1. **Design a system for gathering and analyzing supersystem data to be used for strategic planning and corrective action planning.** Examples of the data from the supersystem that might be gathered are the annual performance goals, operational plan and budget, and actual performance of the total host organization and all major customers.

2. **Design a measurement system that links macro-level measures, end-of-process measures, and department measures** and includes key leading indicators of performance and milestones for strategic initiatives. The goal is a measurement system that makes it possible, for example, to evaluate the quality of a particular product or service and to subsequently evaluate the performance of the processes and individuals who produced that product or service.

3. **Assign review, analysis, and corrective action roles and responsibilities for all organization-level measures.** This is the specification of exactly who is responsible (and accountable) for reviewing/monitoring the quality data

mentioned above, analyzing any deviations from the desired performance, and initiating the necessary corrective action.

This completes the design decisions and work at the organization level.

Process Level

The work at this level is particularly important to the design of a performance department. It is the basic plumbing of the department. Failure to identify the necessary processes, set the requirements properly, design effective and efficient processes, or manage them effectively, will doom the transition effort. (See figure 7.)

FIGURE 7

	Goals	Design	Management
Organization	1	2	3
Process	4	5	6
Job/Performer	7	8	9

Step Four—Process Goals

This is the foundation piece for effective and efficient processes. Here is what is needed:

1. Determine process performance goals that support the organization goals and meet customer requirements. For example, the performance-focused department in a telecommunications company was committed to supporting the performance goals of a major client, the customer service function. One of the operating realities of customer service was the frequent and rapid introduction of new products about which customer service employees had to be experts. The customer service requirement was that all service representatives had to be knowledgeable about new products in advance of the product introduction. As a result, the performance department set a requirement on its training and performance development process that new product training would be delivered a minimum of 20 days prior to product introduction and would take a maximum of 60 days to design.

2. Determine the department goals that support the process and organization goals. Staying with the above example, if the training and performance development process was to produce new product training and support within 60 days, then the instructional design function now has a requirement of completing their work in 30 days.

Step Five—Process Design

Now build those processes identified in Step Two, for which requirements were set in Step Four, by carrying out the following actions:

1. Design the most efficient and effective process to meet the process goals. The most critical process to be created as part of the design of the performance department is the performance improvement process. This is the core process that begins with a general request for help, or possibly a request for a specific solution such as training, and ends with the successful implementation of a solution to the performance problem. The solution most likely will include a number of interventions including process redesign, job redesign, training, electronic performance support, and a change in the performance measurement and feedback system. This process is fundamental to the performance department. Figure 8 contains a macro diagram of such a process (an example, not necessarily a recommendation), showing possible activities in a performance improvement process.

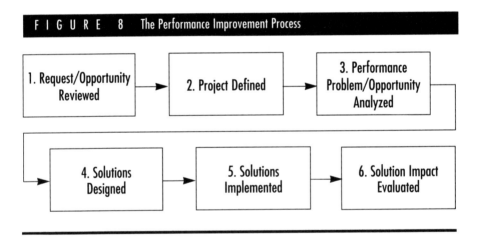

F I G U R E   8   The Performance Improvement Process

1. Request/Opportunity Reviewed → 2. Project Defined → 3. Performance Problem/Opportunity Analyzed → 4. Solutions Designed → 5. Solutions Implemented → 6. Solution Impact Evaluated

The effectiveness of all processes is a function of the design of the process flow, the underlying business or conceptual model(s), and key operating assumptions. Following is an illustration of the latter two variables for the performance improvement process.

Underlying conceptual model, or mental model. If the performance department was being staffed and managed by individuals transferred from the information systems (IS) function, it is safe to assume that IS solutions would be viewed as able to fix almost every performance problem. This IS mental model would influence what was examined and how it was analyzed in the "performance problem/opportunity analyzed" activity (see figure 8, step 3) of the performance improvement process, and subsequently

28

what was proposed and designed as a solution in the "solutions designed" activity (see figure 8, step 4). This brings to mind the old saw: "If the only tool you have is a hammer, everything looks like a nail." There would be comparable limitations on the performance improvement process if the mental model embraced is "culture" or "organization development." For a performance department to be effective in improving the performance of its clients, it is imperative that it operate with a comprehensive mental model or conceptual framework. Experience indicates that the human performance technology discipline forms a solid foundation for a human performance improvement process. It needs to be supplemented with models that deal with economics, organization systems (that is, the three levels of performance), leadership, and culture. The combination of these mental models is a powerful framework that will drive an effective performance improvement process.

Key operating assumptions. A key operating assumption for the performance improvement process has to do with the scope of the performance analysis and design activities that are used. Again, referring to the three levels of the performance model, will the performance department be attempting to improve performance at all three levels (organization, process, and job/performer)? If so, the procedures and skills to be deployed in the "performance problem/opportunity analyzed" activity are going to be quite different than they would be if confined to working at the job/performer level. Similarly, there will be very different procedures and skills involved in the "solutions designed" activity (for example, job redesign versus organization design). So the decision or assumption as to the scope of work will be critical and will drive the specific procedures that need to be developed in each detailed step of the process. And ultimately, this will affect the skills that must be resident in the performance department.

This assumption about scope should change over time, as the performance department develops expertise and credibility. The department should always be trying to increase its scope (that is, at all three levels) in order to have control over more variables that affect performer and organization performance.

In summary, the effectiveness of the performance improvement process will be a function of the following:

● The articulation of a sound process for converting requests for help into effective solution sets.

● The mental model employed regarding what factors have an impact on human and organization performance.

● The levels of performance (as in the three levels) that the performance department will be able to participate in when analyzing and designing.

This will no doubt be the result of a combination of the internal capability of the performance department and external credibility. Both of these factors can be improved over time.

After addressing the question of designing the process to attain stated goals, continue with two more tasks to be performed as a part of Step Five.

2. **Obtain the information technology support for the system and processes.** Do it.

3. **Determine the roles or jobs required to perform the processes.** A critical aspect of process design is determining what roles or jobs are required to effectively perform the process and the activities in it. (Remember, a basic premise of the three levels model is that processes drive jobs and that jobs exist to perform processes.) There are several roles required by the performance improvement process, including the following: account manager, performance analyst, solution designer, solution developer, solution deliverer, and evaluator. Of course, there is also the role of client, which is critical to this process! Make decisions as to how many of these roles are to be performed by each position or job in the performance department. If this is a fledgling performance department organization with a staff of three, then everyone might independently perform all roles for a given request for help. Or there might be specialization, with one person performing the account manager role, another performing the performance analyst and evaluator roles, and the third performing the solution designer, developer, and deliverer roles. If the staff consists of 15 to 20 people, however, each role might be performed by a separate individual. Or most of the roles might be performed by a team of cross-trained individuals, with each team dedicated to a particular client group. There are many options.

Step Six—Process Management

As was done at the organization level, there is now a need to address the management of the processes by accomplishing the following tasks:

1. **Design a process measurement system that allows for tracking the performance of activities within the process.** End-of-process measures were established in Step Three and linked to the macro-level measures. Now those end-of-process measures need to be linked to respective activities and key process steps.

2. **Assign review/monitoring, analysis, and corrective action roles and responsibilities for all process level measures.** Again, this is the action component that goes with the measurement component described above. This is the specification of exactly who is accountable for reviewing/moni-

toring the process and activity performance data, analyzing any deviations from the desired performance, and initiating the necessary corrective action.

This completes the design decisions and actions at the process level.

Job/Performer Level

Establishing the jobs necessary to perform the key processes is applying the glue to hold the department design together. Departments deliver performance through their processes, but in the final analysis, these processes are performed and managed by **individuals performing specific jobs**. (See figure 9.)

FIGURE 9			
	Goals	Design	Management
Organization	1	2	3
Process	4	5	6
Job/Performer	7	8	9

Step Seven—Job Goals

In accordance with the checklist, now it is necessary to **determine job performance goals to support process step, activity, function, and department goals.** For each job, it is important to identify the expected job accomplishments that relate to the processes the job supports. (For example, for the account management, likely accomplishments could be to identify performance opportunities, to define performance improvement projects, or to manage performance improvement engagements). Measures then need to be established for each of these accomplishments.

Step Eight—Job Design

Now, design the jobs so they can achieve the goals established in Step Four. This work is relatively straightforward; just do the following:

1. Based on the roles defined by the process designs (Step Five), **determine the optimal combinations of roles that can be combined into a job.** This must take into consideration required skills or expertise, physical and emotional capability or capacity, and common themes in tooling and the ergonomics environment.

2. **Design the system of consequences (rewards or punishment) that will support achieving the job performance goals.**

3. **Determine the knowledge or skills, tools, and ergonomic environment required for the job performers.**

4. **Design the resource development system that will ensure the necessary expertise for the performers.**

Step Nine—Job Management

Finally, tie the job level together by establishing the measurement and feedback system in the following manner:

1. **Design a job measurement system that links job performance to process activities and process performance.**

2. **Design the performance feedback system by which the performers will receive data on their performance.**

3. **Assign review/monitoring, analysis, and corrective action roles and responsibilities for all job level measures.** This should include performer self-monitoring and correction as well as supervisor roles.

One final action in this whole design process is to step back and make sure that the management system (planning, measures, and management action) of the performance department links all three levels. Ensure that individuals performing jobs can see how they affect the macro-level measures and how the management team of the performance department can troubleshoot poor performance of an organization or group to determine the root cause at any of the three levels.

PART III. PLANNING FOR THE TRANSITION

Fundamentally, the task in transitioning from a training department to a performance department is to move from an "is" performance infrastructure (that is, performance matrix) that supports a *training* organization to a "should" performance infrastructure that supports a *performance* organization. Rebuild each of the cells in the performance matrix to support the new organization. This transition is going to be a complex and difficult task and will take at least three to five years to accomplish. It requires persistence, patience, and a plan. There are four major requirements for successfully deploying a performance department: leadership, performance infrastructure, credibility, and formal charter.

Leadership

Leadership is critical to the journey from training to performance. Two sources of leadership are required for the successful implementation of a performance department.

1. **Leadership within the performance department.** There has to be a leader within the department to get this effort off the ground and keep it moving. This leader needs the following:

- a vision of what needs to be accomplished and why

- the ability to get others (within and outside of the performance department) to believe in this vision and to follow along in its implementation

- an understanding of a focus on performance—what it requires, how to do it

- a lot of energy.

2. **Leadership within the host organization.** There are several possible levels:

- Ideally, the CEO or chief operating officer (COO) of the host organization realizes the contribution a performance department can make and personally sponsors the implementation of such an institution. This happens, but not enough. Still, the goal should be to try to get such sponsorship.

- The next level of leadership/sponsorship is at the business unit or function level. Shoot for general managers, vice presidents, and department heads.

It is assumed that the reader of this book will perform the leadership role for the performance department. For external leadership, identify who are the current leaders and sponsors and determine what is needed to enhance or maintain their support; and identify the desired leaders and sponsors and determine what needs to be done to gain their support (see discussion of credibility).

Performance Infrastructure

It is necessary to make these decisions and build this capability before results can be delivered. Many of the required steps for doing this are provided in this chapter. The components that make up the performance matrix (figure 4 on page 21) can be summarized for purposes of a plan as follows:

- Goals and strategy. Identify the "should" infrastructure goals and then establish appropriate intermediate goals for each time period and related strategic initiatives for achieving them.

- Processes. What processes (primary and support) need to be in place? When?

- Structure. What roles and functions are required in the "should" infrastructure, and when over time are they going to be implemented? What reporting relationships are appropriate as the organization moves from the "is" phase to the "should" phase? (They will need to change as the organization evolves and takes shape.)

- Policies. What policies are required in the "should" phase, and when is each going to be implemented?

- Capability and capacity. How many people, with what skills, will be required at each phase in the transition from training to performance? One challenge may be redistributing existing head count, affecting employee numbers in all levels of the organization—from delivery jobs to analyst and designer jobs.

- Funding. What is the "should" phase source of funding for the performance department? What are the desired approximations to that phase, over the three-year period?

- Management system. Build one early and use it well, or the "should" phase may never be achieved. Historically, management has not been a strength of trainers. A performance department will need strong management to successfully navigate the transition, deliver results, and serve as a model for clients.

Credibility

This work begins as soon as there is capability. Show results and build support ASAP. There are two goals here: to gain acceptance for what the performance department is trying to do, and to create demand for its services. This needs to be planned for and managed; it won't just happen. Identify individuals or organizations that have influence in the host organization and target them for certain projects and results in various blocks of time in the plan. Think of initiating a demonstration project in some influential part of the host organization each quarter.

Formal Charter

This comes last. Such a thing might not even be necessary. The primary reason to put it on the plan is to stress the point that, except in extraordinary circumstances, obtaining a formal charter should not be attempted at the outset of the journey to a performance department. This is something that is earned, that will be bestowed on the department through the results it delivers. This is not to say that the department doesn't want to garner sponsorship and informal support from the outset. It needs that. But do not make a formal announcement that the department is now the grand pooh-bah of the newly formed performance fiefdom. If that happens, more time will be spent fighting turf wars than implementing performance consulting.

Conclusion

Transforming a training department into a performance department is an exciting and crucial journey. If successful, this transition will make major contributions to the improved performance of the host organization. The author hopes that this chapter will improve the probability of a successful transition by providing a framework for aligning the critical three levels of organization, process, and job/performer; and a conceptual, yet practical, road map for the transition. The following chapters offer excellent input on how to execute the steps outlined in this chapter. Good luck!

The Author

Geary Rummler is vice chairman of The Rummler-Brache Group, a research and consulting group specializing in the design and development of organizational performance systems for business and government organizations both in the United States and internationally. Prior to founding The Rummler-Brache Group, he served as president of the Keper-Tregoe Strategy Group, specialists in strategic decision making. He also cofounded and was president of Praxis Corporation, an innovator in the analysis and improvement of human performance. He cofounded and was director of the University of Michigan's Center for Programmed Learning for Business.

Rummler received his M.B.A. and Ph.D. from the University of Michigan. He has served as national president of the International Society for Performance Improvement (ISPI) and as a member of the research and strategic planning committees of the American Society for Training & Development (ASTD). He is currently a member of the board of directors of ASTD. In 1986 he became the seventh inductee in the ASTD Human Resources Development Hall of Fame and was awarded the ISPI Distinguished Professional Achievement Award in 1992.

He has published a wide variety of books including *Improving Performance: How to Manage the White Space on the Organizational Chart* (1990), coauthored with Alan P. Brache, and *Training and Development: A Guide for Professionals* (1988), coauthored with George S. Odiorne.

The author wishes to thank Cherie Wilkins of the Rummler-Brache Group for her contributions to this chapter.

The Process Level
of Alignment

Thishis section of the book provides concepts and best practices for how the human performance improvement process is utilized. This process is organized into four phases of work. For each phase there is a chapter, written by an external consultant, who specializes in that work. In addition, there is at least one case study from a practitioner who provides best practices and lessons learned regarding the implementation of that phase of work.

The **partnership phase** encompasses work that performance consultants do to form and grow strong relationships with key clients in their organization. The chapter is written by Geoffrey Bellman, with a case from PNC Bank.

The **assessment phase** takes place when performance consultants and performance analysts develop performance models and conduct gap and cause analyses. This phase provides the business information required to make informed decisions regarding how to enhance or change on-the-job performance. The chapter is authored by Paul Elliott, while the case is from work completed at Steelcase.

The **implementation phase** occurs when learning and nonlearning interventions, required to ensure that performance is improved, are selected, designed, and rolled out. The chapter is authored by Harold Stolovitch and Erica Keeps; the cases come from Johnson & Johnson.

Finally, the **measurement phase** encompasses work done to determine the results that were obtained from the entire initiative. As noted by chapter author Robert Brinkerhoff, however, measurement is a process that must occur throughout the entire initiative. This is illustrated in the case provided by Arthur Andersen.

3

Partnership Phase: Forming Partnerships

by Geoffrey Bellman

QUICK READ

- There are three primary parts to partnerships: purpose, roles, and partnering.

- Partnerships are formed to create success. It is vital to define success for both the client and the consultant, identifying what each will give and receive from the relationship.

- Contracting is a key element to successful partnering. A contract is "the deal" within which people play out their relationship. It is the present mutual understanding of who will do what to achieve a purpose.

- It is also key to define who the client really is. Broadly speaking, clients are people who work together to reach the agreed-upon purpose. While the majority of time may be spent with management clients, there are also other clients such as the workforce, suppliers, and support staff—people who are invested in the work being done.

- Long-term partnerships are the most valued. They require a personal relationship in addition to the expertise that the consultant can bring. Long-term partnerships generally require that the consultant and client both respect and like each other.

- Knowledge of oneself is a primary source of consulting effectiveness. Knowledge of why one is successful—what one does well when working with clients—gives confidence to propose and confront issues.

Partnership is essential to the success of any enterprise in which people work together. The larger the organization, the more partnership is required. Picture partnership as people linked by clasped hands. Now picture a large and effective organization held together by hundreds of partnerships—hundreds, thousands of people clasping hands, connecting, depending on one another. That image is a better representation of what goes on in our organizations than the boxy charts we so often use to show how the place works. We will explore unique aspects of the client–consultant partnership in this chapter. Much of what we will discuss applies to other work and social partnerships, friendships, and even marriage. We can learn from all forms of partnership as we think about creating a working relationship between client and consultant.

This book's table of contents offers clues to what this chapter is about. The methods and techniques noted in this book are important for performance consultants to learn. Those tools will be used within a context, and that is the focus of this chapter. The context is the workplace partnership with our clients. This chapter emphasizes the essential "softer" side of the performance consultant's work with clients; it is like a recipe ingredient added early in the preparation, hopefully flavoring the whole dish. We will start with the parts of partnership.

THE PARTS OF PARTNERSHIP

A partner is a person who "takes part" with others. So partnership has to do with "parts," as in, "What parts do we play in this work we do together?" That question contains the three primary elements of partnership: purpose, roles, and partnering. Purpose and roles create, and are created by, partners as they interact with one another.

1. **Purpose.** This is what brings us together in the first place. Our continuing contact in a work setting is justified by service to a larger purpose. No purpose? No partnership. That purpose may be quite clear, imposed by a client on a willing consultant. Or it may be only implicit, a mutual exploration for a purpose that is about to be defined. Or it may be buried in a flurry of busyness that never asks the question, "Why?" But be confident: If a client and consultant are working together, there is a purpose behind it.

2. **Roles.** We are particularly interested in two roles: client and consultant. The client role includes all that hard stuff that organizations are so well

known for: products and outcomes; clarity of vision and values; account-ability for results; managing resources (time, energy, money, human talent, materials, equipment, environment); creating structure and systems; making decisions about all of this—and deciding whether they could use the assistance of a consultant. The consultant role has a high emphasis on competence combined with adaptability because it focuses on the needs of the client. This role includes many aspects: clarity about one's own competence and contribution; awareness of the needs of the organization; developing alternatives; bringing new perspective; modeling risk-taking; and knowledge of the consulting process—all while honoring one's personal purpose, vision, and values.

3. **Partnering.** This is what happens when client and consultant decide to pursue purpose together. Partnering is the visible and invisible dynamic between client and consultant and purpose; it is created by the working out of roles and purpose. Partnering is usually focused on the work at hand, but it is much larger than that. Partnering is also about underlying assumptions, trust and risk, shared values, and expectations. Much that is key to partnering often goes unexpressed; much is not rational; and all of this requires attention to succeed in the work at hand. Consultants and clients who attend to roles and purposes but neglect partnering often fail in their work together.

CREATING SUCCESS

Partnerships are formed to create success. We consultants and our clients define success in our own terms. One of our tasks as consultants is to help clients discover what success is for them. Questions like these can be useful:

● If we were successful doing this together, what would our results look like?

● What would have to happen for you to call this effort a success?

● How will you know if this work is succeeding?

● What do you think is working about what we are doing right now?

● How is this meeting giving you what you want?

Notice the pursuit of the positive in those questions. They do not focus on what we wish to avoid in the partnership, but on what we wish to achieve. This positive focus is useful; it establishes the right tone for the work we will do together.

The clients are not the sole determiners of success; we consultants decide as well. When we do not, when we leave successful outcomes determination entirely to the client, we are choosing to put ourselves in a more dependent role. We need to think about what we want from this partnership so that we do not end up saying: "They are the client; they make the rules. Who am I to say? I'm not the client; I just do what I'm told." If you find yourself routinely making such statements, watch out! This thinking is on the passive path to becoming a less powerful consultant—and a less happy person.

So what is the consultant responsibility in defining success? There are at least two perspectives we can take on this: a work perspective and a life perspective. The work perspective involves separately answering the same kinds of questions asked of clients:

- What would make this work successful for me?

- What would be happening that would please me?

- What would the organization have at the end of this work that it does not now have?

- What would I have that I do not have now?

- How will I know the work is succeeding along the way?

Answering these questions gives you a stronger starting point when engaging the client; you know what you are looking for. And having your own answers stimulates discussions as you put your answers beside the client's. Your thoughts will help clients clarify their own success aspirations. Having no answers puts you in a more passive and less powerful position. You have opinions; you have goals; you have expectations; you have purpose. And it is legitimate to share them. You are not there as a tool to be wielded by clients in whatever fashion they choose. Said differently, if you are there as a tool without your own purposes, do not be surprised or complain about how you are used!

All of this can be linked to questions based on taking a life perspective on your work:

- What personal satisfaction do I expect from succeeding in this work?

- When this work succeeds, how will it support what is important in my life?

- What indicators will I get along the way that this is the kind of work I want to do?

You can see how these life success questions fit with those you asked earlier about work success. These new questions enlarge your frame, moving you from work to life. These questions lead to life aspirations you carry from one work endeavor to the next. As you return to them through time, your standards for work that supports your life become clearer; you will do a better job of attracting the work you really want to do. When you don't know what is important to you, it is hard to attract it.

Contracts and Contracting

Everyone working with, playing with, and living with other people is behaving within an implicit contract. All of us are working on how we will relate to, perform with, and interact with the people around us. Even when we are standing silently on an elevator, a dynamic deal is in the making, a deal about how close we will stand to each other and whether we will talk. Here we will talk about contracts between clients and consultants, but as my example illustrates, contracting is going on everywhere. Where there are work partnerships, there are contracts.

A contract is "the deal" within which people play out their relationship. It is about what we each are willing to give and what we want in return. Some form of contract is always there, whether discussed or not, whether mutually understood or not—and that contract is essential to building solid partnerships. Successful and unsuccessful consulting experiences point to the pivotal nature of effective, continuous, visible contracting. We consultants need to understand the importance of contracting; we need to help our partners become more explicit about what they want and what they offer.

The last paragraph mentions both "the contract" and "contracting." The contract is the present mutual understanding of who will do what to achieve purpose. Notice the aliveness of that statement:

> "The present. . .understanding"—not yesterday's or tomorrow's, but today's
>
> "The. . .mutual understanding"—not what the client and consultant might understand separately
>
> ". . .who will do what. . ."—the part of a contract we are most familiar with
>
> ". . .to achieve purpose."—reminding us that client and consultant are together because something larger is being served.

Our understandings and purposes with clients are usually thought of in terms of the current projects and programs; hopefully our contracts and contracting are larger than that. As an internal consultant, you are invested in creating sustained, long-term relationships with your clients; that is what true partnership is all about. In fact, your continuing work and success is dependent on maintaining relationships with clients whether you are working with them right now or not.

This suggests two levels of contracting: an explicit level in which client and consultant are actively engaged in contracting to do current work this week or this month; and an implicit level in which client and consultant are engaged in building and maintaining a work relationship over years rather than months or days. The difference between these two levels is like the difference between a date and marriage! The explicit contract carries a sense of immediacy with it; there is no commitment beyond the task at hand. Of course, there is the possibility of something more beyond this "date," but that is not part of the deal. The implicit contract grows through time on the strength of the explicit work done and contracts completed. Eventually the two parties recognize the potential for a long-term partnership. And, if they talk with each other about this work relationship, they are likely discussing the opportunities inherent in committing more deeply to each other for the long term. This is quite a different discussion from signing up for just another consulting project.

Solid partnerships grow from clear contracting—with emphasis on the contracting. It is the dynamic of contracting on which partnerships thrive. Explicit agreements between partners to keep each other informed allow their living contracts to change. The shifting world requires that the partners adapt to a new reality—a reality that was not present or forecast when they began to work together. Their commitment to contracting anticipates unknown changes. To keep your partnerships alive through contracting, there are a number of actions you should consider:

1. Talk with the client early on about the working relationship between you. For example, talk about how well your initial meeting went and the roles that each of you are taking on. Notice the client's receptiveness to this and adjust accordingly. Do not be surprised if the client has not stepped back from the consulting process to notice how it works. Client focus on task and important work can divert them from thinking about effective ways of building the relationship with their consultants. You are there to help with that.

2. Ask clients what has made for successful partnerships with other consultants in the past. Note this. Then ask the client for their expectations of this partnership with you. Write this down too and return to it in the future.

3. Consciously develop effective ways of making contracting a natural part of the work you do with clients. Learn from client to client. And help them learn too. As consultants with many clients, we usually know more about contracting—or at least we should.

4. The first time you and the client reach and document your agreements about the nature of the work and your roles, write them down—not because this is a legal contract, but because you will forget.

5. Build in regular meetings with the client to talk about how the work is going and how your partnership contributes to or detracts from that.

6. Check regularly and informally with the client: "How is this working for you today?" Always be ready to tell your client how the work and the contract are working for you. Occasionally do this more formally; write it down; put it before them; and take time to talk about it.

7. Hook discussions of the partnership to "real work." Reinforce the client's understanding of the connection between the success you are having in this endeavor and the success you are having working together.

8. If the contract is being bent or violated—if something else needs to be included—if you have nagging doubts about what is happening—if anything is happening that relates to the contract between you and the client, bring it up. And use the contract as the way of bringing it up.

9. Your contracts should show that *both* you and the client are doing the work. If you are doing everything (in your desire to be helpful) and the client is doing little (because they are just too busy), then this contract will not likely work. Lopsided contracts do not demonstrate partnership or effectiveness.

10. Continual contracting keeps the partnership vital and successful. Do not treat the contract and the contracting process legalistically; that will choke the life out of it. Keep the contract alive by regularly revisiting it and never finishing it.

Who Is the Client?

For the performance consultant, the client is a slippery, shifting, multi-headed creature. We talk most often about the client as management—the people formally responsible for the direction, structure, systems, resources, and decisions in the organization. Their sponsorship, perspective, needs, and wants are very important. Without them, you are usually without work! They are the formal focal client, and much of your partnering and contracting is going to be with them. My own mixed results in helping organizations change tells me that contracting with management, though essential, doesn't deliver the rest of the organization. That is where all of our other clients show up: the workforce, the suppliers, the staff support—all of those invested individuals.

Broadly speaking, clients are people you work with while reaching for your purpose. Yes, all those folks! No, they do not all exercise the same client roles, and they do not necessarily see themselves as your clients, but clients they are! Better relationships with them help the work succeed. Confining your focus to the "management client" neglects the "employee client" or the "marketing department client" or the "supervisory client." When trying to decide who your clients are, ask yourself the following questions:

- Are these people invested in the outcome of this effort?

- Can they make a difference in the results?

- Will they be affected by this work?

If they bring investment and contribution, that means they are potential clients. If they will be asked to do something differently, to risk changing, they are probably clients. That change will go more smoothly when you see them as clients, when you create positive relationships with them. Practical considerations often limit how and where you spend your time, but there are consequences for neglecting anyone.

Think about a change project you have worked on recently. Begin listing each of the distinct client groups you can identify important to this change project. As you build the list, notice how different they are, how different their expectations are. Positive results usually mean dealing with the whole array of expectations created by the project. Deal with any one group to the exclusion of the others, and the larger effort is jeopardized. One of the more challenging aspects of being an effective performance consultant is building an array of partnerships with invested parties, each tailored to the agreements that serve this particular client and yourself. It is a lot to keep track of because organizations are complex creatures. If organizations were as simple as some of our efforts at changing them suggest they are, predictable change would happen easily and we wouldn't be needed.

Long-Term Partnerships

One real indicator of consultant success is repeat business. When clients choose to use you again and again, you know they see value in your work. These long-term relationships are the ones that most of us like to cultivate, and that internal consultants must cultivate to ensure their contribution. As mentioned earlier, we can make it more likely that these partnerships develop by paying attention to what we want to create and discussing this with our clients. Support those discussions with strong patterns of accomplishment and you are on your way to creating a long-term relationship. Part of your challenge is to help the client see the value of what you have been doing. Client focus on other priorities often prevents them from seeing what you have accomplished for them. Give them the data they need to recognize your patterns of accomplishment; lay the groundwork for a long-term partnership.

Most of my older partnerships with clients are based on the fact that they value me not just as an expert or as a pair of hands, but as an individual. It is a personal relationship, and I don't know any other way to grow a partnership that lasts many years without making it a personal relationship. You may know how to do this, but I don't. Long-term clients choose to use me again and again not primarily because of expertise; my expertise is available in many other consultants. They choose to use me because of my knowledge of them and their organizations and the trusting, successful work we have accomplished together over the years. You may see this differently; I know some performance consultants do. But if you feel the need to sustain long-term partnerships with clients, consider asking yourself these questions:

1. Is there a pattern of accomplishment in the work you have done with this client? Practical people all, clients want to invest in partners who have demonstrated a repeated ability to succeed. Build that pattern and help clients see it. Since you love that pattern too, all this sequential success builds your confidence with this client.

2. Do you respect your clients? Do you respect what they do? Their intentions? Their aspirations? Their characters? If you do, show it. If you do not, you will not be able to hide this over the long term and you will be caught in your charade. Find other clients or other work.

3. What do you know about the clients' lives? What do they know about yours? What is your reaction to knowing and sharing more? Since long-term relationships thrive on the personal, you will likely need to share more of your life than the work might seem to require. This will likely provoke a struggle between you, the consultant, and the rest of you. A deeper partnership usually includes elements that are definitely outside the consultant role. And learning more about the clients' lives potentially deepens the partnership and complicates it.

4. Do you like your clients? Yes, *like*! Can you imagine being friends with them? Are you open to that possibility? Caring and friendship (not to mention love) are still difficult concepts in many work settings. I am not suggesting that you start inviting all of your clients over to the house for dinner, but I do know the benefits of being partnered with a client that I like. You do too. Liking the people we work with has too many pluses to be ignored as we think about building long-term work partnerships. Though not essential, it is a great addition. It is wonderful to move to the point at which work with someone else yields success, respect, knowledge, and caring—where we are grateful for the ways in which our work partnership feeds a deeper connection. To my way of thinking, it is silly to meet all of our needs for friendship outside the workplace. Our consulting work often gives us the opportunity to get to know people more fully; let's use it.

For those readers doubting the importance of developing this softer side of business partnerships, consider the option quite pragmatically. Most of our work in organizations is about change, about letting go of some of what is familiar in favor of something different. Change requires risk for those who are changing. People are more willing to risk when they trust the people supporting change, and that is often us, the consultants. Trust springs from doing things together successfully through time. And that is just what successful partnerships are all about. So it makes sense to develop relationships with clients in which you and they can succeed, building on the trust you have created together.

Dealing With Management Clients

"People in authority. . .emphasis on hierarchy. . .power brokers. . .control freaks. . .management politics:" Words like these keep coming up when I talk with consultants about what blocks effective partnerships with managers. I struggle with these issues too.

How do we succeed with clients who are caught up in the corporate game? How do we make a difference with people operating from different values than our own? I don't have the easy answers, but I have learned something about what works better. Here is a short list of practical ideas:

There is no substitute for competence. And competence comes first. The people who intend to run things around here, many of them clients, have a greater respect for competence than they do for good ideas. To them, competence means demonstrated ability to solve their corporate problems. Build competence that they value in order to succeed as a consultant in their system. They will begin to see you as a potential partner. A corollary: Do not expect them to listen to your many good ideas until you have shown them that you can do something for them.

Just because you have issues with authority does not mean authority is an issue here. Many of us bring authority issues with us to the workplace. In the process of growing up, each of us develops a stance toward authority and the people who have it. Notice where you stand on this; look back over your life; talk with others who know you well. Yes, childhood is a clue. A corollary: Do not expect management to recognize your expertise until you respect their authority.

Make yourself valuable by having something to contribute to the issues at hand—the issues as identified by the organization. Yes, there are other issues, but go to where the organization is focused. By establishing a pattern of being valuable in solving identified organizational problems, you may earn the right to work in areas that you know are **really** important. A corollary: Do not expect management to be impressed with your understanding of their world until you are impressed with theirs.

Give the respect to your clients that you would like them to give to you. You want to be heard? Listen to them. You want to put forth ideas? Hear their ideas. You want to take risks? Support their risk taking. Too often we find ourselves withholding from our clients the respect we are demanding from them. A corollary: Do not be surprised when others withhold from you what you are unwilling to give to them.

Some of these ideas may run counter to what you feel like doing. If that is so, ask yourself how well your present approach to management clients is working. If you are happy with the results, wonderful! If not, maybe it is time to try another approach.

YOUR UNIQUE, VALUED-ADDED CONTRIBUTION

Partnership has more to do with "doing your part" than equality. Its emphasis is less on whether partners have equal power and more on whether they can each uniquely contribute to results. Too often I have seen myself and other consultants striving for power equal to that of the client, giving too much attention to hierarchy. That just misses the real point, which is found in the answer to this question: "What is your unique, value-added contribution?" When the consultant and the client agree on their answers to that question, the basics for a partnership are in place. This means they have agreement on what each of them brings to the partnership. From the consultant's perspective, you are uniquely qualified to be there based on what you bring that is special. And that concept links to an underlying dilemma I experience with clients.

Clients hire me because of how I am *like* them, and they continue using me because of how I am *unlike* them. I see a parallel to romantic relationships: During early dating, couples often remark on how similar they are, how they experience the world in the same way. Years later, their relationship will likely be enriched by the differences between them. As Sheila Kelly, my local authority and partner for thirty-plus years says, "The reasons we got married and the reasons we stay married are different." And so it is with the "marriages" of clients and consultants. Check to see if this observation fits with your own experience.

Similarities between consultant and client contribute to the comfort and predictability of the relationship—and we certainly need a dose of that! The dissimilarities are the source of creativity and friction, opportunity and risk—we need this too. It takes all the awareness a consultant can muster to stay on top of these conflicting expectations and continue to be a fairly well-aligned professional. When we are most effective as partners, we help our clients understand what is unique about us and how that uniqueness might apply to the work at hand. At the same time, we show our clients that we are interested in them, their work, and their issues; we demonstrate our understanding by the questions we ask, the stories we tell, and the ideas we offer.

The "work" suggested by focusing on our unique, value-added contribution turns us toward the intrapersonal and intraprofessional. Look through the following questions; some of them are worth exploring.

● In what organizations have people remarked on your impressive understanding of them?

● In what organizations do you feel as if you know the feelings, thoughts, and heartbeats of employees?

● What kinds of clients are you more attracted to?

● What have clients said to you about how you are different from and valued by them?

● In what ways are you different from most consultants in the marketplace?

● When a client chooses you, what do they get that is special?

● What do you reliably, repeatedly bring to all clients that they value?

● What kind of work are you regularly attracted to?

● What are you passionate about in life that you can reach for through your work?

● How would you describe the kind of partnership you like to create with clients?

Not easy questions, are they? But with experience and reflection, you will find the answers becoming clearer. Those answers are about your unique, value-added contribution.

Knowledge of Yourself

The primary source of my consulting effectiveness is myself. Knowledge of myself is more important than the techniques and methods I have accumulated, more important than the many models and many years of internal and external consulting experience. After all the seminars and workshops and conferences I have attended, I return to where I started: myself. My patterns of success with clients have involved knowing who I am, what I want to do, what I believe in, what I aspire to. This knowledge gives me the confidence to propose and confront; the ability to know where I stand and to be honest about it; the openness to understand and respect my clients' needs. When I fail with clients, it is often because I literally did not know what I wanted, what I was trying to accomplish.

Being a great partner to a business client means bringing your whole self to the work, not using the consultant role as a mask. It means making consulting an integral part of your life, not just a job that allows you to be your "real self" in your off hours. Yes, you can succeed in the marketplace while playing the role of a consultant. Given that you invest most of your waking hours in this work, however, why not do it in a way that allows you to be yourself?

Here in this chapter on partnership, we are returning to core human dilemmas and giving advice that sounds remarkably like what you might get from a self-help book, a life skills workshop, or a counselor. Given that there is so much help available, here are a few points tailored to the work that performance consultants do:

1. You are not through learning yet; you are still reaching toward your potential. You are an experienced, knowledgeable person partway through life. You have learned a lot, and you have much to learn. Keep yourself open to what is to come. (This is a useful way of thinking about your clients too.)

2. Make regular efforts to understand yourself better. Use reading, workshops, and friends to broaden your perspective on the possibilities that exist for performance consultants. Reading this book is a good example.

3. Fill out instruments and questionnaires that allow you to compare your scores to the thousands of other people who have been through the same materials. Learn about the differences in personality types or leadership styles or communications patterns. Find out how people with characteristics like yours succeed.

4. Think about your work, why it is important to you. Consider what it has to do with your life purpose. If you have not thought about your life purpose, now might be a good time to do that. Find time each day to in some way (reading, meditation, solitude, journaling) remind yourself of what is most important to you. If you don't, you will end up giving all of your time to what is important to others.

5. Talk with clients about these matters. Find out why their work is important to them. Probe a bit to get beyond their first surface thoughts.

Thinking along these lines increases your self-awareness, and that will make you a more effective work partner. You will become a better partner because you know yourself better. You will contract more clearly; you will confront more readily; you will respect and appreciate your clients.

The Good News and the Bad News

As the joke goes, which would you like first? First, what may be—or at least sound like—bad news for internal performance consultants: Internal performance consultants are not blessed with position power in their organizations. Many of us are buried in human resources (HR) or human resource development (HRD) departments and seldom held up as a most-valued, indispensable function. From here, we pursue our noble trade with our clients across the organization marketplace. And back in our home department, we live in short hierarchies with limited potential for upward advancement. To have a "real" future with this company, to climb the corporate ladder, we would have to leave our performance consulting function and role. Think about this in relation to your aspirations as an internal consultant. These ideas have significant implications for your power and success with clients.

The good news in this common reality is that since we have "no future" in this organization, we have less to lose; we have more room to do what we want to do. People burdened with the desire and possibility of moving up four levels and six pay grades think twice before taking action that might jeopardize their progress. We internal performance consultants don't carry that burden because our upward opportunities are limited by the positions we have chosen.

As successful internal consultants, we can play on the advantages of how our limited organizational career growth widens our professional possibilities. We can use the power of this position to speak the truth, to take risks, to establish partnerships focused on the work that needs doing without concern for traditional career growth. We can serve our clients better as we let go of the distractions of traditional organizational success.

Conclusion

Here are some closing thoughts to draw together the ideas in this chapter:

● Start with (and keep paying attention to) your work on yourself—self-awareness, self-knowledge. You are *the* place to start because you bring yourself to every partnership you will ever participate in. The client is not here right now, you are. And you can do something about yourself when you choose.

● Learn about partnering from doing it; there are better and worse ways. Reflect on your experience with working with others. What works in your particular life and work? Look at what you have learned about partnership in friendships, in marriage, in social activities, in civic organizations, and keep track of your learning. Read some of the resources listed below.

● The Golden Rule is a great foundation for all partnerships. Take it seriously and "do unto others as you would have them do unto you." So much of the guidance I give others (and try to heed myself) goes back to first considering and serving the client.

● Said another way, show your clients how you want to work by the way you work with them. They are learning from your actions. When you listen to them, they are more likely to listen to you. When you trust them, they are more likely to trust you. When you are willing to risk and act, they will be more willing. So take the initiative. Whatever you want from them, do it for them first.

Resources

If this chapter intrigues you, here are five sources of complementary ideas:

Bellman, Geoffrey. *The Consultant's Calling*. San Francisco: Jossey-Bass, 1990.

————. *Getting Things Done When You Are Not in Charge*. San Francisco: Berrett-Koehler, 1992.

Block, Peter. *Flawless Consulting*. San Francisco: Jossey-Bass, 1981.

————.*Stewardship*. San Francisco: Berrett-Koehler, 1993. (Quick read)

Henning, Joel. *The Future of Staff Groups*. San Francisco: Berrett-Koehler, 1997.

The Author

Geoffrey Bellman spent the first 14 years of his career working in major corporations (Ideal Basic Industries, AMOCO Corporation, and G.D. Searle) before starting his own consulting business in Chicago in 1977. His consulting work focuses on creating and sustaining positive change in large corporations, including changes in vision, values, purpose, strategy, and ownership. Among his clients are GTE, Booz-Allen & Hamilton, TRW, First Bank Systems, PacifiCorp, Simpson Investment, Anixter, Boeing, and Whirlpool.

Bellman is the author of *Getting Things Done When You're Not in Charge* (Berrett-Koehler, 1992), a book for succeeding from the middle of the organization. It is a Book-of-the-Month Club and Fortune Executive Book Club selection. He also wrote *The Consultants Calling* (Jossey-Bass, 1990), a book for those who want to know what consulting is really like as a career, as a living, and as a life. *FORBES* magazine recently selected this book as one of the country's best-selling small business books. His newest book, *Your Signature Path* (Berrett-Koehler, 1996), explores unique perspectives on life and work and how to do both well.

Bellman is an occasional columnist with *Training & Development*, a magazine dedicated to human resource development. He is a founding member of The Community Consulting Project, a group of volunteer consultants who give their time to nonprofit organizations. He also belongs to the Organization Development Network, the Woodlands Group, and the American Society for Training & Development.

This chapter is based on ideas presented in Geoffrey Bellman's upcoming book on consulting, to be published by Berrett-Koehler in 1999.

Case Study

The Importance of Partnering at PNC Bank

by Robert Leininger

COMPANY NAME: PNC Bank Corporation

INDUSTRY TYPE: Financial services

ORGANIZATION PROFILE

ORGANIZATION SIZE:

26,000 employees; 850 Community Bank offices in six states (Pennsylvania, Delaware, Indiana, Ohio, Kentucky, and New Jersey).

KEY PRODUCTS AND SERVICES:

PNC Bank provides lending, deposit, brokerage, and other financial services to 3.3 million households and 135,000 small businesses. Services are provided on a national basis through online banking, telephone access, and ATMs, as well as a network of Community Bank offices.

NET INCOME:

992 million in 1996.

ASSETS:

73 billion.

DEPARTMENT NAME:

Consumer Bank Performance Improvement and Training.

DEPARTMENT SIZE:

76 employees.

MISSION FOR DEPARTMENT:

To meet and exceed our service partners' expectations in leadership, responsiveness, quality, and performance solutions in the following ways:

● team with our service partners to prioritize and communicate key initiatives and achieve the line of business goals and objectives

● provide consulting services to determine customized solutions to meet business goals and objectives

● assess, design, develop, deliver, and measure high-quality solutions to improve performance

● implement continuous improvement processes to promote quality and assist in the growth and development of employees.

PRIMARY REASONS FOR TRANSITION TO A PERFORMANCE FOCUS:

● the need for a strategic alliance with senior management to develop a proactive approach toward performance improvement

● the need to link business needs with performance needs

● the need to analyze current performance compared with on-the-job performance required to achieve business needs

● the need for a holistic approach to combining training and business measures.

Creating and Maintaining Partnerships

The quality of performance consultants' work is closely correlated with and dependent upon the quality of their relationship with their clients. Consequently, this case study is about how to create and maintain this strategic partnership.

Research has determined that performance consultants spend an average of 25 percent of their time developing and maintaining partnerships with their clients (Dana Gaines Robinson, "Performance Consulting: The Job." Presentation at ASTD International Conference, 1997). Developing true partnerships does not happen by chance. You cannot create one without considerable effort on your part as a performance consultant and on the part of your client. To that end, this case study contains both methods and lessons learned from a real case intended to help you develop and maintain lasting partnerships that are both rewarding and successful.

As the Consumer Bank performance improvement and training manager of PNC Bank, I am responsible for the development and maintenance of strategic partnerships with all executive managers across all business segments within the Consumer Bank. These include the branch system, the National Financial Service Center, credit card, consumer lending, business banking, bank operations, and AAA Financial Services. The focus of these partnerships is on improving performance in the consumer line of business (see table 1 for organization chart).

Early in 1995, the Performance Improvement and Training Department began the transition from a traditional training department to a performance improvement function. It was during this transition that I was contacted by the senior manager of the eastern division branch system to discuss how the Consumer Bank Performance Improvement and Training Department could help the rapid growth of the eastern division and relieve the pain associated with the expansion. This was my first opportunity to put into practice my

T A B L E   1   Community Bank Organization Chart

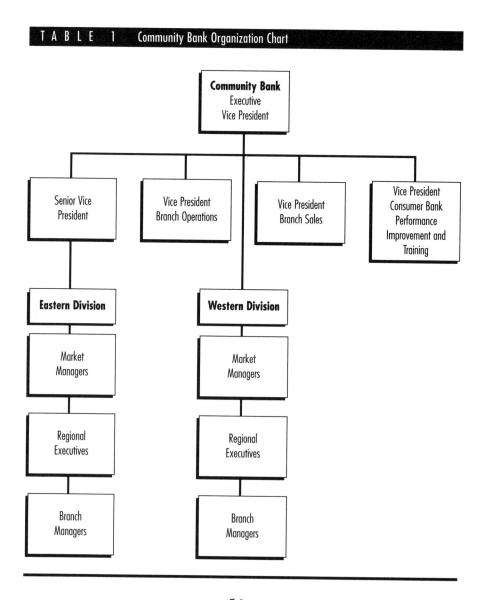

knowledge of human performance improvement, especially by forging a new partnership with the eastern division senior manager and the branch system leadership.

Background Information

During a 14-month period from July 1995 through August 1996, PNC Bank acquired 345 Community Bank offices in the state of New Jersey from two premiere regional financial service providers. These acquisitions positioned PNC Bank as a major force in the financial service industry, particularly in the northeast region. As a result of the acquisitions, the eastern division of the Community Bank was experiencing growing pains, which prompted the request for assistance from Performance Improvement and Training.

Building the Partnership

Building a strong partnership with the client would be critical to the success of the project. My strategy to accomplish this focused on two key areas: communication and education. My objectives for developing communication with the client were to

● build a trust relationship

● develop credibility

● communicate easily and often with the client

● develop a sense of team or partnership

● encourage innovative approaches to performance improvement.

Methods to accomplish these objectives were established. The following were selected and implemented:

● networking (both formal and informal)

● communicating when networking (listening actively, using feedback as a primary tool in overcoming barriers to communication, and framing messages that are clear and concise).

My objectives concerning education were to

● develop a clear vision of what is to be accomplished

● develop a results orientation to the project

● agree on a process and structure within which we would work

● get as many people involved and owning the process as appropriate.

Methods to accomplish the educational objective fell within the formal networking process for the project. A series of meetings would be needed to contract for the performance assessment and to create the vision. I wanted to keep the strategy to accomplish our objectives for both communication and education simple, but very focused. With the strategy in place for the relationship to begin to grow, I now turned my attention to the business need.

The *business need* was defined by the senior manager of the eastern division as the integration of three organizations into a consistent sales and service culture. During the acquisition period, the Community Bank was in the midst of moving from a traditional banking environment to a sales environment and developed a new set of performance needs. One of the objectives was to ensure that the business strategies were supported by a workforce that exhibited the appropriate performance required to optimize desired sales and service performance. Strong sales and service leadership was required for this performance to be exhibited and supported by the work. Because all branch managers reported to the regional executives, the position of regional executive was identified as the critical sales and service leadership position around which the eastern division could begin the integration of three banks into one sales and service culture. An agreement in principle to conduct a performance assessment was reached. This was an opportunity to provide consistent performance across all markets (both eastern and western divisions) to support the sales and service management process. Therefore, the executive vice president of the Community Bank now became the ultimate client, and the project a corporate initiative. Agreement was reached with both the eastern division senior manager and the executive vice president (new client) of the Community Bank that a performance model would be developed for the position of regional executive. This model would describe the best practices required of regional executives to develop consistent sales and service in all branches.

My objectives of communication and education now were broadened to include the new client and to keep the eastern division senior manager in the formal and informal networking process. The objectives and methods to accomplish them remained unchanged. A series of meetings were held with the executive vice president that focused on defining the business goals for the regional executive position. The data collected from these meetings would be the basis for future interviews with exemplary regional executives across the Community Bank. During these meetings, the client vacillated between not wanting to complete the process, wanting to more fully understand the process, and fully embracing the process. This was a critical time for me as a performance consultant. Communication, particularly listening, was key to the success of this period. Providing feedback and acknowledging the client's concerns were paramount. This positive working relationship was developed during informal networking that I initiated between formal project meetings. Gradually a trusting relationship developed, and the project picked up momentum.

The major outcomes of these meetings were the identification of 10 business goals for the position of regional executive; a communication plan to involve key individuals and groups across the Community Bank; and the agreement to develop a performance model for the position of regional executive. During the execution of the communication plan and the model development strategy, I was in constant communication with the client and the eastern division senior manager. I never lost sight of the importance of this responsibility and the need to maintain the relationships with both the client and the eastern division senior manager.

Information for the performance model was gathered from exemplary regional executives, their immediate managers (market managers), and a sample of their direct reports (branch managers). The information was obtained by one-on-one interviews conducted by performance consultants. Each consultant had participated in an interview preparation session. Here they used a customized interview guide while they interviewed an exemplary regional executive. The consultants were provided feedback about how they conducted the interviews.

Our next task was to validate the performance model. We agreed to set up a validation meeting that would include key stakeholders in the model who would need to own the process going forward. This meeting included exemplary regional executives, their managers, the eastern division senior manager, the executive vice president of the Community Bank, and the project team. The objectives of the meetings could be divided into two distinct sets. The first set of objectives revolved around examining and modifying the model. The outcomes of this set of objectives were to agree on the content of the model and determine its future use. The second set of objectives centered on further relationship building and education of the key stakeholders on the process used to develop the model itself. To help accomplish both sets of objectives, I asked the client to play a vital role in the validation process. This role ranged from involvement in the planning process to being part of the agenda. Our shared vision, good working relationship, and continual communication got us to this point in the project.

The validation meeting was successful in that a final draft of the model was now complete and the client sign-off was the last action needed before proceeding to the next step. At this point in the process, the client felt that we had met or exceeded his expectations with the quality of support provided. The development of the performance model was ahead of schedule. The partnership with the client was growing stronger. We were now ready to move to the next phase of the project.

The next task was to reach agreement with the executive vice president to complete a gap and cause analysis. As there was more of a balance between our relationship and tasks to be completed, educating the client became easier with each step. Creating a shared vision and agreeing on the process we would use to accomplish the assessment gave us a feeling of excitement. In addition, we both began to take risks regarding not only what we were going to accomplish but also how we would do it. The level of the client's satisfaction with the gap and cause analysis results exceeded my expectations. He was willing to support both training and nontraining actions to accomplish the vision. His acceptance of the work environment feedback was high. His acceptance of nontraining actions was further evidence of risk-taking behavior on his part. His trust in the process, the data collected, and our partnership contributed heavily in his decision making. We were now ready to move to the next phase of the project—implementation.

The depth of my relationship with the client would have an effect on the actions selected for implementation. We conducted a data reporting meeting with the purpose of reviewing the results of the gap and cause assessment; determining implications on the business and performance needs; and agreeing on actions to be taken. We reached agreement in principle on implementation goals, actions to be taken, and measurement strategy. The ease with which the agreement was reached was the result of substantial information in the report itself and the strong relationship with the client. The client's feedback was that the project was the best work that he had seen by our department and that we had exceeded his expectations for cycle time implementation. He has asked that we initiate the performance improvement process for other positions in the Community Bank. The role of performance consultant in the Community Bank was firmly in place. The objectives of communication and education were the building blocks for the success we achieved. In addition, the hard work on everyone's part resulted in a very useful performance model and valuable gap and cause analysis information.

Lessons Learned

● Close client contact is critical in the partnership phase. Just as in any new relationship, the more communication you have, the faster the relationship can develop and grow.

● Relationship building with the client is proportionate to the speed with which you can move the process. In other words, the better you know each other and the better the client understands the process, the faster the process can move.

● Patience and resilience are core competencies for a consultant. The performance consultant must be skilled at nurturing a relationship and accepting of a client's lack of understanding of the process as a challenge. This lack of understanding of the process cannot be misinterpreted as resistance to you or the process.

● It is important to establish the process of partnering proactively rather than reactively. The performance consultant must maintain the client relationship on an ongoing basis and stay in touch with strategic initiatives. A performance consultant must know the business of the client.

● After the completion of a successful performance improvement project, the performance consultant must work diligently to maintain the partnership with the client. There must be ongoing communication, both informal and structured. The informal communication consists of e-mail, voice mail, corridor conversations, and brief phone conversations. The structured communication includes monthly meetings where business and performance needs are discussed and performance improvement opportunities are identified. The key here is to find "where is the pain" in the client's business unit.

The Author

Robert Leininger is vice president and manager of the Consumer Bank Performance Improvement and Training Department of PNC Bank. As the Consumer Bank performance improvement training manager, he is responsible for maintaining strategic alliances with all business segment senior managers and directing the design, development, and implementation of performance improvement and training initiatives with special emphasis on measurement and impact on business results.

Leininger began his career in performance improvement and training in 1975 and has held a number of training and development positions, including contract instructional designer and management consultant; training director for a private nonprofit health care organization; and faculty member of three Pennsylvania universities. In 1988 he was named manager of the Professional and Leadership Development Department at the Erie Insurance Group and was responsible for the assessment, design, development, and measurement of the supervisory, leadership, and executive development of the management team. In 1995 he moved to his most recent position as Consumer Bank training manager at PNC Bank.

Leininger received a B.A. and an M.A. in education from The Pennsylvania State University. He is the most recent recipient of the Director Award for outstanding leadership for integrating performance consulting, instructional design, and measurement into his line of business at PNC Bank.

4

Assessment Phase: Building Models and Defining Gaps

by Paul Elliott

QUICK READ

● Assessment of human performance in the workplace is the tool upon which human performance improvement is founded. There are two factors that are key to doing performance assessments:

—The focus must be on outputs, which is what workers produce, and not simply on what they do.

—The assessment process needs to include, when possible, observation of exemplary performers. These are individuals whose outputs exceed standards.

● There are two types of performance assessments:

—Performance models, which are used when there is a need to add new outputs to an existing job or when an entirely new job must be designed.

—Gap and cause analysis, which is used when current performance of people is not meeting the organization's expectations.

● Information provided from these assessments is used to select and design the interventions that will be employed to enhance and improve human performance.

As traditional competitive advantages such as access to capital, manufacturing expertise, and research and development prove insufficient in a global marketplace, more companies are examining the role that human performance improvement (HPI) processes and the discipline of human performance technology (HPT) play in providing them with a competitive edge for the organization. HPI is a systematic approach to improving human performance in the workplace through the use of interventions such as skills/knowledge training, work environment improvements, and worker incentives. This chapter will examine the tool upon which human performance improvement is founded: the human performance assessment.

There are two models that the performance analyst can use when conducting an assessment: a performance model and gap and cause analysis. Performance models are used when adding new outputs (what a worker produces) or best practices (what a worker does to produce those outputs) to an existing job or when creating a new job altogether. A gap and cause analysis is done when the performance of workers on the job does not meet a company's expectations. But before describing these two models in detail, we need to consider the underlying factors that shape an assessment.

The person who has most influenced the assessment of human performance is Tom Gilbert. In his classic book entitled *Human Competence* (1996), he points out two underlying factors that should shape an assessment. First, the analyst should focus on what people produce in the work environment, not simply on what they do. It is the contrast between accomplishments or results (referred to as outputs in this book) and the practices used to produce those outputs. Helping workers perform the wrong practices more efficiently does not improve a company's performance. A worker's major outputs and how those outputs contribute to the company's business goals need to be identified up front. Only then can the analyst determine the practices and interventions needed for workers to produce those outputs with a high level of competence. Table 1 illustrates this output-based approach to improving human performance.

Second, what workers produce and what they do to produce it can best be identified by interviewing and observing exemplary performers, that is, workers whose outputs exceed standards. For example, how does a high-performing loan officer select borrowers with a high percentage of paybacks? Understanding how exemplary performers work can reveal ways to improve the performance of other workers. Not all of their high performance will be

T A B L E 1 Output-Based Approach			
Business Goal→	**Output →**	**Best Practices →**	**Interventions**
• Increased profits	• Project plan	• Prepare work breakdown • Assign project staff • Write proposal • Negotiate proposal	• Training in cost analysis • Cash incentive for projects completed above pro-jected gross profit

transferable; however, facets of their performance that can be easily trans-ferred to others will have a significant effect on the success of the company. This idea is in stark contrast to asking managers, policy makers, or subject matter experts what they *believe* workers should be doing.

There is an important preliminary step: Before beginning an assessment, align the purpose of the project with the organization's business goals. A for-mal alignment meeting that includes the client, other key stakeholders, and members of the assessment team is recommended to verify and clarify the request that led to this specific project. What situation prompted the request and who in the organization would be affected the most by the pro-posed project?

It is critical to verify the organization's basic business goals relative to this assessment. My experience indicates that consensus is rare between the client and his or her stakeholders regarding the business goal and how it should be measured. Is it improved customer satisfaction or enhanced prof-its? It is important to spend some time reviewing internal documentation to see how the goal is stated formally prior to the meeting. It is even more important to work through the goal with the team to ensure that the real, operational indicators of the goal have been captured. That is, how do the client and the stakeholders visualize and assess organizational performance on a day-to-day basis? The alignment meeting should also capture parame-ters and constraints of the assessment project. When does the client require the results? How many sites need to be visited? Are there any budget and travel constraints? It is also essential to determine roles within the project and to identify who will be the final authority.

Perhaps the most important part of the alignment process is the clarifi-cation and representation of the organization's goals. This is true for two reasons. First, it determines how the results of the assessment are evaluated. Ultimately, the client wants any assessment and interventions coming out of the assessment to directly affect the achievement of organizational goals. Second, workers perform best when they know what their company is trying to accomplish and how they fit into the big picture. Goals must not only be clearly stated but also clearly communicated to workers. Unfortunately, many workers don't understand the relationship between their work and their company's goals, and this is one of the most significant inhibitors in achieving optimal performance. For example, a colleague of mine recently visited a manufacturing facility on a day that a 30-year employee was retiring. Managers asked the employee how he would like to spend his last day on the job. He said that he wanted a tour of the entire plant; he had never seen the entire operation. Consequently, he probably never understood his role in it.

PERFORMANCE MODELS

There are four major steps involved in building performance models:

- Determine major outputs.

- Collect data on major outputs.

- Produce a best practice list for major outputs.

- Collect data on best practices.

1. **Determine major outputs.** In an ideal environment, data on outputs and best practices can be collected by interviewing and observing exemplary performers. Exemplary performers are individuals who produce outputs, in support of business goals, in an exceptional manner. A task force or focus group will not provide reliable and valid information. Often some of the characteristics or behaviors that differentiate the exemplary from the average performer are subtle and intuitive and will not be self-reported through an interview process alone. It requires observation combined with debriefing following performance to "get inside the skin" of the exemplary performer.

If exemplary performers are not available within the organization, attempt to find them in an organization that permits benchmarking. For example, if the performance model being developed is in support of new technology, work with the technology provider to find noncompetitive organizations that have already implemented the technology. If the performance model is being done in support of a new job, perhaps some of the outputs of the new job are already produced in existing positions. Exemplary performers who are currently performing only parts of the new job can assist in the analysis for the new job. When exemplary performers are not available either inside or outside the organization, other data

66

sources will be required. For example, documentation that supports the new technology can serve as a source. A task force of people performing similar work from within the company can be used. Interviewing the process or technology designer can also be a source of data. None of these alternative sources will provide the quality of data that comes from an exemplary performer, but they will provide close approximations.

To develop a summary statement that captures the overall purpose or mission of the job, ask questions like: "What overall output summarizes this job?" or "What is the main thing produced?" After developing the job summary, begin to create a list of the major outputs that routinely make up the job by asking, "What is produced during a day, a week, or a month?" Further probing will identify those outputs that are produced on a nonroutine basis, particularly those infrequently performed outputs that carry a high consequence of error. Table 2 shows the job summary and major outputs for a project manager.

I am often asked about the relationship between outputs and competencies. Many organizations have invested significant resources in capturing the competencies required to perform various jobs. They have established human resource development systems that are based on providing these competencies to people either for their current positions or as a way of preparing them for future positions within the organization. While this may be a useful model—and certainly a popular one—my concern is that competency does not correlate directly with performance.

Imagine a situation where an athlete practiced all week long and developed competence in each basic skill required to play on a basketball team but at game time chose to sit on the bench. In this environment, no one would consider the individual's capability to play as competence. Instead,

T A B L E 2 Job Summary and Major Outputs

Job Summary, Project Manager: To manage projects within budget and at or above projected gross profit

Routine Major Outputs	• Project plans • Deliverables produced on time and to standard
Nonroutine Major Outputs	• Troubleshooting client complaints to produce maximum client satisfaction and minimum negative effect on project profitability and company reputation

they would focus on how the person actually performed during the game. A competent basketball player is one who applies his or her skills to pass, defend, and score during the actual game. Outputs are the passes, defense, and scoring within the organizational environment. Developing capable employees who don't contribute to the organization is not a desirable goal.

The other concern with competencies that are not tied to results or outputs is the ability of individuals to ascertain where to focus their priorities. The competency list for a particular position can be long and complex and not tied directly to day-to-day performance. The work in competency models is valuable, but it can be leveraged and extended by having the competencies tied to outputs and by measuring the ability of the individual to produce the outputs and not simply being satisfied with competence.

2. **Collect data on major outputs.** After determining the job's major outputs, collect data on each output. First, identify the criteria or standards for the output. As a rule, these criteria can fall under the categories of accuracy, time, productivity, or safety. After identifying the criteria, look for any anticipated changes that could affect the output in the near future. These changes might include reorganizations; new equipment or technology; and changes in policy, regulations, or procedures.

Next, determine what percentage of time is spent producing this output in a typical week or month. Finally, identify the interactions required to produce the output, that is, with whom and with what does the worker interact while producing this output. Table 3 is an example of data collected on one major output of a project manager—a project plan.

3. **Produce a list of best practices for major outputs.** This list is the basis for almost all subsequent work in the assessment, so it is worth the time to be rigorous here. At this point, the assessment of human performance is identical to traditional models of job and task analysis. It may be useful to further define what is meant by a best practice. A *best practice* is a unit of behavior that has been affirmed as desired and as one that contributes to achieving an output. For example, a person caught in a downpour with a flat tire late at night might call for assistance. When the tow truck showed up, the desired output would be a car ready to drive. To achieve that output, several best practices would need to be performed: jack up the car, loosen the wheel, remove the wheel, replace the wheel, and lower the car. Each of those practices has, in turn, a series of steps and a result. For example, the result of jacking up the car is a wheel that can be removed. The customer, however, will not pay for the wheel being removed in isolation from the desired output, which is a car ready to drive.

If a draft list of best practices is available, work with exemplary performers to identify practices that should not be or are not currently done. See if any of the practices should be part of another job or another output. See if

T A B L E 3 Data Collected on Project Plan	
Major Output	• Project plan
Percent of Project Time	• Five percent
Major Criteria	• Plan clearly describes scope of work, deliverables, work breakdown, staffing, schedule, cost, assumptions
Anticipated Changes	• No changes likely in over approach to project planning; however, each project requires specific tailoring of planning steps
Interactions	• Project director, project staff, peers who may be involved with similar projects

there are any best practices that are missing and review the wording of each practice to make sure the terminology is accurate. If a draft list of best practices is not available, the optimum results can be achieved by observing exemplary performers doing the actual work and generating a list in real time. If the practice takes too long to actually observe, ask exemplary performers to simulate the process of producing the output while you observe. Table 4 is a list of best practices for producing a project plan.

This process works effectively even when the work is cognitive in nature. For example, suppose you need to analyze the process of a loan officer reaching a decision concerning whether or not to grant a loan to an applicant. To get the best results, place individuals in their actual work environment and ask them to simulate how they go about making such a decision. They will spend some time reviewing the application, perhaps turning to a policy and procedures manual, and maybe interacting with a colleague. Make extensive notes of the observable behavior as they go through the simulated activity, and then go into extensive debriefing and ask them questions such as, "When reviewing the application, what are the key things you look for?" Suppose their response is, "I review the application to determine the credit worthiness of the applicant." Then ask them, "What data do you use to determine if the applicant is credit worthy?" Ask how they take the various pieces of data and think about them. There are a series of tools available under the label "knowledge acquisition tools" that can be very useful at this point. They were developed to support expert systems, but they are totally applicable to capturing the cognitive performance of experts.

TABLE 4 Best Practice List	
Major Output	**Project Plan**
Best Practices	• Prepare work breakdown. • Assign project staff. • Complete project pricing proposal. • Write proposal. • Negotiate proposal and obtain purchase order. • Set up project baseline. • Write detailed project plan.

After creating a draft list of best practices and confirming its accuracy with exemplary performers, determine the criteria for each practice. You might ask exemplary performers, "How do you know when the practice is complete?" or "How would you judge that the practice has been done correctly?"

4. **Collect data on best practices.** Examine any available documentation and meet again with exemplary performers to capture some critical data on each practice analyzed. These data will be used to make important decisions in the design of interventions. Determine if speed is a factor in performing the practice. Do seconds count? Look at the work environment in which each best practice takes place. Are there any characteristics of the environment that are particularly noteworthy? For example, would it be difficult for a worker to use a job aid?

Determine the frequency of performance for each best practice. In addition, determine what the possible consequence of error is if the practice were performed incorrectly or below standard. Might it result in loss of life or injury? Could it cause intolerable economic costs? Find out the complexity of each practice in terms of number of steps or difficulty in doing any of the steps. Finally, determine what the probability is that the practice will change in any significant way within the next year or two.

Performance Model Case Study

Determination of the major outputs of a job and generation of accurate and valid best practice lists, plus the capturing of critical data on each practice, will provide the data necessary to make critical decisions about how to support superior performance leading to high-quality outputs. It is important to validate the data on hand before proceeding. There are several options for doing this: Take the data to exemplary performers in other parts of the organization to verify and validate; have it reviewed by technical experts and people familiar with organizational policies, procedures, and safety regulations; and, finally, obtain ultimate validation from the client and key stakeholders of the client organization.

The following case study illustrates how a performance model assessment can significantly accelerate the launch of new technology, new work processes, or new organizational designs. A refinery decided to enter the asphalt market, so it began by conducting a detailed human performance assessment. The goal was to process an asphalt delivery truck safely in less than 30 minutes from the time it arrived at the refinery's gate. To ensure a successful market entry, a performance analyst worked with management to identify company goals based on the needs of potential customers. The analyst then analyzed every facet of human performance that would be involved in every step, including blending, testing, certifying, loading, and doing paperwork. The analyst also identified the major outputs and practices required to meet the goal of processing the truck quickly and safely. Finally, the analyst translated these outputs and practices into training, work procedures, and job aids to ensure high performance for all workers involved in the process—from the operators blending the asphalt to the security force controlling truck traffic. The asphalt facility is expected to show a 75 percent return-on-investment in the first year of operation.

GAP AND CAUSE ASSESSMENT

A gap and cause assessment will determine a client's problems, the reason why the problems exist, and what the solutions are. The steps of a gap and cause assessment include the following:

● Identify the deficient output that is triggering the assessment.

● Define the current practices of the deficient output.

● Determine where inadequate human performance is causing the deficient output.

● Generate multiple cause hypotheses.

● Collect evidence to support or deny hypotheses.

● Identify probable causes and make recommendations.

1. **Identify the deficient output.** Determine which major output is not being produced or produced to standard. This is not always a straightforward task. Often the client comes in with a specific solution to the request in mind. The client did not ask for help in improving performance but

requested training on some topic instead. The recommended response to a solution request is to state: "Yes, I can help you with that. Can you tell me more about the situation that led you to this request?" Most requests for training require identification of what is not being achieved in the client's organization. Consider asking questions like: "If this intervention was successful, what would you see changed in your organization?" or "Is there some current goal or product that your team produces that is currently being produced below standard?"

Be sure to identify any current metrics or measurements within the client's organization that deal with the deficient output. Review the data on historic performance and compare it with expected performance. If hard data is not available, explore with the client what anecdotal data would be acceptable. It is essential to achieve consensus with the client at the beginning of the project on what needs to be measured, what data will be acceptable, and how the assessment efforts and later intervention design will be assessed in relationship to any improvements. You can never give credible results to the client at the end of the project unless you have achieved consensus on how to measure those results at the beginning of the project. Clearly define for the client the gap between current performance and desired performance and tie it directly to business goals. Also determine the potential value to the company—in dollar terms if possible—of resolving the problem.

2. **Define the current practices of the deficient output.** After identifying the deficient major output, generate a list of best practices. Begin each statement with a verb and include an object, for example, "troubleshoot installation problems." Then have exemplary performers produce or simulate the production of the major output while you observe with the best practice list. Revise the list as needed.

3. **Determine inadequate human performance.** Distinguish between those practices that are being performed adequately and those that are being performed below standard. You can determine which practices are performed adequately and which are not by reviewing existing data; observing exemplary performance and comparing it to average performance; and interviewing incumbents, managers, and technical experts. Look for the following:

- best practices that are not being performed at all
- best practices that are not being performed fast enough
- best practices in which errors are made in some of the steps
- best practices that are not being performed safely
- best practices in which steps are performed out of order

- best practices in which steps have been added that are not required.

Also try to ascertain whether the deficient performance of practices occurs at a particular time or place. After identifying the deficient practices, generate cause hypotheses for why the practices are not performed adequately.

4. Generate multiple cause hypotheses and collect evidence to support or deny hypotheses. It is useful to cluster possible cause hypotheses into three categories: skill/knowledge, work environment, and incentives (see table 5). For the first category, consider whether workers know how to perform the best practice, when to perform the practice, and what the practice is. For the second category, examine work conditions and the type of equipment workers use. For the third category, consider whether workers are rewarded for performing the practice correctly. Use diagnostic questions to help collect evidence on which hypotheses are valid and which are not.

Data from multiple sources support the fact that when workers are not performing to standard, 80 percent of the time it is not due to a lack of skill or knowledge, but rather to a poor work environment or a lack of incentives. Support for these findings includes a 1994 Conference Board report entitled "Closing the Human Performance Gap" and data from hundreds of front-end analyses performed by members of the Harless Performance Guild. Interestingly, this data aligns with much of the data from the quality movement, which states that 85 percent of the problems reside in the system and not in the individual job performer.

5. Identify probable causes and make recommendations. Based on the answers to the diagnostic questions, identify probable causes for the deficiencies and make general recommendations to the client. I would recommend pulling together the client and the stakeholders who participated in the alignment process for this presentation. The tone of the meeting should be to validate and verify the information, not to simply present the results to be accepted or rejected. A typical agenda would be to provide an overview of the process employed; the sources of data, including sites that were visited and performers who were involved; hypotheses that were generated; and evidence that supported some of those hypotheses and led to the recommendations. At this time, engage the participants in an effort to refine and enhance the report. Do not try to be too specific in identifying solutions at this point unless you are a specialist in the required area.

Concerns in Gap and Cause Assessment

The following are some concerns encountered during a gap and cause assessment:

1. There is distrust and misinformation about the purpose of the analysis.

T A B L E 5 Multiple Cause Hypotheses

Skill/Knowledge	Work Environment	Incentives
Skill/knowledge questions	*Work environment questions*	*Motivation and incentive questions*
• Do workers ever perform the best practice correctly?	• Do workers receive all the needed inputs?	• Is the practice aversive (dangerous, unsafe, difficult, boring)?
• Have workers ever been trained?	• Is the workload too heavy? Do workers have enough time?	• Do workers get any feedback on the output of the practice? If so, is it adequate?
• Are job aids available? If so, are they used?	• Does emphasis on quantity cause quality to suffer?	• What are the consequences of performance?
	• Are there any performance criteria?	• Is there an absence of consequences?
	• Are the criteria too high? Does anyone meet the criteria?	• Is there a positive consequence for incorrect behavior?
	• Are workers and supervisors using the same criteria?	• Is there a negative consequence for correct behavior?
	• Are tools and equipment adequate to do the best practice?	• Is effort greater than positive consequences (not worth it)?
	• Are the physical working conditions adequate in the area?	• Does the practice lack value (no purpose in doing it)?
	• Is the work well designed?	• Do workers disagree about how it should be done?
	• Are process or procedures for performing effective?	• Do workers think someone else should be doing it (not my job)?
	• Do workers have control over the variables influencing the work?	
	• Are elements needed to do the work easily obtained?	
	• Do workers have adequate authority to make decisions?	
	• Are there any other factors that interfere with the correct performance?	

Response: Make an extra effort to ensure that the client organization understands the purpose of the analysis and the expectations for the data collection trips. Send a brief description of the project in advance of any site visits to help explain the purpose of the project.

2. Secondhand opinion is presented as fact.

Response: Present the findings honestly; you may report opinions, but never state them as facts.

3. Access to all the desired or preferred sources of information is denied.

Response: You must be able to define exemplary performance and standards for that performance. Insufficient access to data can prevent creation of a complete description of the desired performance and significantly impede the project. Keep the client informed about any access problems encountered; you may need to identify alternative sources of information.

4. Some topics may be politically and organizationally sensitive.

Response: Before collecting data, become aware of any sensitive issue to avoid discussing. For example, comments about recent downsizing or major organizational changes could cause people to misunderstand the purpose of the current project.

5. Avoid recommending low-value solutions.

Response: Always remember that the worth of the assessment will be tied to the value of improving performance and the cost of the interventions. The potential value of each solution must be higher than the cost to implement the solution.

6. The client organization has too many decision makers.

Response: Be sure that the client understands that he or she is the single point of contact and the only decision maker for the client organization. When differences of opinion arise, the client should be expected to resolve them within his or her organization.

Case Study 1

A performance analyst working for a large manufacturer was given the following challenge: Have those department managers who routinely exceed their budgets by 7 to 23 percent annually keep costs within budget. A gap and cause assessment revealed that managers prepared their budgets without help and then submitted them to their vice presidents for approval. Many of the managers did not know how to estimate costs accurately or justify their numbers to their superiors. The assessment also found that managers were given feedback only twice a year on how much money they spent, and that managers who overspent their budgets were "rewarded" by having their moneys increased the next year.

Several interventions occurred to improve performance. Managers were given training on projecting costs and preparing budgets based on those costs. They could request technical assistance from the financial department during budget preparation, and they received training in how to justify their numbers to their superiors. Monthly reports were adjusted to show actual versus projected spending on each line item, significantly reducing the delay in feedback concerning performance. In addition, the company established a policy that overspending would negatively affect a manager's performance evaluation.

Case Study 2

Recently, I participated in the assessment of the residential customer service operations of a major international telecommunications company. The customer service representatives (CSRs) might use up to seven different existing information systems in response to a customer request. The company had recently moved to a PC/Windows environment, and each system was accessed through a separate window.

In observing CSRs at several locations, I had noticed that they consistently opened and closed windows when they required information from a particular system. This particular morning, I was observing one of the exemplary performers. I happened to be there when he arrived and started up his system. I noticed that he opened all seven windows and arranged them carefully so that he could click on one and bring it forward, without closing the others. That simple procedure, done intuitively and without much planning, cut 15 to 20 minutes of nonvalue activity from his workday. That small amount of time may not seem significant, until multiplied by the company's 3,500 CSRs.

A way to improve the CSRs' performance was to redesign the primary interface screen so that they could access all systems from it, but that was a major, multiyear project. In the short term, I was able to disseminate this technique for "tiling" windows through a one-page job aid. The CSRs could immediately make their job easier and become more productive by arranging their windows in the same way that the exemplary performer did. The moral of the story: By assessing work performance and identifying an area in which it could be improved, the company saved 70,000 minutes of nonvalue activity per day—a savings that translated into better customer service and a more competitive position in the market.

Evaluating the Success of an Assessment

The success of an assessment depends on whether the major outputs of the job now meet the company's standards of quantity, quality, and cost and support the business goals being focused on by the client. If at the end of the project the outputs still do not meet standards, assess which interventions were inadequate and make changes where necessary.

Only through this rigorous assessment of human performance within the workplace can the analyst select appropriate interventions to help workers produce the major outputs needed to meet a company's business goals.

The Author

Paul Elliott, Ph.D., has served as a consultant to business, industry, and government in the area of training program development and evaluation and has provided instructional design support for numerous computer-based training projects. His expertise is in the analysis of human performance, the design of interventions that optimize human performance in support of business goals, and strategies for transitioning from training to performance models. Elliott assists organizations in performance analysis; instructional design; product and process launch support; the design of advanced training systems; and the design and implementation of integrated performance interventions. His clients include RWD Technologies, Inc., General Physics Corporation, General Motors, and the Baltimore Gas and Electric Company.

Elliott served on the board of directors of the American Society for Training & Development (ASTD) from 1993 to 1995 and was recognized as External Technical Trainer of the Year by that organization in 1994. As Executive-in-Residence for ASTD (1988–1995), Elliott's focus was on the paradigm shift from training to performance and its implications for ASTD, its membership, and the profession.

Elliott frequently presents at ASTD conferences. A recent presentation, entitled "Supporting Performance in the Work Setting," was delivered at ASTD's first Executive Forum. He has participated in the organization's Chief Training Officers Workshop for the past two years, focusing on performance models and the appropriate use of new training technologies. He has published multiple articles in journals, including an article entitled "Power-Charging People's Performance" in *Training and Development* magazine (ASTD, December 1996).

The contents of this chapter are based on Analyzing Human Performance, *by Joe Harless, ASTD, 1997.*

Case Study

Performance Analysts at Steelcase

by Michael Wykes

COMPANY NAME: Steelcase, Inc.

INDUSTRY TYPE: Manufacturing and service
(office furniture and environments)

ORGANIZATION PROFILE

ORGANIZATION SIZE:

16,000 employees. Headquarters in Grand Rapids, Michigan. Manufacturing facilities and sales offices in 15 countries. Products and services marketed and sold through a network of more than 675 independent dealerships throughout the world.

KEY PRODUCTS AND SERVICES:

The world's leading designer and manufacturer of office productivity furniture and services dedicated to helping people work more effectively. Products include work settings, systems, seating, desks, and files as well as work tools, services, and information to help improve office productivity.

ANNUAL SALES:

Approximately $2.5 billion.

DEPARTMENT NAME:

Corporate Learning and Development (CL&D).

DEPARTMENT SIZE:

60 people (approximately 15 percent devoted to performance consulting and analysis).

MISSION FOR DEPARTMENT:

"Through collaboration with our business partners we advance the performance of individuals and the Steelcase enterprise. We focus on business results by designing systems to generate, disseminate, and apply knowledge."

OVERARCHING CORPORATE HUMAN RESOURCES (HR) MISSION:

"To enhance performance of employees in support of Steelcase's business goals."

PRIMARY REASON FOR TRANSITION TO A PERFORMANCE FOCUS:

A need to increase corporate business performance in a high change environment.

Performance Analysts and the Integrated Human Resources Process at Steelcase

Organization: Performance analysts are part of the Performance Planning Services segment of Corporate Learning and Development (CL&D). CL&D makes up about one-third of Steelcase's total human resources function. CL&D has two functional tracks: Performance Planning Services (for performance consulting and analysis) and Learning Services (for administration, development, brokering, delivery, and evaluation of learning solutions). See figure 1 for the organizational structure of human resources.

Performance consultants work with human resources line directors to build relationships with internal clients, manage performance enhancement projects, and provide ongoing follow-up services. As part of this team, performance analysts provide measurement, assessment, gap identification, and evaluation expertise.

Process: Performance analysis at Steelcase is done in five phases: partnership, entry, assessment, implementation, and measurement (see figure 2).

A performance analyst's key involvement takes place during entry, assessment, and measurement (indicated by the gray areas on figure 2). Table 1 further defines the analyst's role in each phase.

Outputs from the process are used for performance planning and development and performance management applications such as succession planning, performance review systems, and staffing.

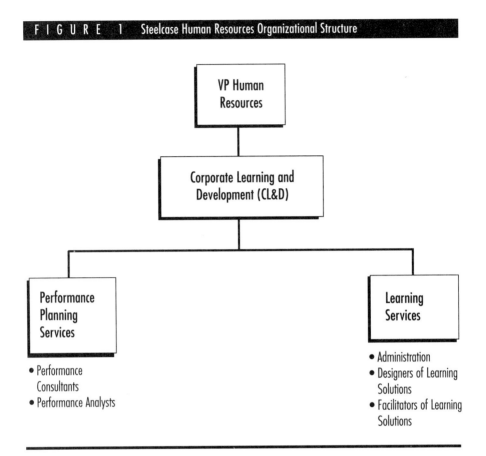

FIGURE 1 Steelcase Human Resources Organizational Structure

The Steelcase Case Study*

Background: Steelcase's products and services are marketed and sold through a network of independent dealerships throughout the world. In the United States, there are about 500 dealers. The Steelcase employees who call upon these dealers are market managers; these people are the direct link between the dealers and Steelcase. Dealers, in turn, sell to the end user or customer. Market managers report to area sales directors, or ASDs; there are a total of 23˙ ASDs within the United States. An area sales director has between 15 and 20 direct reports, the majority of whom are market managers.

Business need: As with many industries, the business of office furniture is rapidly changing. The focus is less on selling furniture and more on space management. This change in focus has tremendous implications for the dealers, the people who have the most direct contact with customers, and

---

*The situation described represents a typical medium-sized engagement. It is a composite that has been revised for proprietary reasons.

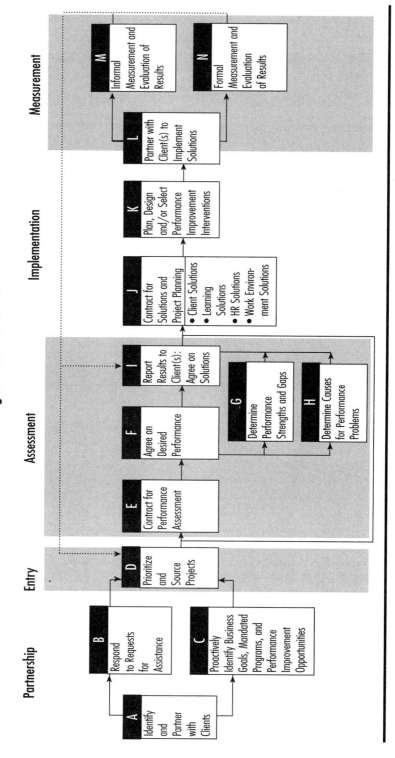

F I G U R E   2   Steelcase Performance Planning and Development

Steelcase Integrated HR Process Phases

T A B L E   1   The Role of Performance Analysts at Steelcase

The Role of Performance Analysts Within the Steelcase Integrated Human Resources Process

Phase and Outputs from Phase	Performance Analyst Responsibilities
Partnership: • Building internal client relationships • Identifying business needs • Responding to requests	• Involved in interviews, discussions, and information gathering sessions
Entry: • Qualifying situations into the next steps of the process for further analysis	• Involved in discussions to qualify situations for further analysis
Assessment: • Identifying performance models and competency models • Determining performance gaps and causes • Reporting results to clients • Gaining agreement on potential solutions	• Architect of the performance assessment contract • Designer, project manager, and performer for specific assessment and reporting activities (represents the bulk of the analyst's work)
Implementation: • Planning, designing, selecting, brokering, and delivering solutions	• Not actively involved in implementation (responsibility owned by the client, and actively supported by performance consultants)
Measurement: • Measuring and evaluating the business and performance impact of solutions • Reporting results to clients	• Architect of measurement and evaluation strategies and tactics

potential customers. Rather than sell furniture, they need to educate customers on the business benefits and returns for effective management of office space. Steelcase created financial models and approaches that could be used with customers to indicate the financial returns that are possible when space is efficiently and effectively utilized.

It was the requirement of both market managers and ASDs to call on dealers and educate them in these financial models, so dealers could, in turn, work with customers using these models. ASDs had an additional accountability: to coach and reinforce the market managers as they worked with dealers. Many resources were expended by Steelcase to research, build, and test the financial models. In addition, training programs were developed for ASDs and market managers to use in educating dealers in these models. The return to Steelcase and to the dealers would be greater sales to more customers.

The implementation of this space management process was measured in several ways, including the number of dealers who were adequately prepared to utilize the financial models. Therefore, number of dealer visits and number of training sessions conducted were key measures. In a meeting with the senior vice president of sales (the client for this business need), it was learned that the results for dealer development and installation of these financial models was inconsistent across the sales offices; installation was 20 percent below expectations overall. Financial results were 15 percent below expectations. It was determined that the ASDs were the key performers for success of this initiative because of the dual accountability they held: to both develop and coach market managers who report to them as well as to utilize the approaches with dealer accounts they called on personally. It was determined that a few ASDs were meeting their operational goals in this area; these were the exemplars. Therefore, it became important to answer the following questions:

1. What techniques and approaches are the exemplary ASDs using to accomplish the goals in this business area?

2. How does this performance compare with what all remaining ASDs are doing? What are the performance gaps?

3. What are the causes for performance gaps? What factors (learning and nonlearning) are contributing to the current disappointing operational results?

Based upon results from these assessments, actions would be taken to address the operational and performance gaps. As a result of these actions, the client anticipated that overall operational goal attainment would be increased by 15 percent and learning goal attainment increased by 10 percent within the next six months.

Assessment Phase—Building a Performance Model

I was called in by the performance consultant to help negotiate and finalize an assessment contract to document key learning and work environment gaps that affect performance related to the financial service program. That information would be used to help develop focused solutions.

83

The client chose to focus performance analysis on area sales directors because measures indicated clear differences among sales areas—even when local market conditions were factored out—indicating that current on-the-job performance of the area sales director behaviors was a key variable. The goal of this assessment was to define what area sales directors of high-performing areas did differently from more typical performers.

As the performance analyst, I worked with some performance consultants to conduct interviews with five high-performing (exemplary) area sales directors—about 15 percent of the total population—and their leaders (area sales vice presidents and the senior vice president of sales) to get the needed information. We asked directors to respond to questions such as the following:

• "Can you tell us what you do to ensure that all of your area's dealers are contacted within the time frame indicated on the implementation plan?" (one of the key result areas related to the financial service program)

• "How do you know you have been successful at doing that?" (to uncover key measures used)

• "What gets in the way or helps you achieve the results?" (to uncover barriers and enhancers to performance).

The interview information was combined with outside research, benchmark data, and selected focus group input from the staffs of high-performing area sales directors. The staff focus groups were informal discussions centering on the general question: "What does your area sales director do that helps you achieve your goals?" I then integrated information from all sources into a performance model (see table 2 on pages 86 and 87), which defined the best practices (behaviors) that high-performing area sales directors used to meet their results. The model also highlighted key measures and barriers and enhancers to performance.

Once the model was formed, it needed to be validated by the client, the area sales vice presidents (to whom the ASDs reported), and a sample of ASDs. Because these individuals were located throughout the United States, the validation process was done in a series of meetings and discussions (rather than by bringing all the people together into one location at the same time). The results from this validation process were both an approved performance model and buy-in from key managers in the sales organization.

Assessment Phase—Gap Analysis

I used the performance model information to design a survey (see table 3 on page 88) to compare behaviors of typical performers against the model and clarify the importance of each barrier and enhancer indicated (see table 3a on page 89). These surveys were sent to all area sales directors. They were asked to do two things: (1) rate the frequency and skill with which they performed each of the desired behaviors (table 3); and (2) indicate their extent of agreement or disagreement with work environment statements (derived from information uncovered during the interviews) (table 3a). For comparison purposes, area sales vice presidents also completed surveys on the area sales directors who reported to them. Feedback from direct reports to the area sales directors was not sought in this case due to time and resource constraints.

Results of the survey showed that one skill in particular—the ability to use financial models—stood out dramatically as the main learning need for typical area sales directors (see figure 3 on page 90). Other key skill needs included coaching skill and the skill to measure results from each dealer.

Respondents felt that a general lack of financial knowledge among salespeople, too many program introductions going on at once, and inconsistent sales tools and marketing materials impeded their ability to perform; whereas factors like excellent executive leadership, high salesperson motivation to learn, and well-designed office environments helped them perform. Together with the performance consultant, I reported these results to the client.

Implementation Phase

Design and implementation teams (client representatives, sales management, CL&D staff, and subject matter experts) used the results to design and deliver a six-part solution mix to address identified learning and work environment needs (see table 4 on page 91).

Learning solutions. The first three parts focused on the following interventions:

1. a personal coaching intervention, using financial experts, to help each area sales director use financial models better and also to be able to effectively coach salespeople on use of the models

2. a distributed learning intervention through development and distribution of a CD-ROM program, to increase the general financial knowledge and skills of the Steelcase and dealer salesforces

3. encouragement of informal learning teams among the field salesforces to leverage their high motivation to learn.

Work environment and management action solutions. The last three elements of the solution mix included the following:

1. a revision of the current financial modeling tools

2. a reemphasis of the financial and cost-saving aspects of the new program with dealers (this would enhance dealer interest in and motivation to use the new program)

3. Communication of senior management emphasis on the office space man-

TABLE 2 Sample Result from Performance Model (with Performance and Competency Language)

Result Areas	Competencies	Best Practices*	Measures and Criteria	Barriers and Enhancers
Clarify financial impact of new corporate programs with dealers. **Definition:** *Ensure that the newest corporate program's financial impact information is fully integrated with dealer business plans and activities.*	**Key competencies used for this result area:** • Economic Orientation • Communication	**Definition:** Ensure that the program's financial impact information is fully integrated with dealer business plans and activities.	**Key measures:** • Clear impact models • Dealer satisfaction	
	Economic Orientation: Analyze, integrate, and use financial data to accurately diagnose business realities, identify key issues, and develop strategies.	1. **Create clear examples to show how the program integrates with dealer business plans.** • Start with dealer business plan and indicate where and how the corporate program specifically affects it.	• Example documented	• Too many programs introduced at once (barrier) • Clear vision of program's power (enhancer)
		2. **Use knowledge of financial models to adjust analysis and presentation to specific dealer needs.** • Adjust depth of your analysis and model reporting to fit specific dealer needs.	• Model adjusted to specific dealer needs	• Low skill levels (barrier) • Motivated salespeople (enhancer)

*The full Performance Model contained approximately 50 best practices.

T A B L E 2 Sample Result from Performance Model (with Performance and Competency Language) (continued)

Result Areas	Competencies	Best Practices	Measures and Criteria	Barriers and Enhancers
	Communication: Use appropriate communication methods to work with business partners.	3. Hold regular, specific conversations to update dealers on status and measures. • Balance your communications with dealer needs.	• Meetings documented	• Many things competing for dealer's attention (barrier)

T A B L E 3	Sample Performance Gap Survey Derived from Performance Model

Assessment of Frequency and Skill

Performance Survey			
1 = Almost Never	4 = Frequently	1 = Little/No Skill	4 = Proficient Skill
2 = Very Infrequent	5 = Very Frequent	2 = Basic Skill	5 = Expert Skill
3 = Infrequent	6 = Almost Always	3 = Adequate Skill	

Frequency of Use	On-the-Job Activities	Current Skill Level
	Clarify financial impact of new corporate programs with dealers. **Definition:** Ensure that the newest corporate program's financial impact information is fully integrated with dealer business plans and activities.	
NA 1 2 3 4 5 6	1. Create clear examples to show how the program integrates with dealer business plans.	1 2 3 4 5
NA 1 2 3 4 5 6	2. Use knowledge of financial models to adjust analysis and presentation to specific dealer needs.	1 2 3 4 5
NA 1 2 3 4 5 6	3. Hold regular, specific conversations to update dealers on status and measures.	1 2 3 4 5
	Measure targets and status. **Definition:** Set clear measures and monitor performance against those measures on a regular basis.	
NA 1 2 3 4 5 6	1. Ensure that measures are clearly written in individual Steelcase salesperson's performance review objectives.	1 2 3 4 5
NA 1 2 3 4 5 6	2. Monitor Steelcase salesperson's use of the program's concept with dealers.	1 2 3 4 5
NA 1 2 3 4 5 6	3. Ensure that the program is part of each person's specific objectives: Example: Set objectives with five target accounts.	1 2 3 4 5
NA 1 2 3 4 5 6	4. Keep updated with training representative measurements by meeting with them at least weekly.	1 2 3 4 5
NA 1 2 3 4 5 6	5. Hold regular management meetings to measure where integration is or is not happening.	1 2 3 4 5
	Model behaviors related to the program. **Definition:** Personally perform exemplary behaviors.	
NA 1 2 3 4 5 6	1. Reinforce that this program is a priority and we need to continue to increase knowledge and skill.	1 2 3 4 5
NA 1 2 3 4 5 6	2. Personally use appropriate language related to the new way of thinking brought on by the program.	1 2 3 4 5

T A B L E 3 A	Sample Performance Gap Survey Derived from Performance Model (Barriers and Enhancers)

Instructions:
Statements relating to potential barriers or enhancers to performance are listed below. Please read each statement and indicate your level of agreement or disagreement with it.

Circle the number that corresponds to the **extent you agree or disagree** with each statement, using the following scale:

NA = does not apply to my situation

1	= Strongly Disagree	4	= Slightly Agree
2	= Somewhat Disagree	5	= Somewhat Agree
3	= Slightly Disagree	6	= Strongly Agree

		Barriers/Enhancers
NA	1 2 3 4 5 6	1. Program introductions are usually done in an evenly paced way, which makes it easy to adequately introduce each one to dealers.
NA	1 2 3 4 5 6	2. Expectations I get from management are consistent; they rarely change.
NA	1 2 3 4 5 6	3. We have consistent, clear measures in place for all initiatives.
NA	1 2 3 4 5 6	4. There is a clear corporate vision of how the newest initiative can positively affect dealer sales and profitability.
NA	1 2 3 4 5 6	5. There is a clear vision of what this program is capable of doing for dealers.
NA	1 2 3 4 5 6	6. Management provides visible support for this program.
NA	1 2 3 4 5 6	7. Our executive staff makes a visible attempt to lead by example.
NA	1 2 3 4 5 6	8. Our salespeople are positively motivated regarding this program.
NA	1 2 3 4 5 6	9. Dealer "share of mind" is usually easy to get because there are usually no competing priorities.
NA	1 2 3 4 5 6	10. Our salespeople are highly skilled in financial analysis and reporting.
NA	1 2 3 4 5 6	11. Financial analysis tools are easy to use.
NA	1 2 3 4 5 6	12. Tools are always ready on time (when a customer says "show me" we have the tools for the "next steps" readily available).

Note: All statements are written as positive statements; barriers are indicated by the extent an individual disagrees with a statement (usually rating it a 3 or less).

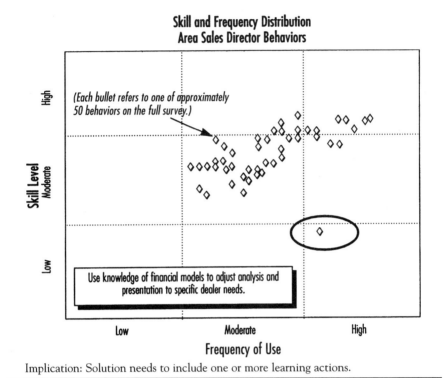

FIGURE 3 Sample of a Results Report from a Performance Gap Survey

Implication: Solution needs to include one or more learning actions.

agement initiatives that were being implemented by the field sales force.

Measurement Phase

After approximately six months of implementation, I worked with members of the client's team, the performance consultant, and the HR line director to measure and evaluate the relative changes in performance and operational goals identified at the beginning of the project. The evaluation was accomplished through a combination of documentation reviews, one-on-one interviews, focus group interviews, and surveys. Results of the evaluation were used to validate the solution interventions, uncover additional potential needs, and make adjustments.

Results Obtained

Operational measures increased by 10 percent. Sales offices reported more consistent performance among areas. The number of dealers who were effectively trained to use these financial models increased by nine percent. While a number of other factors could have contributed to these figures, the client believed strongly that the solution investments generated returns that far outweighed the costs, and he was convinced the revenue results would follow.

Area sales directors felt more able to use financial models and that this

T A B L E   4   Barriers and Actions Taken

Barrier	Action
1. Financial knowledge of ASDs and market managers is deficient for requirements of financial models.	• Provide personal coaching of ASDs, using financial experts. • Create and distribute a CD-ROM-based training program to use with Steelcase sales personnel and dealers. • Encourage formation of informal learning teams among the field salesforce to leverage their high motivation to learn from one another.
2. Tools created for use by ASDs and market managers are inconsistent (across markets) and not easy to use.	• Revise current financial modeling tools.
3. Motivation among dealers to want to use the financial models is inconsistent.	• Reemphasize the financial and cost-saving aspects of the new program with dealers.
4. Too many initiatives occur simultaneously, which makes it difficult to focus on any single initiative.	• Communicate senior management emphasis on the office space management initiatives that were being implemented by the field sales force.

skill contributed greatly to their ability to motivate and coach their sales-forces. They thought that the personal coaching, in particular, met their needs far better than a traditional learning intervention. Salespeople reported increased ability to use the newly enhanced tools with customers.

The client also indicated some additional benefits that arose from the performance analysis process:

● better management decision making: helping leaders focus expenditures on solutions that were designed to address work environment, management action, and learning needs as a total package—rather than spending (and potentially wasting) money on less-focused training solutions that may or may not work

- better clarification of what good performance looks like (and how it can be measured)

- increased general communication among leaders and staff members.

Conclusion

Performance analysis, done correctly, is a valuable tool to help leaders decide where to spend their performance improvement dollars to get the best return-on-investment. At Steelcase, performance analysts contribute to the continued success of this process by providing key analytical and evaluation expertise that works in tandem with the relationship building, consulting, and project management skills of performance consultants and human resources line directors.

Lessons Learned

Each performance analysis project usually has to be adjusted to suit situational needs. Regardless of size or relative complexity, most successful performance analysis projects tend to have the following characteristics:

- There is a client, and the analyst has direct access to that client.

- The client commits to "own" the solutions and to adhere to the process and follow-up.

- The project is the right size relative to available resources.

- There are clearly defined operational or performance problems (or at least the potential to uncover clearly defined gaps).

- The project has sufficient potential impact on the corporation (visibility, cost saving, revenue generation—it is not a "so what" project).

The Author

Michael Wykes has been a practitioner of human performance technology, human resource development, and instructional design for more than 20 years. After several years as a community schools director, Wykes joined Foremost Insurance Corporation in 1979 as a trainer and instructional designer. In 1982 he became the manager of sales training at Blue Cross & Blue Shield of Michigan, where he led the revision of sales training and leadership development systems. In 1986 he joined Steelcase, Inc.

As the principal performance analyst at Steelcase, Wykes provides performance analysis direction, coaching, and outputs for a team that offers performance planning and development services to Steelcase corporate audiences. The team—part of Steelcase's Corporate Learning and Development function—helps internal clients clarify operational and performance gaps and implement appropriate solution mixes.

Wykes has an M.A. in educational leadership and is completing a second M.A. in human resource development from Western Michigan University. He has developed and facilitated numerous successful performance and learning interventions and has presented at events sponsored by both the International Society for Performance Improvement and the American Society for Training & Development. He has published in journals such as *Human Resource Development Quarterly* and *HRD Review* and has received national recognition for computer-based learning systems from *CBT Directions* magazine.

5

Implementation Phase: Performance Improvement Interventions

by Harold Stolovitch and Erica Keeps

QUICK READ

● Interventions are selected after completion of a performance assessment.

● An intervention is a solution or solution component specifically designed to bridge the gap between actual and desired state. There are two types of interventions: learning and nonlearning.

● Within the nonlearning interventions, there are three categories:

—environmental, which are adjustments made within the work environment

—incentives/consequences/motivation, which are interventions taken to motivate desired performance

—job aids, which assist performers in using information that they do not have to learn or remember

● A primary role for a performance consultant is to assist clients in selecting the appropriate and necessary interventions to achieve the desired results. It is vital to consider multiple interventions; learning will rarely be sufficient.

● During the process of intervention selection, the performance consultant plays a central role in identifying and building the rationale for the entire set of interventions that will be required.

● During the phase of work in which interventions are designed, developed, and implemented, the performance consultant may become more of a facilitator and supporter of work; often the work itself is done by others.

● Performance consultants must build resource banks of suppliers (internal to the organization and external) to whom work can be brokered when required.

One of the most difficult requirements for the performance consultant is never to lose sight of the ultimate performance goals and best interests of the client. The transition from training to performance demands a resolve that organizations constantly test. Documentation and training are listed tasks that clients know must get done. The traditional assumption is that somehow these will result in competent performance. From the client perspective, there is a compulsion to check off the boxes showing task completion. The last thing they want is for someone to complicate their already overburdened lives with excessive demands for time and resources. Yet by focusing on performance, this is exactly what the performance consultant may appear to be doing.

Life is so much simpler when training is the default solution to address performance problems. Proposing a systemic view of performance and offering up an array of interventions to achieve desired results may be relevant— but also apparently complex. Suddenly, what seemed to be straightforward—training—has become far more burdensome. To the client, this presents unanticipated demands. Why are the rules of the game changing? Isn't this beyond the bounds? To the performance consultant, this creates strong professional challenges.

This chapter is designed to help meet these challenges in a systematic, structured, and professional manner. It focuses on three performance consulting activities: selection, design/development, and implementation of interventions. It presents an overview of the process that leads the performance consultant from assessment to implementation. It then describes a range of interventions, including those that extend beyond training, and provides both models and examples. The chapter adopts a *system* view of performance improvement and offers a "basket of solutions" approach to achieving optimal human performance results. Along the way, the chapter introduces a process and steps for developing performance improvement systems. It describes essential roles and responsibilities of the performance consultant during the selection, design/development, and implementation phase with particular emphasis on the consultant's brokering function. The chapter also includes tips for managing clients during this very active phase and describes client responsibilities. The chapter concludes with a review of key points and a transition to evaluation of interventions and monitoring of results.

FROM ASSESSMENT TO IMPLEMENTATION

As described in an earlier chapter, during the assessment phase the performance consultant diagnoses the situation and identifies performance improvement opportunities. The diagnosis naturally leads to prescription, design, development, and implementation of performance improvement interventions. By *intervention*, we refer to a solution or solution component specifically designed to bridge the gap between actual and desired states. It is a deliberately conceived act or system that is strategically applied to produce intended results.

Performance consultants play many roles: facilitator, diagnostician, designer, project manager, resource finder, and a host of others. They do this for the purpose of meeting client needs, sometimes despite obstacles that the organization, in its desire to meet short-term goals, strews in their path (insufficient budgets, lack of accessibility to experts or target populations, impossible timelines, impatience with process). Essentially, given the resources and constraints, the performance consultant's objective is to engineer within this environment the most effective and efficient performance improvement system possible. The term *engineer* suggests systematic application of scientific and organized knowledge to achieve practical results. It implies skillful, methodical, and artful management of information and resources to build solutions that are based on solid, data-based foundations rather than on tradition, enthusiasm, or intuition.

Engineers work with both conceptual and process models to create and build their solutions. So, too, does the performance consultant. Figure 1 presents the Engineering Effective Performance Model that has been applied to many organizations and projects (Stolovitch and Keeps, 1997). The model consists of 10 major steps, the first five of which are related to the assessment phase. The remaining five deal with selection; design and development; implementation; and finally, monitoring and maintenance of performance interventions. What follows is a brief explanation of the model. The purpose for presenting this here is to place all of the performance consultant's engineering activities into a coherent flow and system. A secondary purpose is to clearly show the relationship of this chapter's content (selection, design/development, and implementation) to that of the earlier one dealing with the assessment phase and a subsequent one that focuses on the measurement phase.

Performance consultants operate to help organizations meet business requirements. These are generated as a response to the external environment with its opportunities, challenges, resources, regulations, and other characteristics. Consequently, the first step in engineering effective performance is to identify what these business requirements are. The performance consultant does this either by proactively scanning the organization or by

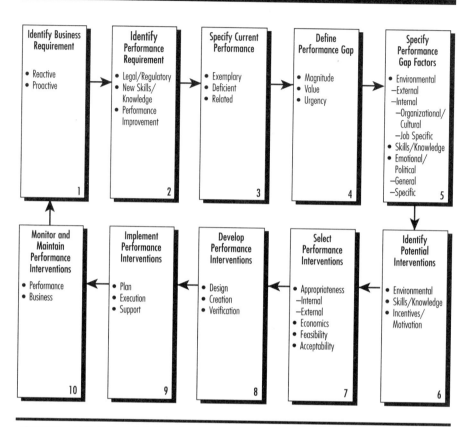

FIGURE 1   Engineering Effective Performance Model

Identify Business Requirement	Identify Performance Requirement	Specify Current Performance	Define Performance Gap	Specify Performance Gap Factors
• Reactive • Proactive	• Legal/Regulatory • New Skills/ Knowledge • Performance Improvement	• Exemplary • Deficient • Related	• Magnitude • Value • Urgency	• Environmental —External —Internal —Organizational/ Cultural —Job Specific • Skills/Knowledge • Emotional/ Political —General —Specific
1	**2**	**3**	**4**	**5**

Monitor and Maintain Performance Interventions	Implement Performance Interventions	Develop Performance Interventions	Select Performance Interventions	Identify Potential Interventions
• Performance • Business	• Plan • Execution • Support	• Design • Creation • Verification	• Appropriateness —Internal —External • Economics • Feasibility • Acceptability	• Environmental • Skills/Knowledge • Incentives/ Motivation
10	**9**	**8**	**7**	**6**

©1997 Harold D. Stolovitch & Erica J. Keeps

reactively receiving requests. By far the most common, although not necessarily desirable, scenario is the latter. In organizations transitioning from training to a performance orientation, the usual request is for some sort of learning event. If a department or service carries in its name "training," "education," or "learning," it is not surprising that the expectation is for it to produce some type of educational intervention. Regardless of title or expectation, the major activity in this step is to document the request in a collaborative and open manner. This allows the performance consultant, in subsequent assessment steps, to analyze and determine the true nature of the requirement.

The remaining assessment steps lead to discovery of whether the requirement is to meet regulatory or other mandated conditions; new system demands or performance improvement expectations; current performance levels, if relevant; size, urgency, and value of the gap between current and desired states; and factors affecting the performance gap whether environmental, skills/knowledge, or emotional/political. Taken together, the five major steps of the assessment phase form a process, the outcome of which is a series of findings and conclusions. These offer a rich portrait of the opportunity for improved human performance. When conducted systematically, the result of the assessment phase naturally points to potential performance interventions.

Solution selection, which includes the next two steps in the model, is also a process with its own specific outcomes. Based on the conclusions of the assessment phase, the performance consultant first draws up a list of potential interventions that fall into three main categories: environmental, skills/knowledge, and incentives/motivation. These mirror the performance gap factors identified during assessment.

Because many interventions may be possible, the selection process requires further refinement. The performance consultant then examines potential interventions for *appropriateness* (Will it help close the gap internally and smoothly integrate with other departmental activities and conditions?), *economics* (Can we afford it?), *feasibility* (Can it be done within constraints?), and *acceptability* (Will the client organization and target groups accept/implement the intervention?). Through collaborative analysis and discussion with the client group, the performance consultant produces recommendations for an integrated basket of interventions that will lead to desired performance results.

Once recommendations are approved, the next step in the Engineering Effective Performance Model is to develop each of the interventions. The development process can be brief or lengthy, depending on the type of intervention. Each intervention may also require a separate and distinct development process. For example, the creation of a new compensation system is considerably different from the creation of a job aid. Commonalities exist, however, of which the performance consultant should be aware. These are treated later in this chapter.

The final two steps of the model include implementation, chronologically divided into planning, execution, and support; and monitoring/maintenance, which involves evaluation, measurement, fine-tuning, and updating. All combined, the model outlines the steps of systematic human performance improvement. Table 1 presents the processes and outcomes embedded in the model.

With the complete process illustrated first, we will focus in this chapter on steps six through nine. First, however, we will turn our attention to the range of interventions for achieving desired performance.

LEARNING AND NONLEARNING INTERVENTIONS

Earlier, we defined the term intervention as "a solution or solution component specifically designed to bridge the gap between actual and desired states." Concretely, an intervention is anything the performance consultant

T A B L E 1	Steps, Processes, and Outcomes in Engineering Effective Performance	
Steps	**Processes**	**Outcomes**
1 to 5	Assessment	Findings
6 and 7	Intervention selection	Recommendations
8	Design and development	Interventions
9	Implementation	Performance improvement
10	Monitoring and maintenance	Efficiency and effectiveness

can conceive of that is currently absent and whose presence will result in performance improvement. Table 2 contains some examples to help illustrate the concept.

In each case, something is done to intervene in the current situation that leads to a favorable change in results. Please note that the final example in table 2 is different from the others. In this instance, the intervention is not an addition but rather an elimination of something (interfering tasks). Removal of obstacles is an excellent and often inexpensive means for improving performance.

It is essential for the performance consultant to keep in mind that a wide range of performance interventions is available. Information gathered during the assessment phase is the key to identifying appropriate interventions. Only when the data clearly indicate lack of skills and knowledge are learning interventions appropriate.

Learning Interventions

These are the range of actions or events designed to help people acquire new skills and knowledge. Learning is a change in cognitive structures that results in the potential for behavior change (Gagne, 1985; Gagne, Yekovich, and Yekovich, 1993; Stolovitch and Yapi, 1997). It takes place within the individual. There are many forms of learning interventions from which a performance consultant may select to facilitate such an internal change. Table 3 offers a continuum of these.

Current State	**Intervention**	**Improved Performance**
Lagging sales	Increased commission	Soaring sales
High error rates	Feedback on error rates with comparisons across work teams	Low error rates
Waiting customers	Increased number of customer service representatives	No waiting customers
Inefficient use of new software	Training and job aids	Efficient use of software
Late reports	Removal of interfering tasks	Reports on time

T A B L E   2   Examples of Performance Improvement Interventions

This list represents traditional training interventions. Organizations, once they reach a critical size for their industry, generally realize that there are benefits to spending time and money on training. Their reasoning is that employees must continue to learn in order to keep up with changes. This is especially true of knowledge-based enterprises. As the organizations grow, so do their training systems. Over time these take on a life force of their own, promoting learning interventions not only as a benefit to the company but also for their own survival. Eventually, the learning services they offer become expected activities. For client groups seeking to change work processes, restructure, launch new products and services, meet regulatory requirements, improve performance, or move into new markets, training also becomes a natural intervention of choice. Training has turned into the default selection for improving human performance. Even the harsh economic contractions and downsizings of the early 1990s scarcely affected training budgets. Over the past five years, training expenditures in corporate America have surged 21.5 percent, or from $48.2 billion to more than $58.6 billion. (*Training*, 1993 to 1997).

All learning interventions have as their prime mission the generation of new skills and knowledge. The assumption is that these will lead to improved performance. Numerous studies (Baldwin and Ford, 1988; Broad

T A B L E 3 Continuum of Learning Interventions

Learning Interventions	Description
Natural experience	The individual is placed in the natural environment and learns through real-life, trial and error events. This might also be labeled life experience.
Experiential learning	As above, but the individual also participates in structured debriefing sessions to reflect on experiences and draw conclusions.
On-the-job training	The individual assumes an apprenticeship role while working in an operational setting. Guidance on how to perform is provided by co-workers and supervisors as needed.
Structured on-the-job training	As above, except that the operating work environment has been systematically organized for learning. The individual has a learning plan and acquires knowledge and skills with assistance from trained lead workers, sometimes called structured-on-the-job trainers.
Simulation	The individual performs as he or she would in real life, but, the setting is a re-creation (low or high fidelity) of the natural environment.
Role play	The individual assumes the role of another or of himself or herself in a different setting and acts out feelings, reactions, responses to various scenarios.

(cont'd. on page 103)   *(cont'd. on page 103)*

TABLE 3 Continuum of Learning Interventions *(continued)*	
Learning Interventions	**Description**
Laboratory training	Similar to simulation training except that the laboratory does not necessarily re-create the work environment. The individual can practice a broad range of work activities not necessarily in normal job sequence.
Classroom training (live or virtual)	The individual acquires skills and knowledge through guidance from an instructor in a formal class setting removed from the workplace.
Self-study	The individual acquires skills and knowledge through self-learning, guided by structured materials ranging from print to highly sophisticated multimedia systems.

& Newstrom, 1992; Ford & Weissbein, 1997) suggest the contrary. They point out that little more than 10 to 20 percent of training transfers to the job. The reasons for this are many: poor selection of trainees, insufficient or no preparation of trainees for the learning event, no explicit expectations from supervisors on application of training to the job, no incentives to apply learning, lack of support posttraining, and many more (for example, Stolovitch & Maurice, in press). This suggests that learning interventions, while apparently appropriate for building skills and knowledge, do not necessarily result in significant on-the-job application and performance change.

In addition, research (for example, Stolovitch and Keeps, 1992) suggests that while learning plays a role in improving performance related to skills and knowledge, a host of other factors strongly influence how people perform in the workplace. A prudent performance consultant must carefully analyze assessment findings before selecting appropriate interventions. It is likely that learning interventions alone will not solve complex performance problems.

The consequences of the above points for the performance consultant are great. Clients approach the training group for "training" interventions. Their expectation is that some form of learning event will be produced and will result in desired performance. Challenges for the performance consultant include accounting for training transfer as well as the other factors identified in the assessment phase. Training may be necessary, but it is rarely sufficient. To achieve success requires implementation of other, nonlearning interventions.

Nonlearning Interventions

These are actions or events designed to change conditions that facilitate attainment of desired performance. Anything that removes an obstacle or adds a facilitative element to the performance system qualifies as a nonlearning intervention. The possibilities are limitless. However we can set some boundaries around them. Essentially nonlearning interventions fall into three major categories: job aids, environmental, and incentive/consequences/motivation.

Job aids: Job aids are external memories. They contain information that the individual does not have to learn and remember. Much has been written about job aids (Harless, 1981; Elliott, in press; Rossett and Gautier, 1991). They may come in the form of a task list, an algorithm, a cookbook recipe, a decision table, or a sophisticated electronic performance support tool (Gery, 1991, 1995; Stone and Villachica, in press). As learning is not always easy or efficient, job aids can guide the individual to perform an operation rapidly and without error. The efficiency of the job aid resides in the rapidity and accuracy with which a task can be performed. A simple example illustrates this.

The public transit authority of a large city employs former bus and subway operators to sell monthly passes to public transit users. This is to help the operators work until pensionable age. Most have been forced to give up their bus or subway driving for health reasons (sight, heart condition, diabetes).

Each month, riders purchase monthly passes in subway stations to obtain a highly favorable rate. Let us say an adult pass costs $42, a child's $26, and a senior citizen's also $26. A user may request two adult, one senior, and three child passes. The seller must total the amount rapidly (there are long lines early in the month) and accurately. Error rates are high (5 percent) and transactions take too long. At the moment, the transit authority has no funds for an automated system. Trials with calculators were not successful; sellers were slow and made many entry errors.

The transit authority decided to train the pass sellers on rapid math. Trials still showed a high error rate although transaction speed improved slightly. While considering various training options, the performance consultant to the team devised a simple job aid shown in figure 2.

F I G U R E   2   Monthly Public Transit Pass Job Aid

Number of Adult Passes

		0	1	2	3	4	5	6	7	8
Number	0		42	84	126	168	210	252	294	336
of	1	26	66	110	152	194	236	278	360	362
Special	2	52	94	136	178	220	262	304	346	388
Passes	3	78	120	162	204	246	288	330	372	414
	4	104	146	188	230	272	314	356	398	440

With this, the seller listens to the request, "two adults, one senior, three children," and groups the information as "two adults, four specials." Locating the intersection of the "2" column and the "4" row, the seller requests $188. A large laminated card and some practice resulted in high acceptance by sellers, high speed (less than one-fourth the previous time) and a virtual "0" error rate.

The limits of this chapter do not permit detailed explanation of how to develop job aids or electronic performance support tools. The references cited earlier, however, contain guidelines and examples for creating these.

Environmental: This category of nonlearning interventions is extremely large. It encompasses all the adjustments one can make within the work environment, either by eliminating barriers that prevent performance or increasing support mechanisms for obtaining and enhancing desired accomplishments. Table 4 presents a convenient means for classifying environmental interventions. It includes the general class of intervention, an explanation, and examples of specific interventions.

Incentives/consequences/motivation: Incentives are stimuli the environment provides that, when perceived as meaningful and valued, increase motivation to perform. Somewhat akin to incentives, consequences occur after performance. A promised commission on a sale is an incentive; receipt of the commission for a sale is a consequence. A fine for speeding is also a consequence (a negative one) that may dampen motivation to speed.

Motivation is an internal response to outside events. According to cognitive psychologists (for example, Clark, in press), motivation is greatly influenced by two primary factors: *value* (how highly a person values the desired performance) and *confidence* (how strongly a person believes he or she will be successful). The greater the value one attributes to performance success, the greater the motivation. Confidence, however, must be bal-

T A B L E 4 Types of Environmental Interventions

Type of Intervention	Explanation	Specific Intervention Examples
Provision of information	Lack of clarity of performance expectations and insufficient feedback on how one is performing according to expectations combine to form the number one cause of performance deficiencies in the workplace. Other information factors that decrease performance are lack of access to required information; unclear or unavailable policies or procedures; inaccurate and out-of-date information; lack of communication about products, events, decisions.	• Create standards for doing the job. • Harmonize conflicting standards. • Set unambiguous performance expectations. • Provide current catalogs and price lists. • Provide timely and specific information to the individuals on how they are performing. • Develop a company policy on ethical practices.
Provision of resources	Without sufficient resources, including material and human, the individual cannot perform as expected.	• Provide appropriate tools and equipment to perform the job as expected. • Provide sufficient time for task completion. • Provide access to supervisors, specialists, and resource personnel. • Create workable, efficient procedures.
Redesign of the work environment	Inadequate organizational structure, communications systems, work processes, and physical/administrative infrastructures create delays and inhibit optimal performance.	• Break down barriers between departments to increase cooperative, mutually beneficial decision making and resource sharing. • Introduce e-mail. • Redesign work flow. • Eliminate bureaucratic procedures. • Introduce better lighting and sound buffers to decrease ambient noise levels. • Create networks to share files and peripherals.

(cont'd)

T A B L E 4 Types of Environmental Interventions (continued)

Elimination of task interferences	The work environment creates conflicting priorities or requires execution of tasks that may decrease performance on essential tasks. As an example, filling out sales and contact reports may decrease time with customers and, hence, sales.	• Create weekly work priority sheets with a procedure and verification/approval process. • Assign tasks to individuals most capable and desirous of performing these and free up others to focus on other required tasks. • Audit tasks being performed and eliminate or reassign nonessential ones. • Set policies that reward accomplishment of priority tasks. • Increase support personnel. • Automate routine tasks. • Remove trivial tasks from essential workers.
Selection	Persons who do not have essential prerequisite skills and knowledge or appropriate characteristics and talents to perform drain the organization's resources. Training may improve performance somewhat but will rarely achieve desired results. The negative consequences to the individual, work colleagues, and customers can be dramatic and costly when selection is inappropriate.	• Establish competency and characteristics requirements for the job along with performance-based measures for selection. • Create a performance-based assessment center. • Set clear performance goals (both behavior and accomplishments) with set checkpoints during a specified trial period. • Target recruitment to the widest range of high-probability sources for appropriate candidates. • Train selection committee members on performance-based selection methods and provide clear examples of poor selection.
Provision of support	Performance, especially during early stages of acquisition, requires encouragement, monitoring, and support. Research shows that when early performance attempts fail, individuals soon return to previous patterns of behavior.	• Create initial meetings that cooperatively define expectations. • Encourage and reward initial performance attempts. • Build regular monitoring and support systems that include coaching. • Create a performance tracking system with specific supervisor intervention menus. • Recognize and publicize accomplishments. • Build in regular meetings to review performance and provide support. • Provide adequate resources to demonstrate support.

anced. Under- or overconfidence decreases motivation. Motivation, therefore, is the result of perceiving a performance as having high value while posing a sufficient degree of challenge.

Table 5 presents incentives/consequences/motivation as two classes of performance interventions with explanations and specific intervention examples.

What emerges from the foregoing discussion and descriptions is that many forms of interventions are available to the performance consultant. Improving human performance seldom emerges from a single intervention. Performance systems are complex. It is only natural then, that means for improving performance will require an array of learning and nonlearning interventions.

SELECTING PERFORMANCE INTERVENTIONS

The assessment phase resulted in a series of findings: desired state, actual state, feelings of all parties and stakeholders involved, causes, and perhaps some initial thoughts about solutions. How do we translate findings into recommendations? A performance consultant, operating within a training to performance transition context, must address three important issues when the initial client expectation is for training.

First, there is a strong likelihood that training will be insufficient (if it is even necessary) to achieve desired results. This means that the performance consultant will have to prepare the client early in the process for this eventuality. Secondly, there are a limitless number of performance intervention possibilities. The initial set of selected interventions may be large and varied, with many falling far outside the normal purview of the training community. If clients are unprepared for this, they may be shocked, uncomfortable, and resistant to recommendations. Members of the performance department itself also have to deal with what may be "uncomfortable" and certainly unfamiliar selections. In the past, discomfort in the training group may have arisen from lack of familiarity with a training strategy (case study method, listening teams), medium (CD-ROM, high fidelity simulator), or delivery system (bi-directional television, internet). Now the stakes have risen much higher with many of the potentially relevant interventions clearly outside the traditional training department's sphere. In reality, there is little to fear as we will see when we later describe the roles and responsibilities of the performance consultant.

The third issue is one that should bring a sigh of relief to performance consultants. Following the 80/20 rule, the majority of interventions that apply to most performance improvement cases is small in number. Although performance improvement problems or opportunities come in many varieties, the range of interventions generally required to close the

T A B L E   5   Types of Incentive/Consequence/Motivation Interventions

Type of Implementation	Explanation	Specific Intervention Examples
Provision of incentives/ consequences	People perform well when they see what is in it for them as well as for the organization. Clear, meaningful, equitable rewards for performance and consequences for lack of performance result in improved performance. Incentives may be both monetary and non-monetary. It is essential that the incentive/consequence system be seen as fair—no rewards for inadequate performers.	• Pay for performance system • Team-based pay • Bonuses for outstanding achievements • Realignment of commissions on sales • Career enhancement opportunities • Recognition for superior performance • Enhanced status system (pins, titles) • Positive reports placed in file • Time off • Additional resources provided
Enhancement of motivation	People perform better when "motivated." Operationally, this means that they value what they do, feel secure in their work, yet are challenged by it and believe that with reasonable effort they can achieve success.	• Value of required performance shown through meaningful explanation of impact • Links established between performance and personal growth • Value of performance tied to incentives/consequences • Unnecessary threats to job security eliminated • Desired performance made challenging, yet attainable • Meaningful "contests" that stimulate self-challenges • Impact of performance clear • Support systems that build confidence

gap is relatively narrow. This means that over time, the ability to identify appropriate interventions rapidly and accurately improves as do the skills to explain and "sell" them.

As described in the Engineering Effective Performance Model introduced earlier in the chapter, the initial activity in the solution selection process is to identify potential interventions (step six in the model). After examining the findings from the assessment phase, the performance consultant develops a list of these interventions, which correspond to the performance gap factors identified.

The job aid in table 6 assists in matching the list of findings with the appropriate intervention types. While not exhaustive, it covers most performance improvement situations. The performance consultant can always add other causes of performance deficiencies discovered during the assessment phase. Suitable matching interventions are usually obvious.

As stated earlier, the job aid covers a significant number of causes and interventions drawn from numerous performance improvement cases. The following simple example illustrates its use.

Harry's Diner

Harry is your brother-in-law. He owns a diner in an industrial park. His major trade is breakfast and lunch, with some traffic flow-through during the morning and afternoon (coffee, toast, sweet rolls). Harry has been lucky in that there hasn't been much competition. But rumor has it that some fast-food franchises are eyeing the area. Harry is worried. If he doesn't keep his customers satisfied, he could lose them to a glitzy, nationally known fast-food place. So Harry has been analyzing his operations, listening to customers, and watching for problems.

One glaring problem is the toast. The short-order cooks prepare the main parts of the meals. The servers make the toast. Harry buys his bread from an Italian bakery. He has an "exclusive" with them in his area. The bread arrives in full loaves (raisin, raisin-walnut, seven-grain, ciabatta). Servers slice the bread, place the slices on the conveyer toaster (heated by gas flames for a toastier flavor), and pick the toast up when the slices drop into the receiving pan.

When the toast is done right, customers love it. However, customers often send toast back (10 to 15 percent of the time) because the slices are too thick, too thin, too dark, too light, too cold, or uneven. Complaints and rejections increase during peak periods. Rejected toast holds up orders; slows down service; makes customers late; creates tensions; increases costs; waste, and rework; and is a major sore spot because Harry's toast is a big draw for the diner.

Harry's Diner experiences a 40 percent annual turnover in serving staff. So training is an important issue. Training is done on the job. A new server is teamed with an experienced one. The new server shadows, assists, and after two to three days, is given a section. Servers have other tasks besides making toast. They

T A B L E   6   Performance Intervention Selection

Based on the data collected during the assessment phase, identify relevant performance interventions:

If performers. . .	Consider. . .
Lack skills or knowledge essential for the job	Training ☐
Lack job relevant skills or knowledge but may refer to readily accessible information, procedures, decision tables, or information systems to perform at desired levels	Job Aids ☐
Lack clear performance expectations	Setting performance expectations ☐
Lack unambiguous performance standards	Setting performance standards ☐
Lack timely information on how well they are performing	Feedback systems ☐
Lack appropriate prerequisite skills, knowledge, background, or personal characteristics to rapidly meet performance levels	Selection ☐
Face interferences that discourage or prevent desired performance	Elimination of task interferences ☐
Have to work outside the accepted way the job has been structured to achieve desired performance levels	Job redesign ☐
Face organizational obstacles (structural, communications, climate, administrative, infrastructural) that inhibit performance	Organizational redesign ☐

(cont'd. on page 112) *(cont'd.on page 112)*

T A B L E 6 Performance Intervention Selection *(continued)*	
If performers. . .	**Consider. . .**
Face physical obstacles that inhibit performance	Environmental redesign ☐
Work with inefficient processes that inhibit desired performance	Process redesign ☐
Are not meaningfully rewarded or are even punished for desired performance or do not perceive the reward system as fair and equitable	Incentives/Consequences ☐
Do not value the desired performance, do not feel confident they can perform, or do not feel challenged to perform	Motivation systems ☐
Lack required tools, materials, supplies, or support systems	Provisions of resources ☐
Lack access to information necessary to perform	Provision of information ☐
Are not encouraged or supported by supervisors or management	Increased management support ☐
Are not supported by appropriate specialists	Increased technical support ☐

serve, make coffee, fill salt-and-pepper shakers, clean ketchup bottles, check bathrooms, prepare bills, and assist busboys in table cleanups and setups. They are also supposed to chat with the customers to build relationships and encourage repeat business.

Harry feels that the toast issue is a really serious one and that servers need better training in making toast than they are currently getting. He has asked you to develop this training for him.

In the Harry's Diner case, the assessment phase findings showed that personnel knew how to slice and toast appropriately. Job pressures, especially at peak periods, were the primary causes of rejected toast along with insufficient resources (toasters) and crowding around the toaster area. Sometimes, only by asking a short-order cook or a colleague to help, could orders be filled on time. The job aid helps to identify five interventions likely to assist Harry with his performance problem. (See table 7.) Please note that training is not among them.

A Basket of Solutions

The Harry's Diner case, while not corporate, illustrates the systemic nature of performance problem solving. Rarely is a single intervention sufficient to solve even mildly complex problems such as Harry's. The job aid in table 6 helps identify potentially suitable interventions. However, system constraints such as resources, time, budget, and personnel generally do not permit implementation of all selected interventions. The performance consultant, in collaboration with the client, must narrow these down to a workable few. The result is a basket of solutions appropriate for implementation.

The performance consultant must be a *system* thinker. This means that he or she views performance improvement as the outcome of a number of interrelated elements operating within a specific context. Just as an automobile engine is a system comprised of spark plugs, pistons, fuel injection, cylinders, and other elements all operating interrelatedly to power the car, so too the performance interventions function together within the work context to produce improved performance. There must be harmony and alignment among all elements to achieve desired results. In the performance system, the following five criteria apply both for selecting the final basket of solutions and for verifying alignment:

1. **Appropriateness.** The intervention will help close the gap. It responds perfectly to a major cause for not achieving intended results and has a high probability of leading to desired outcomes.

2. **Economics.** The budget permits us to do this. The cost of the intervention is less than the cost of the performance problem.

3. **Feasibility.** The capability, resources, and timelines make this intervention possible.

4. **Organizational acceptability.** This is an intervention that is culturally acceptable and will not be rejected because of its nature or characteristics.

5. **Individual performer acceptability.** This is an intervention that the targeted performer group can live with and will not reject.

Using a 0 to 4 scale, the performance consultant and representatives of the client group can assess each of the potential interventions, total the

T A B L E   7   Harry's Diner Performance Intervention Selection

Based on the data collected during the assessment phase, identify relevant performance interventions

If performers. . .	Consider. . .	
Lack skills or knowledge essential for the job	Training	☐
Lack job relevant skills or knowledge but may refer to readily accessible information, procedures, decision tables, or information systems to perform at desired levels	Job aids	☐
Lack clear performance expectations	Setting performance expectations	☐
Lack unambiguous performance standards	Setting performance standards	☐
Lack timely information on how well they are performing	Feedback systems	☐
Lack appropriate prerequisite skills, knowledge, background, or personal characteristics to rapidly meet performance levels	Selection	☐
Face interferences that discourage or prevent desired performance	Elimination of task interferences	☑
Have to work outside the accepted way the job has been structured to achieve desired performance levels	Job redesign	☑
Face organizational obstacles (structural, communications, climate, administrative, infrastructural) that inhibit performance	Organizational redesign	☐

(cont'd. on page 115)   *(cont'd. on page 115)*

T A B L E   7   Harry's Diner Performance Intervention Selection *(continued)*

If performers. . .	Consider. . .	
Face physical obstacles that inhibit performance	Environmental redesign	☑
Work with inefficient processes that inhibit desired performance	Process redesign	☑
Are not meaningfully rewarded or are even punished for desired performance or do not perceive the reward system as fair and equitable	Incentives/Consequences	☐
Do not value the desired performance, do not feel confident they can perform, or do not feel challenged to perform	Motivation systems	☐
Lack required tools, materials, supplies, or support systems	Provisions of resources	☑
Lack access to information necessary to perform	Provision of information	☐
Are not encouraged or supported by supervisors or management	Increased management support	☐
Are not supported by appropriate specialists	Increased technical support	☐

scores, and select the highest scoring interventions. Table 8 shows how the ratings are done.

Using the Harry's Diner case, table 9 illustrates what a completed rating table would look like.

The retained interventions can now be translated into the specific performance intervention solutions found in table 10. The Harry's Diner example also illustrates how the retained interventions smoothly fit together to form an integrated basket of solutions.

T A B L E 8	Performance Intervention Rating

- List all selected performance interventions.

- Rate each intervention for each criterion using the scale

   4 = Excellent fit
   3 = Good fit
   2 = Could fit with some difficulty
   1 = Very poor fit
   0 = Unacceptable

- Eliminate any intervention that contains even one "0."

- Total scores for all criteria and rank, with rank of "1" allocated to the intervention with the highest total score.

- Select the combination of highest ranking interventions. Retain the most efficient (time/resources) combination given the total available budget.

Intervention	Appropri- ateness	Econ- omics	Feasi- bility	Org. Accept- ability	Indiv. Accept- ability	Total	Rank	Retain (✓)

DESIGNING AND DEVELOPING PERFORMANCE IMPROVEMENT SYSTEMS

The most important point to keep in mind about designing and developing performance improvement systems is that the performance department does not have to create all the interventions. Performance consultants are responsible for helping to select systematically the appropriate combination of interventions. Subsequent roles will vary based on the nature of the interventions. The next section of this chapter elaborates on roles and responsibilities. Suffice it to say here that design and development should be done by qualified persons and teams with the performance consultant facilitating and monitoring the process. As an example, selection and purchase of new toasters are obviously not areas of performance consultant expertise. Harry can do a better job.

TABLE 9 Performance Intervention Rating: Harry's Diner

Intervention	Appropri-ateness	Econ-omics	Feasi-bility	Org. Accept-ability	Indiv. Accept-ability	Total	Rank	Retain (✓)
Elimination of task interferences	4	2	3	3	4	16	3	✓
Job redesign	4	2	2	3	4	15	4	✓
Environmental redesign	2	0	1	0	3	6	5	
Process redesign	4	3	3	4	4	18	2	✓
Provision of resources	4	4	4	4	4	20	1	✓

TABLE 10 Performance Intervention Solutions

Type of Intervention	Specific Intervention
Provision of resources	Purchase additional toaster.
Process redesign	Slice breads for toasting prior to peak demands.
Elimination of task interferences	Eliminate interfering server tasks.
Job redesign	Assign a dedicated person to slice bread during peak periods to alleviate demands on servers.

To state that there are different design/development processes for different interventions is an oversimplification. For example, environmental redesign and process reengineering have well-established models and processes for producing their outputs. These may differ dramatically in approach and detail. However, some overall models and sets of tools are necessary for performance consultants to monitor or help manage and coordinate the creation of all retained interventions. The authors of this chapter have found the systems approach to be a helpful conceptual framework for building a performance system. Essentially, it breaks into five basic components as shown in figure 3.

Analyze. Each intervention requires a careful reexamination of the assessment and selection data. Based on this review, the development team must analyze the specifics of the situation, especially desired performance outcomes, time, budget, resources, and constraints, and integrate these with other performance improvement system components.

Design. Based on the analysis outputs, the development team produces design specifications that lay out all the components of each proposed intervention. Appropriateness, economics, feasibility, and acceptability once more become critical criteria for ensuring that the design will work within the organizational context. What emerges are detailed blueprints for the interventions along with a rationale and, where appropriate, proposed verification/test points.

Develop. In this phase, design blueprints are converted into prototype interventions that can be verified by experts for accuracy and technical feasibility as well as tried out by intended performers to assess whether or not they will work. Sometimes, microcosms of the interventions (a module or a simulation) are built to derive feedback on usability and to produce "feedforward" for creation of new components.

Evaluate. At each step, the performance consultant, client organization, and appropriate internal specialists verify to ensure that the performance goals are being met. Once more, the criteria of appropriateness, economics, feasibility, and acceptability come into play. To these, compatibility with other initiatives or interventions is added. In the development phase, eval-

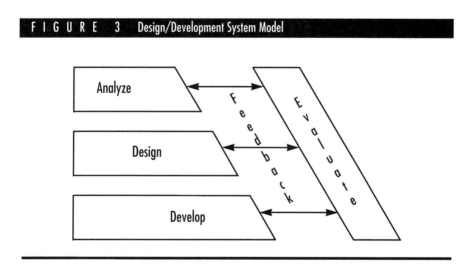

FIGURE 3   Design/Development System Model

uation includes actual tryout testing of increasingly more complete versions of each intervention.

Feedback. Based on evaluation findings, information is fed back to the development team for purposes of revision.

Two tools that performance consultants may find useful to apply during design and development of interventions are some form of "timelining" instrument and what is familiarly called a RASCI chart. The timeline tool most often used in performance consulting is the familiar GANTT chart. Other more detailed and refined systems exist for planning and monitoring development (PERT, Critical Path Method). For most performance improvement projects, however, the authors have found the GANTT chart with its list of activities and projected start and end dates to be a usable tool that communicates well to clients and work teams. An example of one for the Harry's Diner case appears in figure 4.

Both projected and actual times can be displayed on the GANTT chart. Software programs (for example, Microsoft Project) permit automation of timeline planning and monitoring. This is especially useful for complex projects.

The RASCI is an excellent, though less well known, tool for planning and monitoring design and development of interventions. RASCI stands for *Responsible, Approve, Support, Consult,* and *Inform.* For each intervention (unless it is a small one like the Harry's Diner case), the performance consultant, with all relevant parties, creates a two-dimensional matrix. This matrix lists all activities to be performed along the vertical axis and all parties involved in the performance improvement interventions along the horizontal. Cells are labeled with *R, A, S, C,* or *I* depending on the role each party assumes for a particular activity. Every activity must have an *R.* Many activities require an *A. S, C,* and *I* are entered as needed. A highly useful variation is to include time estimates for each party for each activity (except *Inform*). This permits parties to plan for required design and development time. Table 11 shows part of a sample RASCI for a performance project at an insurance company that decided to centralize its customer service function.

Design and development of specific interventions generally require a team approach involving all stakeholders. The more all parties are actively engaged in this process, the greater the likelihood of acceptance. This will also facilitate the implementation of interventions later on.

To repeat an earlier statement, the performance consultant does not have to possess design and development expertise for all selected interventions; in fact, it is virtually impossible for one person to have all these skills. As the sample RASCI chart in table 11 indicates, the performance consultant's level of involvement is one of supporter and facilitator. This leads us to the next section on roles and responsibilities.

FIGURE 4 Timeline for Harry's Diner

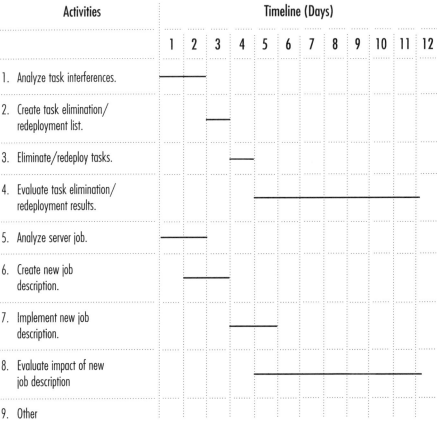

Activities	Timeline (Days)
	1 2 3 4 5 6 7 8 9 10 11 12
1. Analyze task interferences.	
2. Create task elimination/ redeployment list.	
3. Eliminate/redeploy tasks.	
4. Evaluate task elimination/ redeployment results.	
5. Analyze server job.	
6. Create new job description.	
7. Implement new job description.	
8. Evaluate impact of new job description	
9. Other	

Roles and Responsibilities of the Performance Consultant in the Selection-Design/Development-Implementation Phase

The roles and responsibilities of a performance consultant during this very active phase are varied. A lot depends on the project size, degree of complexity, and range of interventions involved. Assuming that the performance consultant does not have deep technical skills and knowledge with respect to the client's operations but possesses strong instructional, project management, and facilitator competencies, his or her major roles and responsibilities can be placed on a continuum. Table 12 lays out this continuum of involvement, which ranges from prime actor to occasional participant.

As table 12 points out, roles and responsibilities vary considerably. A consistent theme does emerge, however. The performance consultant remains

TABLE 11	Sample RASCI Chart—Consolidated Life Insurance Centralized Customer Service

Activities	Participants							
	Client	Perform. Consultant	Devlopment Team (2)	Customer. Serv. Reps. (4)	Field Mgrs. (2)	Desktop Pub.	Graphic Designer	Union
Analyze mandate for client services.	A 2	C 4	R 20	C 10	C 10			I
Develop new mandate.	S 2	S 2	R 16	C 4	C 4			I
Verify new mandate.	A 2	I	R 16	C 4	C 4			C 2
Analyze total inventory of client services and tasks.	C 4	C 8	R 24	C 36	C 10			I
Create new task inventory.		S 2	R 24	C 10	C 8	S 8		C 3

Cell numbers represent estimated number of hours to complete activity.

an interested party throughout the entire phase, regardless of role. To be successful in fulfilling any or all of these roles, he or she must create and maintain a collaborative work style with client and performance improvement team members. This is the hallmark of the successful consultant.

Brokering In and Brokering Out

One of the most important sets of tasks the performance consultant performs during the selection-design/development-implementation phase is that related to brokering. The previous section mentioned that the consultant frequently identifies and obtains resources for the project. We now explore this further.

We have stated several times that the performance department does not have to be able to do it all. But a key and valuable role the group can and should play is that of resource broker. What a broker does is act as an intermediary between client and performance intervention resources. This requires the performance department to spend time identifying potential

T A B L E   1 2   Performance Consultant Roles and Responsibilities—Selection-Design/Development-Implementation Phase

Role (Identifying level of involvement)	Explanation	Responsibilities
Selector-Designer/Developer-Implementer	The performance consultant possesses sufficient expertise to select, create, and implement the interventions. The consultant has received a clear mandate from the client to perform all tasks. This usually occurs in small, self-contained projects, usually dealing with familiar or easily understood content and solutions.	• Select interventions. • Design/develop interventions. • Implement interventions in collaboration with the client. • Act as the main resource, drawing from support services, technical specialists, and outside vendors as appropriate. • Manage the complete project.
Project Manager	The performance consultant assumes primary responsibility for gathering resources, managing all the activities of the phase, verifying and monitoring progress, and in general, acting as the client's agent.	• Establish resource selection criteria. • Identify and select resources. • Establish timelines and responsibilities. • Manage all aspects of the project. • Obtain client support and approval. • Mediate. • Facilitate. • Consult. • Verify and approve. • Negotiate with development team(s) and client changes in scope, timelines, and budget. • Ensure successful implementation.

T A B L E   1 2   Performance Consultant Roles and Responsibilities—Selection-Design/Development-Implementation Phase *(continued)*

Role (Identifying level of involvement)	Explanation	Responsibilities
Consultant	As the person most familiar with the performance improvement requirements, the performance consultant offers information, reviews development team work, and makes recommendations. The key role as a consultant is to act as project memory.	• Assist development teams with activities. • Communicate project vision. • Identify internal resources. • Provide inputs as appropriate. • Review draft ideas and materials. • Interpret client needs and goals to developers.
Facilitator	This essentially assumes that the client or his or her agent has taken over this phase of the project. The performance consultant plays a backseat role, stepping in when requested to help the project proceed smoothly.	• Identify resources on request. • Explain to client or development/implementation team members requirements of each that are not clear. • Facilitate meetings. • Mediate. • Monitor and assist as appropriate.
Monitor	The performance consultant is accountable for the project and the client even though others are now doing all the work. The performance consultant acts as an interested account manager, verifying activities and maintaining contact with client and work teams to ensure all is going as planned.	• Make periodic contact with client to verify degree of satisfaction. • Make periodic contact with work teams to verify progress and quality of output. • Provide information to the project as appropriate. • Keep performance consulting department informed of project status.

resources, verifying capabilities and track records, maintaining an ever-expanding data base of internal and external resources, matching resources with client needs, and in some cases, actually contracting for services.

The aware performance consultant constantly scans the organization's internal resources for *insourcing* possibilities. Many companies encourage departments to "broker in" or initiate internal servicing contracts (for consulting purposes, to provide technical or legal expertise; to develop specific products such as videos or software; to execute tasks such as reproduction). The advantage of these resources is that they are familiar with company culture and are often less expensive than external vendors.

The world outside the organization offers a limitless array of expertise and services, however, many of these are relevant to the performance department's expanding repertoire of potential interventions. To "broker out" or obtain skilled, reliable, external resources that can be offered to client groups requires the performance consultant to attend conferences, scan pertinent journals, contact professional associations, obtain referrals, and build networks of competent individuals and groups.

The brokering role is filled with opportunities and obstacles. From the opportunity perspective, a broad bank of in-house and external resources allows the performance consultant to meet client design/development and implementation needs rapidly and with assurance. Some degree of responsibility does attach itself to the broker, however, to ensure that the resources proposed are of high caliber and then to "sell" the resources to the client. Finally, regardless of the role the performance consultant plays in the design/development and implementation phase, there still remain some management responsibilities. Insourced or outsourced, the performance consultant has to introduce the resources into the client organization, smooth the way for their integration, and facilitate communication. Occasionally the performance consultant will also have to mediate between client and resources, all the while ensuring that the performance improvement goals are never lost from view.

Because interventions can differ markedly, the nature of the resources the performance consultant brokers will also differ in many ways. Nevertheless, there are some general criteria that apply for selecting internal or external resources. Table 13 provides a list of these criteria with explanation and suggestions for verifying how well a resource meets them.

In addition to the general criteria listed in table 13, other selection criteria specific to a project may also be considered, such as quality of proposal, feasibility of proposal timelines, or responsiveness to client needs. The brokering role contains many dimensions. Qualifying resources, maintaining a resource bank (internal and external), and matching resources to client needs are important ones.

The broker-performance consultant role may also include contracting with resources, managing them, and monitoring performance. Much depends on the degree of involvement the performance consultant is called upon to demonstrate. Regardless of role, however, the brokering in and out of resources remains a usual task for most performance departments and a useful set of skills for the consultant.

Managing Clients

It would be wonderful if all clients viewed the relationship between themselves and the performance consultant as one of equal partners. In reality, this is not often the case. The performance consultant faces difficult challenges in managing clients to act in ways that are ultimately "for their own good." This has a manipulative ring to it, but it is not something sneaky or unethical. Many clients still perceive the performance department as a training service that produces and runs courses. This can be especially true if the group is transitioning from a training to a performance orientation. The department has a responsibility to educate clients about its role, the appropriate expectations the clients should have, and the optimal relationship for achieving the results they desire. Below are some suggestions for helping clients make the best use of the performance department's services.

1. Inform clients of what performance consulting is. Explain the roles and services they should expect. Provide concrete examples.

2. Show samples of what the performance department has done for other internal clients.

3. Explain clearly the responsibilities clients must retain during selection, design/development, and implementation. These generally include the following:

● reviewing selected interventions with their rationales and providing input on economics, feasibility, and organizational acceptability

● legitimizing the change initiative, through communications to the performer groups involved

● approving the retained basket of solutions

● participating in or approving selected resources

● providing information and content expertise (personally or through appropriate specialists); facilitating access to required content information/subject matter experts

● facilitating access to targeted performers for tryouts

● participating in budget and timeline reviews

T A B L E 1 3	Criteria for Selecting and Brokering Resources	
Criteria	**Explanation**	**Suggestions for Verification**
Expertise	The resource must possess qualifications and demonstrated knowledge/skill to perform. These may include technical, content, or process competencies sufficiently advanced to allow the resource to perform with minimal support. The expectation is that the resource's expertise will be greater than that of the client group.	• Review qualifications (for example, certifications, degrees) for credibility. • Verify via references past performance. • Verify work samples. • Conduct performance-based interviews using interviewers with relevant backgrounds.
Track record	The resources should be able to provide references and examples of previous work. Length of time performing the required work and evidence of success with similar projects are important elements of this criterion.	• Verify references and previous clients for process and outcome success. • Review work samples. • Verify professional organizations and informal network for work experience. • Verify any awards or recognitions received for accomplishments.
Resources	Particularly for large projects, the persons or groups selected must be able to supply sufficient human and material resources to complete the job within the time frame.	• Verify size of operation. • Verify quantity and quality of human and nonhuman resources to determine if these are sufficient for the job. • Verify availability of resources.
Knowledge/experience working with the industry	Previous experience with or sound knowledge of the industry makes it easier for the resource to come up to speed on the project. Although not always essential, this type of experience can also decrease length of learning curve.	• Verify past performance to identify work experiences with industry. • Interview to determine knowledge of industry. • Verify industry references for quality of work.

126

T A B L E 1 3 Criteria for Selecting and Brokering Resources *(continued)*

Criteria	Explanation	Suggestions for Verification
Cost	Similar resources may vary considerably in cost. However, higher-priced resources may be worth additional expense due to capability, experience, and less rework. Cost, all other things being equal, is a factor to consider.	• Benchmark costs with other organizations or professional groups. Select and compare cost estimates. • Discuss costs with desirable vendors and verify flexibility. • Compare cost to quality of output.
Credibility	Clients must have confidence in the resources they engage for their projects. In addition to qualifications and experience, resources that project competence and present information well facilitate client acceptance.	• Interview to determine how well the resource projects credibility. • Performance test in role play situations that are confrontational and demanding. • Verify with previous clients degree of perceived credibility.

- participating in planning, decision making, and as appropriate, troubleshooting

- providing feedback and reinforcement for successes

- removing obstacles once identified

4. Guide clients to protect the performance improvement team so that it may focus on critical tasks.

5. Help clients to produce communications, activities, and accomplishments concerning performance improvement that they can take to senior management or to internal staff.

Overall, managing clients means ensuring that they do all that is necessary to achieve results they themselves value.

The Client's Role in Selection, Design/Development, and Implementation

Performance consultants are major players in the selection of performance interventions. While remaining interested parties, they may or may not be as active in the design/development and implementation stages. However, the client remains the owner of the performance improvement venture from beginning to end. In this final content section of the chapter, we return to the main reason for all of the selection-design/development-implementation activities.

A business need triggered a requirement for a change in human performance. As a result of proactive scanning or as a recipient of a request, the performance consultant became involved in the change requirement. If the organization is one that in the past has primarily turned to training as **the solution** to performance change, the initial client contact most likely took the form of a request for an educational intervention. Assessment analyzed the request and produced findings suggesting multiple factors influencing the gap between desired and actual states. Selection transformed findings into a proposed basket of solutions. During design and development, these were created and formatively tested. Implementation, the next major step, has seen the interventions disseminated to the operational setting to bring about the desired change. Throughout, the client has remained responsible although he or she may have occasionally forgotten this. It is the client's project. There is no one else who can replace him or her in the roles and duties associated with this responsibility. The performance consultant can certainly help in the execution of these. Table 14 lists some of the major client responsibilities during the selection-design/development-implementation phase and ways the performance consultant can assist.

T A B L E 1 4	Examples of Client Responsibilities and Ways Performance Consultants Can Assist

Client Responsibilities	Ways Performance Consultants Can Assist
Approve selection, design/development, and implementation outputs (intermediate and final)	• Review materials for approval prior to client. • Verify that all approval materials are clear and accompanied by credible rationales. • Ensure sufficient lead time for client review and approval. • Facilitate approval meetings. • Mediate between client and performance team.
Provide resources	• Verify for reasonableness of resource requests prior to client submission. • Coordinate resource requests. • Identify and qualify resources beforehand. • Help prepare rationales for resource requests. • Identify alternative solutions to resource requests (simulations as opposed to early trials with actual performers).
Support performance improvement team	• Explain to client need for constant support to facilitate performance improvement team's work with internal staffs. • Obtain authority to act on behalf of client. • Schedule and facilitate periodic meetings to update client on progress and transmit support needs.

(cont'd. on page 130)   *(cont'd. on page 130)*

TABLE 14 Examples of Client Responsibilities and Ways Performance Consultants Can Assist *(continued)*	
Client Responsibilities	**Ways Performance Consultants Can Assist**
Facilitate payments	• Inform client of payment issues and consequences. • Prepare files on payment problems (delays in purchase orders or invoice processing). • Intercede with legal, accounting or client payment processing to speed up payments.
Contract	• Help prepare contracts for signature. • Explain contract terms to contracted resources. • Facilitate processing of contracts.
Monitor progress and results	• Provide client with progress updates and implementation results. • Create or build in an ongoing evaluation system. • Report to client meaningful data. • Bring to client attention significant milestone achievements, problems, or data.
Reward/reinforce	• Bring to client attention opportunities for recognition. • Suggest appropriate means for recognition. • Create recognition symbols and events.

The performance consultant is an influencer, facilitator, and partner in performance improvement but does not replace the client. Nevertheless, clients are generally operational persons consumed by numerous demands on their time. The performance consultant can make the performance improvement process so much smoother and efficient by working with clients to help them attend to their responsibilities and fulfill their appropriate roles.

Summary and Conclusion

This chapter addressed the selection-design/development-implementation phase of the performance improvement process. It presented a model that links assessment, selection of interventions, design, development, implementation, evaluation, monitoring, and maintenance together. The chapter focused specifically on the central phase in which the bulk of the performance improvement activity occurs. It also provided numerous suggestions and guidelines to the performance consultant on what to do at each stage. During selection, the performance consultant plays a central role in identifying and building the rationale for the retained basket of performance improvement interventions. During design, development, and implementation, the role may remain primary (if the consultant actually goes on to create the interventions and participate in carrying them out) or switch into a management or support mode. Regardless of role, the performance consultant still remains actively engaged and interested, facilitating where appropriate, providing resources where necessary. An ongoing activity for the performance consultant with respect to this phase is the creation of resource banks, built up from both internal and external resources and prequalified by the performance department.

The closer the performance project moves to implementation, the greater the involvement of the client. Throughout the entire phase he or she has important responsibilities and tasks to perform. The performance consultant, discretely or directly, intervenes as an influencer or guide to smooth the process. As implementation arrives, the client takes final ownership of the performance interventions and their results. Evaluating, monitoring, and maintaining the performance change become the next set of challenges for both client and the performance consultant.

References

Baldwin, T.T., and J.K. Ford. "Transfer of Training: A Review and Directions for Future Research." *Personnel Psychology 41*, (1), 1988, pp. 63–105.

Broad, M.L., and J.W. Newstrom. *Transfer of Training: Action-Packed Strategies to Ensure High Payoff from Training Investments*. Reading, MA: Addison-Wesley, 1992.

Clark, R.E. "The CANE Model of Motivation to Learn and to Work: A Two-Stage Process of Goal Commitment and Effort." *International Journal of Educational Research*, (in press).

Elliott, P. "Job Aids." In *Handbook of Human Performance Technology*. 2d edition. Edited by Harold D. Stolovitch and Erica J. Keeps. San Francisco: Jossey-Bass, (in press).

Ford, J.K., and D.A. Weissbein. "Transfer of Training: An Updated Review and Analysis." *Performance Improvement 10*, (2), 1997, pp. 22–41.

Gagne, E.D., C.W. Yekovich, and F.R. Yekovich. *The Cognitive Psychology of School Learning*. 2d edition. New York: HarperCollins College Publications, 1993.

Gagne, R.M. *The Conditions of Learning*. 4th edition. New York: Rinehart and Winston, 1985.

Gery, G. *Electronic Performance Support Systems*. Cambridge, MA: Ziff Institute, 1991.

————. "Attributes and Behaviors of Performance-Centered Systems." *Performance Improvement Quarterly* 8, (1), 1995, pp. 47–93.

Harless, J.H. *Job Aids Workshop: Collection of Self-Instructional Lessons and Practical Exercises*. Newnan, GA: Harless Performance Guild, 1981.

Rossett, A., and J. Gautier-Downes. *A Handbook of Job Aids*. San Diego: Pfeiffer, 1991.

Stolovitch, H.D., and E.J. Keeps. *Handbook of Human Performance Technology*. San Francisco: Jossey-Bass, 1992.

————. *Front-End Analysis*. Montreal: HSA Publications, 1997.

Stolovitch, H.D., and J.-G. Maurice. "Calculating the Return on Investment in Training: A Critical Analysis and Case Study." *Performance Improvement*. (in press).

Stolovitch, H.D., and A. Yapi. "Use of Case Study Method to Increase Near and Far Transfer of Learning." *Performance Improvement Quarterly* 10, (2), 1997, pp. 64–82.

Stone, D.L., and S.W. Villachica. "Electronic Performance Support Systems." In *Handbook of Human Performance Technology*. 2d edition. Edited by Harold D. Stolovitch and Erica J. Keeps. San Francisco: Jossey-Bass, (in press).

————. *Training, 31* (10), 1993.

————. *Training, 34* (10), 1997.

The Authors

Harold Stolovitch is president of Harold D. Stolovitch & Associates Ltd. (HSA). He earned a Ph.D. in instructional systems technology from Indiana University and has been a teacher, trainer, researcher, and consultant for more than 35 years. Stolovitch has authored more than 100 books, reports, chapters, and articles on various aspects of instructional and performance technology. He has produced countless training materials, games and simulations, and other interactive activities using a wide variety of media. Until his recent retirement, Stolovitch was full professor and program chair at the Université de Montréal where he taught and conducted research in instructional and performance technology. He is also a clinical professor of human performance technology at the University of Southern California. Stolovitch is a consultant to business, industry, government, the military, and the police. He is a past president of the International Society for Performance Improvement (ISPI), former editor of the *Performance Improvement Journal*, editorial board member of several human resource and performance technology journals, and editor of the *Handbook of Human Performance Technology*. He is a frequent keynote speaker and presenter for major companies and professional associations and has won numerous awards for his contributions to instructional and performance technology, including ISPI's highest award, Member for Life.

Erica Keeps is executive vice president of HSA. She has an M.A. in educational psychology from Wayne State University, Detroit. In her 27-year training and development career, she has been a consultant to business and industry and managed two large corporate training functions. She has produced and supervised the production of numerous instructional materials and performance management systems. Keeps also has provided staff development for instructional designers, administrators, and performance engineers. She has managed large-scale projects and conferences. Keeps is a former executive board member of ISPI and a past president of the Michigan Chapter of ISPI. She has a number of publications to her credit in the training and human performance arenas and is coeditor of the *Handbook of Human Performance Technology*. Among her many awards for outstanding contributions to instructional and performance technology are the Michigan ISPI and the Montreal ISPI Chapter Member for Life awards and ISPI's 1993 Distinguished Service Award.

Case Study

Implementing Performance Change

by Gail Judge, Sean Stevens, and Uneeda Brewer

COMPANY NAME: Johnson & Johnson

INDUSTRY TYPE: Health care products manufacturer

ORGANIZATION PROFILE

ORGANIZATION SIZE:

90,200 employees—Johnson & Johnson has manufacturing operations around the world.

KEY PRODUCTS AND SERVICES:

Johnson & Johnson markets personal care and hygiene products, prescription and nonprescription medications, and medical equipment, instruments, and devices used by doctors in hospitals, clinics, and other health-care settings.

ANNUAL SALES:

Worldwide sales in 1997 were $22.6 billion.

DEPARTMENT NAME:

Learning Services.

DEPARTMENT SIZE:

35 Employees.

MISSION FOR DEPARTMENT:

Help build a stronger Johnson & Johnson by

● maximizing the performance of organizations, through the creation of work environments that allow people to do their best work and consistently meet high performance standards

● enhancing the capabilities of individuals, in assigning people from all Johnson & Johnson companies, levels, and functions to acquire the skills and knowledge needed to meet the business challenges they face

PRIMARY REASONS FOR TRANSITION TO A PERFORMANCE FOCUS:

● Formation of a shared service concept for training and other human resources (HR) services provided an opportunity to do things differently.

● The leader of the Learning Services Department strongly believed that greater linkage to business needs and performance requirements was critical to achieve.

● Interviews with leaders in the various companies affirmed their interest in having a greater connection between work of Learning Services and business requirements of the companies.

Background Information

Learning Services, an internal performance consulting group, was created in 1993 as part of Johnson & Johnson's efforts to increase operating efficiency and reduce redundancy. Until then, each of the decentralized operating companies in the United States and Puerto Rico had its own training and development department housed in human resources. It made sense to bring together a select group of highly skilled individuals to create synergy among the 28 operating units with the objective of enhancing organizational performance.

Somewhere in the journey from separate training departments to a shared service of internal consultants, it became apparent that more than a structural change was necessary if the new group was to achieve its objective: to help Johnson & Johnson remain a worldwide leader in health care business. Early in its evolution, Learning Services directed its efforts at becoming performance consultants, recognizing that training alone could provide only a partial solution to the organization's continuous efforts to improve performance.

Among the many challenges this change presented was the need to integrate the department's work processes with the human resources staffs in the decentralized operating companies. Hence, Learning Services operates within an account management framework, which means all work is begun within a partnership relationship of the Learning Services consultant, the company human resources person, and the client, who is the business owner of the project. From beginning to end, the company human resources person is either actively involved in the work or, at a minimum, kept apprised of the status of the project.

At the start of a project, the Learning Services account manager meets with the client to discuss business needs, expected outcomes, and performance measures. At the end of the assessment stage, when the performance gap has been identified, the Learning Services consultant makes recommendations for closing the gap. This may require management actions, learning actions, work environment changes, or a combination of these. Implementation can be provided with the assistance of Learning Services, with or without the company human resources representative, or by bringing in an external consultant.

The decision whether to bring in an external consultant is based on two considerations: Is the work to be done within Learning Services' areas of expertise, and can the work be done within the time frame desired by the client? If "No" is the answer to either of these questions, an external consultant is selected from the network developed by Learning Services according to specialty.

Learning Services carved out seven areas of expertise: change, competencies, leadership, mergers and acquisitions, performance management, strategic planning, and team development. Any interventions that fall into any of these areas utilize the resources of Learning Services, when possible.

Among the challenges facing Learning Services was the need to stay on top of the knowledge, skills, and practices that the consultants need to do their work. Three practice teams were created to accelerate the learning curve in the areas of leadership, change, and mergers and acquisitions. Team members quickly assimilated learning and have been able to provide the expertise required in these frequently requested project categories. Another challenge is to transfer the learning of the practice teams to human resources and line managers in the Johnson & Johnson companies. This is most easily done by working together during implementation of the various projects.

Two case studies follow that demonstrate projects in which Learning Services provided implementation services. Since each project fell within one or more of the specialty areas for Learning Services, the consultants were integral to the design and implementation of the required interventions. All cases are projects done in United States-based companies of Johnson & Johnson.

Case Study 1

NEED: Implementing Employee Involvement Practices into a Manufacturing Environment

Presenting need. A manager of a Johnson & Johnson manufacturing site phoned to request training for his employees on how to be a self-directed team. This site manager had read about self-directed work teams and was certain that his site would benefit from this approach. In initial discussions with the client, the business needs that prompted this request were identified. This site manager (who became the client for this performance change initiative) wanted to increase both productivity and the quality of the product being produced at his facility; the goal was that quality, productivity, and safety would increase by 10 percent. The client believed a key factor in accomplishing these goals was to tap the ideas of the employees in a more systemic and reliable way than had been done in the past. He was confident that employees had ideas that could serve as "breakthroughs" in terms of how to achieve these goals. He also thought that a training program was the action required to achieve this enhanced employee participation and involvement.

Assessing need. The consultants assigned to this project began to ask substantive questions of the client: "What actions had been taken previously, if any, to promote teams within the site? How successful were these attempts and what problems, if any, were encountered? Specifically, what did the client want employees to do more, better, or differently in the future?" In addition, the consultants provided the client with materials to read, and a video to view, which contributed to the client's knowledge of what self-directed work teams actually were and what was required to achieve this type of performance. During this educational process, the client's expectations were modified as he realized the magnitude of this type of change and that, to be done successfully, it would require between three and five years to fully implement.

Part of the diagnostic phase was to conduct focus group interviews with associates at the site. As a result of the diagnostic work, the consultants learned that there were several potential barriers to the success of this initiative.

1. *Pay-for-performance system.* The current compensation strategy focused on achievement of individual, not team, results. There was a comprehensive system in place to monitor and track individual performance within the plant environment; there was no such system in place to monitor and track contributions of a team of people. Therefore, the rewards were distributed primarily based upon what an individual, not a team, had contributed. Clearly this system was unaligned with the intended performance change.

2. *Subgroup of disgruntled employees.* The consultants learned that there was a small but influential clique of employees within the site who resisted any change and were ready to challenge this one. Thought needed to be given as to how to align this group with the initiative.

3. *Lack of motivation to work in a self-directed manner.* While employees wanted to have their opinions and suggestions solicited and implemented, the consultants learned that most employees did not want to work in a

completely self-directed manner. There was limited enthusiasm for this approach.

Implementation strategies. From the initial work done with the client, his expectations were modified. Rather than seek self-directed work teams, the client established a goal of creating a work environment in which employee ideas that would enhance quality and productivity would be offered freely and acted upon whenever possible. Employee involvement became the performance change that was sought—not self-directed work teams.

With the goal clearly stated, several interventions were taken to ensure success.

1. *Interventions of the client.* One of the most important client actions was to hold general meetings with all associates to discuss the transition to employee involvement. He also invited and responded to questions by employees at these meetings. Throughout the initiative, this client took actions to keep employees informed of the goals and results that were being accomplished. He ensured that each employee was provided time to attend training sessions; this included the site supervisors, who were being held accountable for reinforcing and guiding this initiative in their respective areas. Finally, the client personally managed some discipline situations (noted later) when they occurred. Overall, the client was a continual source of reinforcement for the project and its goals.

2. *Learning interventions.* Clearly, employees required skills if they were to effectively present their ideas, reaching consensus as a team on the ideas to be acted upon. Therefore, training programs were provided in skill areas such as:

- team dynamics
- conflict resolution
- team decision making
- communication
- effective team meetings.

Training was also provided to supervisors at the site on how to effectively coach for the needed performance.

3. *Nonlearning interventions.* There were several actions taken both to gain support for this change and to modify work environment barriers that would negatively affect it.

- The consultants were from Learning Services, a company shared service function at the corporate level. There was an HR generalist who had accountability for this specific site. It was vital to engage this individual in the initiative from the beginning to ensure her support and to gain her insights as to how to successfully implement this change. She became a part of the consultant team, specifically addressing some of the nonlearning issues that were identified (such as pay for performance).

● A design team, made up of employees, was formed. Employees volunteered for this assignment and were asked to become actively involved in identifying actions that needed to be taken during the implementation phase. The design team became a small-scale model of the type of employee involvement that was being sought as a result of the entire initiative. The client attended many of these meetings, which continued to evidence his support and interest in the change initiative.

● The pay-for-performance system needed to be modified. This was an action that the HR generalist was particularly helpful in addressing. This system was redesigned to include ratings and feedback on demonstration of teamwork behaviors; and enlarge the percentage of the annual increase that was dependent upon meeting site goals, not just individual goals.

● The shift structure was not conducive to formation of employee involvement. The shifts were staggered in such a manner as to make communication across shifts difficult. The design team was instrumental in identifying ways to modify shifts in order to facilitate team involvement.

● The small clique of dissatisfied associates did "push" the boundaries as a way of resisting this change. This was an undercurrent during the implementation, but it was brought to a head with a specific incident. The client took the necessary disciplinary action that resulted in the termination of one employee. This action proved to be a strong affirmation of the client's commitment to increased employee involvement in the site.

Results. This project is still a work in progress. It is already evident, however, that the skeptical and passive employees are actively engaged in the process of enhancing employee involvement. The communication is much stronger within each team, although there is still work to be done in enhancing communication across teams. In addition, other sites have learned of this initiative and are now seeking support in making a similar change in their environment.

Case Study 2

NEED: Enhancing the Engineering Process

Presenting need. The vice president of national engineering contacted Learning Services to discuss some needs regarding his engineering group and the work they do to support a Johnson & Johnson business unit. He indicated that there were pressures from both within and without the engineering group that indicated a change was required. Specifically, they included the following:

1. The business unit (referred to in this case as the "client") needed to respond to increased competitive pressures; these pressures required that manufacturing and distribution of products be made more efficient and cost effective. A major part of the solution to this situation was to engineer alternative processes and equipment; thus, the client was drawing upon the services of the engineering group and evidencing higher expectations for their performance.

2. The client believed that the work process of engineers could be strengthened. Currently, there was inconsistency in how engineers worked with internal customers. This created both inefficiencies and, at times, confusion, because the engineering process experienced by an internal customer was dependent upon which engineer was assigned to the project. In addition, there was agreement that innovation needed to be enhanced while still maintaining the critical need for complying with FDA requirements.

3. The finance department needed to work closely with engineering when making proposals for capital investments, because many engineering designs required new equipment to be built or purchased. Currently the internal customers within the finance department were dissatisfied with the level of partnering that occurred when making these proposals.

Assessing need. The client had done a significant amount of assessment prior to contacting the consultant. In fact, he had interviewed all 39 people in his department. He learned that the engineers were technically strong but that they needed to enhance the partnering they did with their internal customers. The consultants assigned to this project contributed to the diagnostic phase by obtaining feedback from approximately 60 customers of the engineering group. Customers responded to a survey that helped to identify both the performance they sought from engineers and their opinions of the current performance they were experiencing. In this manner, performance gaps were identified.

All findings were discussed with the client and decisions made as to what actions were required to ensure the changes required. These actions included the following:

1. *Redesign the engineering work process.* The ultimate goal was to have a work process that would be used consistently by all engineers and would result in increased partnering with customers, and an engineering process that would yield more innovative solutions in an efficient manner. The current process was not providing these results, so a process model needed to be formed.

2. *Form and use measures for work process.* It was important to have measures that could be used to monitor the quality and effectiveness with which the redesigned engineering process was being utilized. Currently there were limited measures in place that were tracked in a systematic manner; such measures were to be formed.

Implementation strategies: With the goals for the initiative clearly established, a number of interventions were taken.

1. *Interventions of the client.* The client provided leadership throughout the initiative and was involved in completing three types of actions to accomplish the following:

● gain support of both the customers and of managers within the engineering department

● communicate the change and work being done in support of it

● remove obstacles to achievement of the ultimate goal.

Specifically, the client formed a team of executive sponsors for this initiative, composed of some of the department's customers as well as some stakeholders to the change initiative (for example, the vice president of human resources). The client met with each of these individuals to explain the change initiative and to seek their input and support. In addition, the client met with his direct reports (the managers in the department) to explain the initiative and to clarify the accountability for each manager to support the change.

In order to ensure both buy-in for the change and to gain valued input to it, a design team was formed. Members of this team were selected by the client. Approximately half of the team were from the department; the remainder came from stakeholder groups such as operations manufacturing, finance, and quality. On an ongoing basis, the client ensured that updates regarding the change were provided by this team to the entire department. And when obstacles were encountered, the client worked in an active manner to remove them. For example, one member of the design team was having difficulty obtaining time off from his work to attend meetings and complete tasks. The client met with the manager of the individual to resolve the situation so that the team member's time could be freed up. The client also met with stakeholder group managers to encourage the allocation of people from these groups to the design team. Again, the client's leadership was critical to success of the project.

2. *Learning interventions.* A team was developed to work on the new design. During this design process, the team acquired additional skills and knowledge and experienced firsthand how change affects the people who must imple-

ment it (for example, the team needed to address resistance to change when it occurred). They also were provided skill enhancement in team process and in how to reach consensus. Another developmental action occurred with the engineering management team to ensure they were fully prepared to implement their role as leaders and reinforcers of the change. Throughout the change process, "lunch and learn" sessions occurred during which employees within the engineering group could come to learn about the status of the change process and be provided a venue for asking questions.

3. *Nonlearning interventions.* The major work involved mapping the current work process and then designing a new work process. This was work completed with the design team in partnership with the consultants. First, the current process was mapped. It was posted in a public area; engineering employees were invited to note and post their comments and reactions to what they observed. Once agreement was reached on how work was currently completed, a new process was designed. Again, this desired work process flow chart was posted in a public area with employees being invited to make comments. Once agreement was reached on the process as it needed to be, a department-wide meeting was conducted to inform and educate employees about it. In addition, validation meetings were held with key customers to gain their support for the new process and to identify the implications of this process for the customer's operation.

Goals were established for each major phase in the new process. Work is now being done to create the measuring processes so that reliable information is obtained regarding the degree to which the process phases and goals are being achieved; and to identify obstacles that are occurring in the implementation process, so that these barriers can be minimized or removed.

Results. Several customers have acknowledged a noticeable change in how engineers are working with them. Some of the specific changes noted include better identification of true customer need, increased responsiveness to customer requests, and strong evidence of working in partnership with customers to support the customer's business goals.

The finance department has experienced some "wins" with the engineering group since implementation of the process. Recently there was a co-presentation by finance and engineering for the need to support 14 capital investments; 13 of these proposals were approved, which is the highest approval percentage ever obtained. There is general agreement that this was due in part to the manner in which both groups worked together to prepare for the presentation; once again, partnering is much stronger.

Another result is evidence of strong ownership and enthusiasm for this change by the engineering employees themselves. The support to use, and continually improve, the work process is strong. This result is due, in part, to the work of the consultants who acted as facilitators and enablers of the change without assuming responsibility for it; that ownership remained with the client and the employees throughout the initiative.

The client was so pleased with the work of the internal human resources and Learning Services consultants that he honored them with an award at a luncheon. He acknowledged that the manner in which the consultants partnered with the client and his team, providing expertise when needed but also facilitating others to share and leverage their skills, had resulted in a real success. Not only did the engineering group have a redesigned process, yielding higher results, but the engineering employees themselves had acquired skill in how to design and implement changes.

Lessons Learned

● To successfully implement performance change, the situation must be assessed to affirm the true causes for the situation (go below the symptoms that are in evidence).

● When selecting and implementing interventions to promote performance change, it is important to consider what actions must be taken in each of these categories:

—actions the client will personally take

—actions that enhance the skill and knowledge of the performers (learning actions)

—actions that address work environment obstacles.

● Gaining and maintaining ownership for the change within the client and the performer group is important. Techniques for accomplishing this ownership include the formation of a design team in which members of the performer group are selected to partner with the consultant in designing and implementing the change initiatives.

● If there are members of other training or human resources groups within the client group, these individuals need to be invited to participate as members of the consultant team; their perspective can be leveraged, and it avoids feelings of competition or conflict.

● Continually remind yourself and your client group that change is an iterative process; the desired results will rarely occur as the result of one set of initiatives. Rather, information must be obtained to monitor progress so that additional interventions can be implemented in a timely manner when required.

● It is not possible to have expertise on staff to deliver all interventions that may be required throughout a year to address performance needs of clients. Determine those interventions for which expertise will be maintained on staff; all others will be brokered. Form a list of qualified suppliers with whom you can work when these interventions are needed.

The Authors

Gail Judge joined Johnson & Johnson in 1972 after a career as an educator on both the secondary and college levels. Starting in human resources, she has spent time in marketing and management training and development. She served as vice president of human resources and as a member of the management board at McNeil Pharmaceutical for 12 years. In her current role, Judge has been responsible for the design and implementation of Learning Services, an internal consulting service to the Johnson & Johnson operating companies in the United States and Puerto Rico.

Judge is a member of the St. Francis Medical Center Foundation and on the School Advisory Committee of Sacred Heart School. She has a B.S. from Georgian Court College, an M.S. from Rutgers University, and an M.A. from the University of San Francisco.

Sean Stevens has worked in the training and organizational development field for more than 10 years. During that time he has held positions as an independent consultant, an assessment and development specialist for British Petroleum, and, currently, a consulting director for Learning Services at Johnson & Johnson. In his present position, he serves as an internal organization development (OD) consultant for the operating companies of Johnson & Johnson. He consults in areas such as performance management, competency-based development, teams, leadership, and change management.

Stevens has a B.A. in psychology from Louisiana State University and an M.A. and Ph.D. in industrial/organizational psychology from the University of Akron.

Uneeda Brewer has worked in the training and organizational development field for more than 17 years. During that time she has held positions as a management trainer at Maryland Blue Cross & Blue Shield and at CoreStates Financial Corp.; as a senior instructor at Squibb College; and, currently, as a consulting director for Learning Services at Johnson & Johnson. In her present position, she serves as an internal OD consultant for the domestic operating companies of Johnson & Johnson. She consults in areas such as performance management, competency-based development, change management, team building, leadership development, and individual coaching.

Brewer has a B.A. in American studies from Goucher College in Towson, Maryland, and a M.A. in social work from Atlanta University School of Social Work. She is also certified as a practitioner of psychodrama, sociometry, and group psychotherapy.

6

Measurement Phase: Evaluating Effectiveness of Performance Improvement Projects

by Robert Brinkerhoff

QUICK READ

● Evaluation of performance improvement projects serves three major purposes:

—Promotes learning, so that performance consultants and their clients can improve their capability to plan, design, and conduct effective performance improvement projects in the future.

—Establishes formal accountability to ensure that investments in performance improvement are carefully thought through, professionally conducted, and achieve worthwhile results.

—Serves a quality improvement and assurance role to ensure that principles of good practice are thoughtfully applied and that results are achieved as the project unfolds.

● A five-phase model for evaluation of performance improvement projects is described:

—Phase 1: Goal Setting

—Phase 2: Performance Analysis

—Phase 3: Design for Improvement

—Phase 4: Implementation

—Phase 5: Impact.

This chapter presents practical guidance to help performance consultants and other professionals use evaluation as a strategic tool for leveraging continuously improved value from performance improvement project efforts. The first section of the chapter reviews the function of evaluation in performance improvement, provides a discussion of some fundamental concepts, and provides an explanation of how evaluation strengthens the impact of performance improvement initiatives. The second section presents a systematic five-phase model for designing and using evaluation measurement and data collection methods to improve performance improvement project results and demonstrate business impact. This second section contains an expanded discussion of each phase in the model, explaining the phase in more depth, listing key evaluation questions for each phase, and outlining some of the typical evaluation methods used in each phase. The final section of the chapter provides guidelines for designing a practical and effective evaluation of performance improvement projects. A list of references and additional resources that readers can use to get more information on evaluation procedures and tools is appended to the chapter.

DESIGNING EVALUATION AND THE EVALUATION FUNCTION

Evaluative thinking and data collection are a routine and natural part of performance improvement projects. For that matter, a human being cannot even cross the street without using evaluation. Data collection: Are there any cars coming? How fast is that truck moving toward me? Evaluative judgment: Can I cross safely now? Am I far enough across that I can slow my pace?

Since data collection and measurement are already a part of a performance improvement project, the reader might wonder why we bother to set aside "evaluation" as a separate function. There are three primary reasons for doing so. First, planned and careful evaluation promotes learning, which enables both performance consultants and their clients to be smarter about and more capable in future performance improvement efforts. Second, formally planned evaluation serves important accountability purposes. It helps assure clients, and consultants, that their investments in performance improvement initiatives are carefully thought through and most likely to yield worthwhile results. Third, carefully conceived and structured evaluation serves quality assurance and management purposes. Planning and committing to evaluation also ensures that the principles of good practice will be systematically applied, not unconsciously neglected in the all-too-normal frenetic pace of typical organizational life. Evaluation that is conceived as a "total quality management" function focuses attention on the critical junctures in the process of performance improvement so they can be managed to produce the most effective and valuable results.

Defining Evaluation

Evaluation can be simply defined as *systematic reflection*. Evaluation is reflective in that it requires us—and the clients and other stakeholders in our performance projects—to pause occasionally and ask how things are going, to determine whether we are achieving expected results, to notice other outcomes of actions that may not have been anticipated, or to figure out why some things may not have worked as we expected so we can learn from them. When our efforts work, it is important that we notice them and nurture further success. When things do not work, it is equally important that we notice them and make changes.

Evaluation is systematic in that we make plans for it and that we commit resources to implementing evaluation actions. This chapter presents a five-phase model that calls for formal reflection at especially critical junctures in the design and implementation of a performance improvement project. Using a systematic approach to evaluation ensures that "pauses" are planned to collect data, ask questions, think critically, and consider the course of subsequent performance improvement project plans and actions.

Purposes for Evaluation

The overall purpose for evaluation is learning. Evaluation promotes learning about what works and what does not. This in turn helps clients become better performance managers, and it helps performance consultants build capability to more effectively serve future clients. Evaluation also serves quality assurance and accountability purposes. Evaluation data collected and used during a project help steer the project toward worthwhile results, and evaluation data collected near the completion of a project demonstrate impact and help stakeholders assess the results of their efforts and investments.

The Evaluation Process

Evaluation is a process of asking key questions, then collecting and using data to answer the questions. Some of the questions will represent internal concerns, such as whether a needs analysis procedure has uncovered valid needs, or whether a team of performers can efficiently use a draft job aid. Other questions will represent external stakeholder concerns, such as whether the project has met interim performance objectives, or whether a business goal has been affected.

Each phase in a performance improvement project, from analysis of needs, to forming partnerships with clients and designing improvement interventions, to carrying out plans, entails several vital evaluation questions. These include questions such as the following:

● What is the business need for the performance improvement project and how important is this need?

● How much does performance need to improve to justify the costs of an improvement project?

● What are the comparative merits of one alternative performance improvement approach to another?

● How well would intervention "X" work?

● How well is our performance improvement effort proceeding; is it on track and headed for success?

● How effectively are interim performance improvement objectives being met, and what revisions are needed?

● Has the original business need been met? Are more, or different, performance improvement interventions needed?

● Are the performance improvement project clients satisfied with the results achieved?

● Of the choices for what might be done next, what alternative is best?

Accurate and valid answers to these (and other) questions will lead toward effective performance improvement project design and delivery that meets clients needs. Inaccurate answers, or failures to thoughtfully raise the questions in the first place, will almost surely lead to wasted efforts and frustrated performers and clients. In a nutshell, the job of evaluation is to help performance improvement project leaders ask the right questions, and then collect the data they need for accurate answers to them.

The right questions come from a carefully articulated and systematic approach to performance improvement evaluation design. Accurate and useful answers come in the form of data (information) in and about the organization in which performance improvement project leaders are working.

A Little Goes a Long Way

Evaluation need not be extraordinarily technical, formal, or complex to be effective. Neither does all evaluation have to involve sophisticated data collection and elaborate measurement. Sometimes a few systematically collected opinions from key stakeholders are as useful and valid, if not more so, than fancy statistics from a broad survey, or return-on-investment formulas and charts. There is a place in evaluation of performance improvement for so-called hard data, but there is also a place for thoughtful opinion, professional judgment, and even anecdotal information.

The key to effective evaluation is to use methods and procedures appropriate to the information needs at hand and the complexity of the project being pursued. Every performance improvement project, no matter how small or large, should be subjected to the same thoughtful evaluation process recommended in this chapter. But the level of evaluation effort should be appropriate to the circumstances and guided above all by criteria of usefulness and practicality. Evaluation is a waste of time and money if it uses aloof technologies that no one can understand or make use of, especially when simpler approaches could have been useful and would have taken fewer resources away from the primary performance improvement effort.

A Framework for Evaluation of Performance Improvement Initiatives

Effective evaluation of performance improvement projects must always be more than an afterthought. Evaluation is decidedly not simply checking, with a survey or a performance metric, for example, to see whether some performance improvement project had any results. Assessing performance increases is always a part of a systematic evaluation approach, but it is nowhere near sufficient to address the needs of performance improvement project leaders who must consistently design and deliver performance improvement projects that add value to organization products and services. Effective consulting practice requires thinking about evaluation concurrently with the performance improvement project design and applying evaluation methods throughout the entire performance improvement project cycle.

Using Evaluation to Avoid Five Critical Errors

Like any human effort, performance improvement initiatives can be more or less successful, or they can fail entirely. When considering all of the things that might go wrong with a performance improvement effort, it is possible to group all of the potential causes for error into five fundamental categories. The five fundamental errors are as follows:

1. **Error of direction.** Pointing the performance improvement project in the wrong direction, such as trying to correct a performance deficit that is not worthwhile to the business, or being mistaken about the presumed value of an apparent business need.

2. **Error of analysis.** Aiming to achieve the right business goal (direction), but mistakenly identifying the wrong causes for performance deficits, or failing to connect the right performance objectives to the business goal.

3. **Error of design.** Having the right business goal and analysis, but failing to construct the right performance improvement tools, incentives, aids, and so forth.

4. **Error of implementation.** Having the right goals, analysis, and plan, but failing to implement the plan, so that the right performance improvement tools never get to the right performers, or fail to get installed, used, and supported correctly.

5. **Error of impact.** Having everything appear to have gone right, but for some reason, performance does not improve as planned or the business goal is not achieved.

Notice that the final error (impact) could not logically occur if in fact there had been absolutely no error of the first four types. If, for example, the performance consultant appeared to have done everything right, but performance did not actually improve, then one of two causes for this failure is true: (1) A mistake was in fact made in analysis or design or implementation; or (2) something "new" happened since the analysis was completed to undermine it so that it was no longer valid. Likewise, if performance improves, but there is no worthwhile business impact, then again something was wrong—but was missed—in goal setting, analysis, design, or implementation. Or, something changed in the business environment to undermine the business goal's value or its connection to the presumed performance causes.

Organizational and business contexts never stay the same, of course, so performance consultants must continually revisit their earlier analyses and assumptions, and ensure that they are still valid, or make revisions as needed. This fact of performance improvement life is a primary driving force for continuous evaluation. If performance environments were simple, not complex, or if things stayed the same, or if getting things done in organizations was easy and never went wrong, there would be no need for evaluation—and probably no need for performance improvement consultation either, for that matter.

THE FIVE-PHASE FRAMEWORK

Figure 1 presents a five-phase framework for evaluation that parallels the five fundamental errors. Performance consultants can use the five-phase framework to guide their initial thinking about performance improvement projects, and also to monitor the evolution of a performance improvement initiative, continuously checking to see that their work is accurate and that it remains valid. While each phase defined by the framework entails different sorts of evaluation questions, and likewise involves different sorts of data collection and measurement methods, together the phases provide a practical guide for ensuring performance improvement quality and enhancing accountability.

The following pages provide a more detailed discussion of each of the five phases for evaluation. First, the rationale and function of the phase are explained in more detail. Following this discussion, key evaluation questions for that phase are listed, and common evaluation and data collection methods for that phase are outlined. Readers should note that the methods listed are presented in order, from more simple and cursory, to more complex and in-depth. Readers should also note that the methods listed are not necessarily limited to any particular evaluation phase, because the same method can be used to address evaluation questions in more than one phase. Further, it is suggested that performance consultants employ evaluation methods that combine inquiry from several evaluation phases at once.

While the phases are roughly chronological, they are not pursued in a strictly linear fashion, nor are they pursued one at a time. Evaluation should typically begin at the first phase (goal setting), for example, because this first phase represents to some extent a "go or no-go" choice. If performance consultants discovered that the business objective lacked sufficient support,

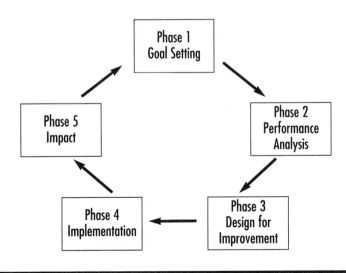

F I G U R E   1   Five-Phase Model for Evaluation of Performance Improvement Projects

then they would be advised to terminate the project at this early point. Yet not all of Phase 1 evaluation should be completed before moving on to later phases. It would be necessary, for example, to collect performance needs data and conduct some project planning before making a final judgment as to the viability of the overall project. Or, it may be that senior management support existed early in the project, but conditions (a replacement of a senior manager, for instance) could change such that Phase 1 would need to be revisited. So, while the evaluation phases are roughly chronological, there is recycling among them as a performance improvement project evolves. And evaluation methods can focus on several phases at once. A survey questionnaire, for example, could ask stakeholders to give their opinions about their commitment to performance improvement goals (Phase 1), the validity of the analysis (Phase 2), and their concerns with the design of performance improvement tools and methods (Phase 3).

Phase 1: Goal Setting

All good performance improvement projects are directed at goals beyond performance. The performance that is to be improved is intended to serve a business purpose, such as increasing market share in a sales area, reducing production costs, increasing product quality, improving customer satisfaction, or any of several other important business outcomes. It is the value of the business goal that determines the potential value of the performance improvement effort. Thus, to judge the merits of a potential performance improvement effort and to help senior management decide whether and how much to invest in performance improvement efforts, it is necessary to weigh the potential business value that could be achieved by improving the performance of specific individuals or groups.

Improving performance alone is not enough. Consider this example, based on the experience of a performance audit team charged with assessing needs for performance improvement. The setting was a travel service business that operated through a network of branch offices. During the site visit to a branch office, a clear performance issue emerged and was vociferously attested to by the office staff. The staff were spending inordinate amounts of time struggling to complete record keeping and other business forms that were evidently poorly designed. Inspection by the audit team of the record-keeping system and forms, and observation of the staff behaviors, indicated that indeed a problem did exist. Further analysis showed that some relatively simple redesign of the forms and some job aids for the staff could cut record keeping time in half, saving the company many hours of needless labor and thus many thousands of dollars at this one branch alone. The bulk of the audit team members, several young and freshly trained industrial psychologists, eagerly prepared a proposal to the management, easily cost-justifying a recommendation to improve performance in an area that would clearly save time and money, and that also was a pet peeve of the staff.

But one member of the team, a veteran with considerable experience in customer service, had noted during the site visit that the branch office staff had spent considerable time with some customers, but little time with others. Further, the customers who were not adequately served represented potentially highly profitable accounts, while customers more thoroughly served represented accounts with far lower profit potential; these lower-profit potential customers were easier to deal with because their problems were less complex. Further analysis by the veteran showed that there were, in fact, about five to seven high-profit sales opportunities per day in the branch. If all, or nearly all, of the opportunities were not turned to sales, the branch's overall business performance would dramatically suffer. If these few high-leverage opportunities were converted to sales, the profits of the branch would more than double, an outcome with financial impact worth many times more than the time savings available through fixing the record-keeping performance. Further, time pressure was not an issue, as the staff had plenty of time available to serve these few customers. Saving time through the record-keeping intervention would provide virtually no business improvement leverage and would even deflect attention from the far more serious business issue of lost profit opportunity.

The correct performance improvement project for this business could be weighed and judged only by thoughtfully reflecting on and assessing the potential business (versus performance) goal merits and value of the alternative approaches. Had the business analysis process not been thought through, it was very likely that both the performance audit team and the branch manager would have been seduced by the easily calculated performance improvement projections showing how much time (and apparent money) could have been "saved" by fixing the record keeping performance. Yet the real business need had nothing to do with saving time, but required a leverage sales and customer analysis approach. Of course the record-keeping problems should have been (and were) eventually addressed, but not at the expense of the more strategic performance focus.

This example demonstrates the need for careful goal identification and evaluation. While improved team or individual performance is the immediate objective of a performance improvement effort, the longer-range goal of business value is always the determinant of whether improving performance is worthwhile.

Business goals are driven largely, of course, by external environment factors, such as competition, technological advances, shifts in market characteristics, and so forth. Because this external environment is changing at an ever more rapid pace, evaluation of the business goal is not done just once at the beginning of a project, but should be revisited as the performance improvement project proceeds. It is entirely likely, though not always true, that a business goal for a performance improvement project could be very important and valid, but that as the project proceeds, factors change such that the project needs to be drastically reconfigured, or even abandoned. Frequent and regular reflection on the current validity of the goal at which a performance improvement project is aimed is advised.

Key Questions for Phase 1 (Goal Setting) Evaluation

- How important and worthwhile is the business goal for the performance improvement project?

- Does the economic value of the business goal justify the likely costs of a performance improvement project?

- To what extent is the business goal aligned with overall organization strategy and values?

- To what extent are business goals supported by reliable and valid data?

- Is the business and organizational context sufficiently stable that this goal will still be valid by the time a performance improvement initiative is planned and installed?

- How thoroughly has the business goal been communicated, understood, and committed to by all key stakeholders in the performance improvement project?

- Is there sufficient senior management support and buy-in to justify a performance improvement project?

- Are there alternative business goals that warrant more attention than the goal aimed at by this performance improvement project?

Phase 1 (Goal Setting) Evaluation Methods

- Compare the business focus of the performance improvement project with information about the organization's business strategy, plan, and goals.

- Make a checklist of the key questions (and others, if needed), and have clients review the performance improvement project plan, providing their opinions and reactions on each point in the checklist.

- Construct a survey questionnaire covering the key questions and administer it to stakeholders in the project.

- Conduct a "panel review" of the plan for the performance improvement project and discuss and critique the key questions.

- Have external experts review the goals and provide both comments and opinions.

Phase 2: Performance Analysis

Analysis is, of course, a major and vital phase of a performance improvement project. In this phase, the performance consultant identifies the critical performance roles and factors that must be improved in order to achieve the business goal. Evaluation at this phase is critically important. If the analysis is flawed, then the wrong performance might be improved, or the wrong performance improvement factors could be addressed. If the analysis is incomplete, then critical improvement factors might be overlooked.

The analysis phase typically identifies three levels of performance improvement needs: primary needs, secondary needs, and tertiary needs. These three levels and some examples of needs at each level are listed in table 1.

As shown in table 1, primary needs are those defined as specific improvements in performer behavior or results. That is, these are performance improvements that are needed to have an impact on the desired business objectives, such as an increase in sales for salespeople, or a decrease in data entry errors for tax information processing technicians. Often the performance analysis reveals that performers cannot just increase their performance on their own, but that they need some sort of tool or other useful support, such has a new customer data profile form to help a salesperson better understand customer needs, or a job aid to help information processing clerks keep track of changing tax regulations. These are examples of secondary needs: performance support tools and aids. In cases where the performance support is not readily available, there may be third-level needs discovered by the analysis process. The job aid that summarizes changes in tax regulations, for example, might require that the company subscribe to a new online information service.

As can be seen by these examples, the performance environment is typically complex, and performance improvement efforts often require a number of interventions and changes across several layers and levels in the organization. Almost never does a performance improvement effort require just one simple fix. Most typically, the performance that needs to be improved has fallen below necessary standards for a variety of interconnected reasons. The changes needed to bring performance up to new levels spread like ripples across a pond, each particular change causing a need for another change.

As complexity increases, so do the opportunities for mistakes and oversights in the performance analysis process. Consultants can use the three-level framework to help themselves, their clients, and other stakeholders understand all of the needs tied to a particular performance improvement effort, and to keep track of the linkages among them. The three-level

TABLE 1 Levels of Performance Improvement Needs

Performance Need Level	Description	Examples
Primary Needs	Needs for improvement in direct performer tasks or results	"Sales representatives need to close 15 percent more sales." "Account technicians need to reduce errors on billing statements to less than 2 percent." "Physicians need to file medical notes within three hours of patient visits."
Secondary Needs	Needs for improved support, tools, training, or resources to directly assist the performer	"Sales representatives need training in how to overcome objections that prospects raise about the product." "Incentives for sales representatives need to be increased." "Upgraded accounting software is needed to help reduce errors in statements." "The medical notes format needs to be integrated into the electronic protocol."
Tertiary Needs	Needs that will help or support providers of assistance to performers	"Supervisors need training in how to accurately award sales incentives." "Additional funds for software development need to be allocated to accounting." "A systems engineer needs to be hired part-time to redesign all medical procedures protocols."

framework also helps consultants assess the relative importance of needs at each level.

The purpose of Phase 2 evaluation is to focus attention on the analysis process and to help ensure that accurate and complete needs are identified. Each need, regardless of its level, should be scrutinized to be sure that it is logically and validly connected to the desired primary performance improvement objective. Performance consultants will spend a good deal of resources to design their performance improvement initiatives to address all of the needs they discover in the analysis phase, and their clients will spend even more in implementing these new initiatives. To be sure they are right so that their interventions have the greatest chance for success, wise performance consultants will systematically revisit and reflect on the analysis process, double-checking for errors and oversights.

Key Questions for Phase 2 (Analysis) Evaluation

● Have sufficient primary performance improvement needs been identified?

● Are the performance objectives clearly and specifically linked to the business goals?

● How valid, reliable, and complete are available performance data?

● How likely is it that the performers identified could improve performance to the levels needed to have an impact on the business goals?

● Have all of the right performers and performance improvement objectives been identified?

● Are the projected performance improvement objectives sufficient to accomplish the business goal?

● Have sufficient secondary and tertiary needs been identified?

● Is there sufficient reason to believe that external factors (acquisition of the company, changes in competition, political shifts, economic climate) will not overwhelm efforts to improve performance?

● How clear, specific, and complete are performance improvement objectives?

Phase 2 (Analysis) Evaluation Methods

● Conduct literature research on effective performance of the type your project is aiming to produce and confirm that you have identified the correct performance improvement factors and needs.

● Make a checklist of the key questions (and others, if needed), and have clients review the analysis, providing their opinions and reactions on each point in the checklist.

● Construct a survey questionnaire covering the key questions and administer it to stakeholders in the project to gather their opinions about the completeness and feasibility of the analysis.

● Have the analysis reviewed and confirmed by external, third-party experts.

● Conduct a panel review of the analysis for the performance improvement project and discuss and critique the key questions.

● Identify other organizations that are currently achieving business goals as targeted by your performance improvement project. Confirm that performers in these organizations match your primary, secondary, and tertiary analyses.

● Conduct a study of performers (if any) who are currently performing at the levels targeted by the performance improvement project. Confirm the validity of the secondary and tertiary analysis by assessing the performance environment of these exemplary performers. Validate that they are making the right and sufficient contributions to business goals.

Phase 3: Design for Improvement

Once needs have been identified, performance consultants design interventions to assist performers in improving performance. These designs typically include a number of elements. A relatively simple plan to help tax information processing technicians reduce errors, for example, could include the following actions and tools:

● a computer-produced job aid, revised monthly, containing summaries of changes in tax codes and regulations

● a subscription to an online updating service and funds to pay for the subscription

● software to produce and revise the job aid

● training for the technicians in how to use the job aid

● a new compensation system for tax technicians based on performance

● an incentive bonus for supervisors of technicians who exceed monthly standards

● an observation checklist for supervisors to use in coaching technicians whose performance is deficient

● training for supervisors in how to use the coaching checklist.

Behind each of these elements in the plan are a number of nested implementation planning steps and decisions. Consider, for example, just the subtasks that lie behind the behavioral observation checklist that is intended for supervisors to use in working with their technicians. The checklist behaviors will need to be identified and validated; someone will have to design this checklist; the checklist will need to be reviewed and approved by managers of supervisors; a trial of the checklist will be needed to be sure that it is workable; training will need to be designed, planned, delivered, and evaluated; checklists will need to be duplicated and distributed to all supervisors in the system; a method for supervisors who have problems in using the checklist, or who want help, will need to be designed and provided for. Each of these subtasks will involve different members of the organization, some to provide approval and oversight, some to supervise the subtasks, and others to implement it. Gaining the buy-in and involvement of these people, and providing them assistance as needed, is likewise a necessary part of a thorough implementation plan.

In sum, performance improvement projects entail complex plans typically involving a broad cross section of people from many levels in the organization. Evaluation of the plan itself is useful in two respects. First, evaluation of the plan helps ensure that it is thorough and adequate, that nothing crucial is omitted, and that nothing superfluous is included. Second, an evaluation of the plan that involves stakeholders in the evaluation process helps achieve the critical mass needed for effective implementation. By reviewing the plan and giving their critical input, stakeholders have a chance to recommend changes, understand their role in the context of the larger plan, and be psychologically more confident and "bought in"—all of which helps increase the probability of success. Finally, a formal assessment of the plan, even if it is relatively cursory, helps assure the client that all reasonable alternatives have been considered and that the final plan is worthy of their investment.

Key Questions for Phase 3 (Design) Evaluation

● Have correct and sufficient performance improvement methods, tools, and other support aids been identified?

● How likely is it that the organization will provide the necessary methods, tools, and other support aids?

● To what extent do senior and mid-level managers agree to and support the targeted performance improvement objectives?

● To what extent do performers themselves agree with the targeted performance improvement objectives?

● How likely is it that the support of key persons (as identified in tertiary analysis) will be provided as needed?

● How politically and economically feasible is the performance improvement plan?

● Is the performance improvement plan the most cost-effective alternative for achieving the needed performance improvement and business impact?

● Is there sufficient senior and mid-level management support to enable a successful project?

Phase 3 (Design) Evaluation Methods

● Make a checklist of the key questions (and others, if needed) that define criteria for an effective performance improvement project plan. Have clients review the plan, then discuss with you their opinions and reactions on each point in the checklist.

● Construct a survey questionnaire covering the key questions and project criteria and administer it to key stakeholders in the project to gather their opinions about the completeness and feasibility of the plan.

● Conduct "hearings" on the plan at which groups of key stakeholders listen to a presentation of the plan, then discuss their reactions to it.

● Have the project plan reviewed by external, third-party experts.

● Conduct research on effective performance improvement project plans, then systematically compare your plan to these exemplary models.

Phase 4: Implementation

Evaluation at this phase is the parallel of effective project management. There are three key purposes for evaluation during implementation of the performance improvement project: (1) assessing usage of tools, (2) steering the project, and (3) providing accountability and documentation of project activities and results.

The first purpose is to discover and assess the nature and extent of usage of the performance improvement tools and aids that the project provided to performers. This information is vital for project management purposes, since if there is low or improper usage of these aids and tools, then the performance improvement project is likely to fall short of its goals. Notice that performers not making sufficient use of the tools and aids provided to them is in itself a performance problem. The performance consultant would need to discover the causes for this failure to use the tools (poor design? lack of opportunity? not enough feedback?), then intervene to correct the low-usage problem. The usage information is also important for assessing impact, as will be discussed in the fifth and final evaluation phase. If the tools and aids are truly effective, then those who use them more, or more effectively, should likewise achieve greater levels of performance improvement.

The second purpose for evaluation of implementation serves a "steering" or quality management function. Evaluation is used to compare actual project implementation and progress to projected milestones and stakeholder expectations for achievement of interim objectives. If, for example, the performance improvement project plan called for a meeting of senior management to review and approve some new performance and quality standards, it might be very important to pause at this point in the project and assess the reactions and feedback of these senior managers to ensure that it has been fully expressed, accurately communicated, and fully understood. The risk at this juncture in the project is potentially high, for if senior manager expectations are not adequately expressed or understood, the project could veer dangerously off track.

Third, evaluation serves a documentation and accountability function, assessing the extent to which project accountabilities are, in fact, delivered and achieved. That is, do staff carry through on assignments? Do managers who promise support deliver on their promises? Do suppliers deliver? This purpose for implementation evaluation is relatively simplistic, limited, and typically cursory. Except in large and highly complex performance improvement initiatives in which there are many real or threatened political liabilities, evaluation to serve this purpose will be very briefly attended to.

The general process for implementation evaluation follows a classical discrepancy analysis approach. First, the evaluator helps the performance improvement project leader (and perhaps staff) review the overall project and identify critical events (milestones) where the project faces some sort of relatively high risk. These are points in the project where a failure to perform as expected represents a serious threat to project progress or results. Next, a method for measuring or otherwise assessing progress at this key point is planned, then carried out.

If there is a discrepancy—the performance improvement project milestone has not been achieved as expected—then the project staff must intervene to remove the discrepancy. Addressing the discrepancy involves either (or both) controlling project performance so that it meets expectations, or renegotiating or otherwise reshaping expectations so that the current level of performance is now acceptable. Imagine, for instance, that the performance improvement project plan called for a pilot test of a computer-driven measurement system that tracked the duration of a call and provided a visual display to help the operator track call duration. The purpose of this job aid was to help operators shorten calls, thereby completing more calls per hour. The expectation was that the aid should help operators trim an average of 30 seconds from each call. Now imagine further that the trial test of the aid reveals that the performance expectation was unrealistic, that it easily trimmed 20 seconds per call, but that almost no one could shorten a call beyond that point. It might be that this level of performance turned out to be good enough, and that trimming call duration beyond this level would be too expensive and stressful. Thus trying to control performance (still aiming for the 30 seconds) was not advised; rather, the evaluation showed that the wiser course of action was to replan the process to take advantage of the 20-second reduction, and look elsewhere for further gains in efficiency.

In a typical performance improvement project, there are three simply defined points in the overall project plan that should be considered for implementation evaluation. These points or elements in the plan are as follows:

1. There is an especially critical event or function (such as a management review of performance standards) upon which many subsequent project operations depend. Failure to meet this particular project milestone would pose considerable threat to the rest of the plan.

2. There is a part of the performance improvement plan that will be especially hard to manage. The experience of the performance improvement project manager (or lack of experience) tells him or her that "if any part of this project is likely to go wrong, it is right *here!*" In other words, this event or project milestone is notoriously hard to manage, and typically goes off track.

3. There is an event or function in the performance improvement project plan that draws exceptional external scrutiny, for political reasons, or because of legal, union, or regulatory requirements.

The project plan should be reviewed in light of these three critical descriptors. Wherever a particular performance improvement project event or milestone meets one, or especially more than one, of these descriptors, it is likely that some implementation evaluation attention should be directed toward it.

Key Questions for Phase 4 (Implementation) Evaluation

● To what extent are clients providing the support and involvement needed for successful results?

● Are important project milestones being achieved on time, with needed quality, and within budget?

● Were all performer and manager expectations considered and addressed in the design of the performance management tools?

● How user-friendly and helpful are new job aids?

● How well and completely are performers making use of job aids and other performance improvement tools and techniques provided to them?

● How accurately does the new measurement system track performance?

● Have costs for the development (or testing, or review) of performance support tools and methods remained within budget?

● Is the use of trial job aids helping to improve performance?

Phase 4 (Implementation) Evaluation Methods

● Systematically review and monitor project objectives, progress, and revision needs at regular project review (evaluation) meetings. Track progress against quality, schedule, and cost criteria.

● Gather and review data on interim performance improvement objectives.

● Gather and analyze performance records (audio tapes, written records, reports, work samples) to assess progress.

● Survey project clients and stakeholders to gather their opinions about project progress.

● Interview samples of performers and ask them how things are going, if they are getting the support they need, how useful the tools they are using are, and so forth.

● Observe performers using new methods to assess their progress.

Phase 5: Impact

The fifth phase of the evaluation model focuses on the results of the performance improvement project. The essential question at this phase is: "Did the performance improvement initiative achieve the impact expected on performance and business goals?" This phase usually also assesses the extent of client satisfaction with results of the performance improvement project. It may also be advisable for this phase to explore what the performance consultants themselves have learned from their experience: What worked well? What did not? What should be done differently in a future project? What skills do they need to learn or improve to do an even better job in the future?

This final phase brings the evaluation cycle back to its beginning. The first evaluation phase assessed the validity, accuracy, feasibility, and worthiness of the business goals that the performance improvement effort was to meet. At the final phase, the question is not "Were these the right goals?" but "Were these goals achieved?"

The impact evaluation question contains some level of a concern for causation. That is, it may not be sufficient to simply assess whether performance at the performer or at the business goal level has improved. When clients invest in a performance improvement effort, it is because they feel that the performance improvement effort is needed in order to achieve a business goal; the performance consultant reinforces this perception by agreeing to take on the project, and thus an implicit and mutual assumption about causality is made. If the client or consultant expected that performance might improve simply on its own, with no intervention, then there would be no need for a project.

Thus it is not enough to just assess changes in performance. Rather it is implied that there should be some evidence that the performance improvement interventions designed by the consultant and paid for by the client played some causal role; that is, these interventions had an impact. And, of course, performance consultants cannot have it both ways. If performance does not change despite their greatest work, performance consultants might like to claim that "outside" factors caused no change, rather than a failed performance improvement project. On the other hand, when performance does improve, these same performance consultants would love to claim credit!

There can be, of course, no indisputable proof that any sort of organizational intervention caused any sort of result, since there is always a certain degree of uncertainty, and the interplay of unknown factors is always a possibility. So no evaluation should seek to "prove" that the performance improvement intervention caused a change. But reasonable evidence that the performance improvement interventions played a role in improving performance is a reasonable expectation, and also one that can be met without a great degree of effort.

The business need or goal (for example, reducing costs, increasing quality, reducing cycle time) that necessitated the performance improvement project is considered the ultimate level for evaluation. Since this business need was the reason for the performance improvement effort in the first place, it is important to know whether there is progress toward it. For instance, imagine a performance improvement project in an automobile service garage that was conducted in order to improve the speed (cycle time) with which repairs were completed and autos were ready to be picked up by customers. In this example, the final evaluation measure should assess improvement in this cycle time.

Impact on the final business metric (cycle time in our example) is driven, however, by prior improvements in performance results. In the service garage, the performance improvement effort may have focused on several performance elements, such as (a) increasing the effectiveness of scheduling to ensure adequate time to complete repairs; (b) increasing the speed of completing the service order when the customer drops off the car on the scheduled day; (c) improving the accuracy of diagnosis by using new diagnostic tools and job aids; (d) reducing delays in waiting for parts by using a computer-tracked ordering system; and (e) reducing rework by assigning repair teams according to diagnostic needs, thus ensuring that repairs are conducted by the most qualified mechanics. Notice that these more immediate improvements must be achieved in order to create the targeted impact on the business goal (cycle time). Evaluation should also be directed at these prior (first-level) impact variables, because if they are not achieved, the business target is at risk.

Evaluation of these first-level, immediate performance improvement objectives helps interpret business impact gains and also helps the performance consultant guide the project to greater impact. Imagine that the performance improvement project was only partially effective; for example, it was unable to achieve the aimed-for reduction in time needed to order parts, though all of the other performance improvement objectives were met. Imagine further that this one performance improvement failure was enough to prevent any significant reduction in cycle time, the overall business goal. The performance consultant can investigate the causes for failure to achieve the reduction in parts ordering time—perhaps an unexpected price increase in software needed that the client decided was too expensive and thus did not authorize an upgrade. Armed with this causal data, plus information about the consequences of the parts ordering performance objective shortfall on the overall business goal, the consultant can make a persuasive cost-benefit argument to the client to justify spending more for the software upgrade.

Key Questions for Phase 5 (Impact) Evaluation

- To what extent has performance in key performer objectives improved?

- To what extent have business metrics and goals improved?

- What evidence is there that performance improvement efforts have "caused" performance improvement?

- How satisfied are clients and other key stakeholders with the performance improvement initiative?

Phase 5 (Impact) Evaluation Methods

- Survey performers and others (for example, their bosses) to have them assess and report on improvements in performance.

- Survey key stakeholders and ask them whether they observe improvements in key business indicators.

- Analyze records of performance (work samples, job data) to track and report changes in performer outputs and achievements.

- Analyze business metrics to assess changes and improvements.

- Conduct pre–post comparisons. Track individual and business performance metrics before the performance improvement intervention took place, then assess again after the performance improvement intervention has had a chance to take effect. If there is a significant change after the performance improvement intervention is implemented, then the assumption of impact is strengthened. This is particularly so when there is a long enough track record before the intervention to establish a stable trend line or baseline of performance to determine whether a change after an intervention is just a normal fluctuation, or a real change upward.

● Make internal comparisons based on extent of usage of support tools. Assess individual and business performance metrics, then compare these among subgroups of performers who made variable use of the improvement tools, or who were exposed to more or less assistance. The assumption tested here is whether people who received and made use of more assistance achieved greater results than those who used less assistance. Where performance improvements align with degree of use, there is evidence that the performance improvement intervention had impact.

Conduct comparison group studies. Provide the performance improvement tools and other support to some groups of performers before you provide them to others. Changes in the performance levels and results of people who participated in and used the performance improvement project tools and methods are compared to performance levels and results of people who did not receive performance improvement assistance. If people who received assistance perform more effectively than those who did not receive any assistance, then the assumption that the performance improvement intervention had impact is supported.

DESIGNING AND MANAGING EVALUATION OF PERFORMANCE IMPROVEMENT PROJECTS

Evaluation design, like good performance consultation, is a continuing design process, since evaluation designs also must be continuously improved. And because evaluation is a learning activity (we learn how well performance improvement is meeting needs, and how to make it better), the evaluation should move through iterative design-implement-redesign cycles to redirect it as learning results indicate. Despite this iterative nature of evaluation design, it is possible to identify several discrete steps in the design process. These steps may be approached in varying sequences and feed into one another, but each step must always be attended to. Thus managing and designing an evaluation go hand in hand.

Design Step 1: Identify the performance improvement initiative to be evaluated

This step entails becoming clear about the performance improvement goals and strategy. Describe the initiative fully: What are the goals and objectives of the performance improvement project? How is it supposed to influence business needs? Who is involved? How, and when?

Design Step 2: Identify and clarify the purposes for the evaluation

Evaluation can serve several specific purposes. Evaluation could be used to assess a pilot performance improvement project, to determine how well it works, what makes it work or keeps it from working, whether it produces the desired results, and so forth. Sometimes evaluation is used to select the better of two alternative performance improvement designs being considered. Sometimes evaluation is done to judge whether an already implemented performance improvement initiative is still needed. At other times evaluation is used to identify revision needs in an existing, but new, performance improvement effort. Or evaluation can be done to demonstrate accountability and to prove results to a client. Evaluation can also be done for purposes of marketing, to assess whether performance improvement initiatives work and how much impact they help clients achieve to demonstrate the value of performance improvement efforts to others. Purposes for evaluation may vary, but what does **not** vary is the need to be very clear about why the evaluation is to be done.

Design Step 3: Identify all clients and stakeholders and clarify their needs

Clients for performance improvement, and the evaluation of performance improvement initiatives, vary according to the purposes of the performance improvement and the evaluation. The client of performance improvement is always the person who authorizes and guides the project. Of course, managers who supervise employees who are the recipients of performance improvement efforts are stakeholders, as are the performers themselves. Higher levels of management are clients, for they are responsible for business performance and the efficient use of resources. External customers may also be stakeholders, when the performers who are being aided by performance improvement efforts (such as bank tellers) work directly for them. In any case, there are always stakeholders for evaluation. They must be identified, and their needs must be carefully and correctly analyzed and confirmed.

Design Step 4: Determine the key questions that the evaluation must address

Evaluation questions focus the evaluation purpose more specifically. The evaluation questions break the overall purpose down into a more specific list of inquiries that respond directly to the information needed by the stakeholders in the evaluation. For example, imagine a pilot project to improve the selling performance of tellers and other platform personnel that has been implemented in one branch office of a large bank. Imagine further that the overall purpose for evaluating this project is to decide whether the performance improvement methods used in this one branch have been successful enough to warrant their extension to all of the other branch offices. Here are some evaluation questions that might have been identified for this particular evaluation.

169

- What gains in performance have been achieved for tellers, customer service representatives, and loan officers?

- What job aids have been most effective?

- What problems have employees encountered in improving their performance?

- How have employees reacted to the new sales incentives?

- What revisions are needed to job aids to make them more useful?

- What are the critical supervisory behaviors needed to support performance improvement?

- How much has sales performance improved?

- What is the projected per-branch cost for replicating the project in 150 branch offices?

- How much sales improvement value is needed on a per-branch basis to offset the cost of the performance improvement tools and training?

Design Step 5: Determine the best data collection plan

The plan chosen must be the one that will best address client needs as reflected in the evaluation questions. There are a range of evaluation designs to consider and choose from, and their applicability varies with the purposes for the evaluation and the information needs of stakeholders. Following is a brief review of a few of the major kinds of design approaches, which may be used singly or in combination. Readers who are unfamiliar with research and evaluation methods and design are encouraged to read further, using the references provided at the end of this chapter.

Descriptive. When causal claims are not needed but it is sufficient to simply describe the performance levels at the end of the performance improvement project, the evaluation should aim to define key measures, then provide data that describe performer and business performance results.

Pre–post measures. Measures of performance are taken before the performance improvement project, then compared with parallel performance measures taken afterward. Changes are attributed to the effect of the performance improvement project (assuming that no other significant factor, such as an infusion of new technology, acted during the performance improvement project).

Experiments. True experiments, where rigorous controls are used, are almost never done in organizational settings. But rough experiments can serve very well. It may be useful, for example, to compare the performance of some employees who received only training, with another group who received training and some additional performance support, such as job aids and incentives, to see which approach is more powerful. Or, the pre- and post-performance of employees who received the additional support can be compared with parallel measures for employees who have not yet received any assistance.

Case studies. This evaluation design focuses on only a few performers and aims to describe and analyze, in rich detail, the experiences of this small sample. This approach is useful when it is important to know, with a depth of understanding, just how performers used their assistance, what their feelings and reactions were, what factors influenced them, and so forth. The aim of a case study design is to achieve understanding, versus solely to demonstrate accountability or proof of impact.

Design Step 6: Identify the best data collection sources and procedures

For some evaluation questions, special instruments will need to be constructed to collect the data needed, and relevant data collection and analysis procedures will need to be designed. Almost always, when performers' learning, reactions to tools, opinions about assistance they are receiving, or other personal characteristics are the focus of the evaluation question, evaluators will need to develop (or select) specialized tools, such as tests or performance checklists.

As the focus of inquiry moves closer to job behavior and business performance, using existing data (such as scrap rates, production output numbers, error rates, telephone call completion records, sales records) is advised. Existing data are preferable for two solid reasons: (1) Existing data are cheaper to collect, and (2) businesses usually already measure the performance that matters.

Design Step 7: Plan reporting and communications actions

Evaluation is driven by client needs for information, thus performance consultants need to think about how they are going to get evaluative information to these people who need it. A key principle of reporting is to "segment" the evaluation market. Consultants should not simply prepare an evaluation report, then give it to everyone who may have an interest. Rather they should plan to provide concise and targeted evaluation summaries that are specifically focused on the needs of the clients, stakeholders, and performers. Consultants also should not restrict themselves to providing only formal, written reports. Reports can take the form of brief memoranda, presentations, workshops, discussions, and so forth. The more interactive the format the better, as clients and stakeholders typically need and want assistance in interpreting evaluation findings and applying them in solving performance problems.

Managing the Evaluation Process

Evaluation, like any other complex activity, must be managed effectively, or it is likely to go astray. Evaluation will always work best when it is planned and conducted in conjunction with the overall performance improvement design process, as depicted in the five-phase model shown earlier. Because evaluation activities consume precious resources and are often fraught with implications for making decisions about resource allocations, evaluation should be carefully planned and managed. Some guidelines for managing evaluation activities are as follows:

Use project management tools and principles. Evaluation tasks should be clearly specified and defined, and should be assigned to a single person or group so that responsibility is clear. Schedules of tasks and key events should be made and followed. The evaluation process should be monitored and redirected when necessary. Evaluation tasks should be budgeted so that cost projections are clear and so that actual costs can be tracked.

Use professional technical expertise when and where appropriate. Not all of the skills needed for effective evaluation will be available in the organization. Measurement experts may be needed, for example, to design or select assessment instruments. A professional evaluator may be helpful in planning an overall evaluation strategy. Data collection and analysis experts may be needed for technical tasks within the evaluation. Whenever evaluation experts are used, it is always a good idea for internal performance consultants to stay closely involved, so that the organization's needs and constraints are responsively considered. It is also a good idea to include training as a part of any performance improvement evaluation effort, so that the evaluation technology can be transferred to the organization, avoiding excessive dependency on external experts.

Implement the evaluation in iterative steps. Like performance consultation, evaluation works best when it is undertaken as a successive learning process. Good performance improvement cycles through several iterations, as organizational needs change and as increasingly more is learned about the results and impact of interventions. Evaluation inquiry should be tuned to the phases of the performance improvement initiative. Some measurement data should be collected soon after performance improvement activities are implemented, then these data should be analyzed and interpreted. Following this, depending on the implications of the data, successive evaluation inquiry can be planned and implemented. In a performance improvement project in which data entry clerks were using a new data system, for example, a few of the first performers were interviewed on the job soon after they received job aids. The experiences reported by these early "pioneers" were then used to refine the next round of tools, which in turn led to a more formal evaluation follow-up using a survey questionnaire. The questionnaire items were developed from responses in the preliminary interviews. The questionnaire data were then used for discussion in a series of focus group interview sessions with yet a later group of performers. These successive data collection-performance improvement intervention-data collection events provided rich and increasingly accurate information about how the tools were being used and pinpointed weaknesses in the performance improvement project design.

Closely involve and stay in touch with clients and other stakeholders. Evaluation information will have the greatest impact on clients and stakeholders when these parties are kept regularly informed and involved throughout the training process. Evaluation findings are never absolutely certain and often raise many questions. For these reasons, it is not a good idea to wait until a performance improvement effort is fully complete before informing interested parties about its results. More understanding, and a greater ability to interpret and use the information, will be created when communications are regular and ongoing. Further, because there are always a range of interests and viewpoints among clients and stakeholders, keeping everyone informed ensures that all viewpoints can be heard and considered.

Implement interactive interpretation and reporting events. Written evaluation reports, like other lengthy documents and reports, are notorious for the extent to which they tend to go unread and ignored. Long evaluation reports will not receive the attention and cooperation that performance consultants need from clients and stakeholders. Great success can be achieved, however, when using interactive formats, such as meetings, discussion groups, and workshops, to help stakeholders understand and use the findings of evaluations. A meeting can be designed, for example, to make a brief presentation of the key findings of an evaluation, and then meeting participants can work in small groups to discuss the implications of the findings and possible actions for improvement. This format helps surface and resolve concerns about uncertainty in the findings and helps clients and stakeholders reach agreement on action steps that must be taken to incorporate evaluation findings into further performance improvement initiatives.

References

Brinkerhoff, R.O. *Achieving Results from Training.* San Francisco: Jossey-Bass, 1987.

Brinkerhoff, R.O., and D.E. Dressler. *Productivity Measurement.* Thousand Oaks, CA: Sage, 1989.

Denzin, N.K., and Y.S. Lincoln (eds.). *Handbook of Qualitative Research.* Thousand Oaks, CA: Sage, 1994.

Phillips, Jack J. *Accountability in Human Resources Management.* Houston, TX: Gulf Publishing, 1996.

————. *Return on Investment: In Training and Performance Improvement Programs.* Houston, TX: Gulf Publishing, 1997.

Rust, R.T., and T.L. Keiningham. *Return on Quality: Measuring the Financial Impact of Your Company's Quest for Quality*. Chicago: Probus Publishers, 1994.

Worthen, B., and J. Sanders. *Program Evaluation: Alternative Approaches and Practical Guidelines*. New York: Longman, 1997.

The Author

Robert Brinkerhoff is an internationally recognized expert in training effectiveness and evaluation. He has provided consultation in training effectiveness and evaluation to dozens of major companies and organizations in the United States and around the world.

Brinkerhoff earned his Ph.D. at the University of Virginia in 1974 and is currently a professor of counseling education at Western Michigan University, where he coordinates graduate programs in human resources development.

He is the author of 10 books on evaluation and training, including his most recent works, *The Learning Alliance: Systems Thinking in Human Resources Development* and *How to Evaluate Training*.

Case Study

Applying the Evaluation Process

by Constance Filling and Rose Setze

COMPANY NAME: Arthur Andersen

INDUSTRY TYPE: Professional services

ORGANIZATION PROFILE

ORGANIZATION SIZE:

50,000 employees.

KEY SERVICES:

Economic and financial consulting; business consulting; tax, legal, and business advisory services; assurance and business advisory services.

ANNUAL SALES:

$4.6 billion.

DEPARTMENT NAME:

Performance Consulting.

DEPARTMENT SIZE:

90 employees.

MISSION FOR DEPARTMENT:

To develop and deliver high-value performance enhancement consulting, tools, training programs, and research studies to support management decision making, and organizational, team, and individual growth. Integrating these high-quality products and services will enable us to fill the needs of an ever-expanding niche of markets.

PRIMARY REASONS FOR TRANSITION TO A PERFORMANCE FOCUS:

Requests from clients for evidence of impact on individual and organizational performance; ability to integrate full complement of services while demonstrating impact; consistency with the evolution of the field.

Background Information

Performance Consulting was contacted in 1997 to work with Arthur Andersen business developers. The managing partner of the Business Development Organization wanted Performance Consulting to recommend and implement a strategy for leading and measuring performance improvement within his group. At that time, the Business Development Organization was, in the words of their managing partner, "on the verge of collapse." Partners within Arthur Andersen who had initially created the group to help them increase revenues were disappointed at the *perceived* value they were receiving from the business developers. The generally held view was that the investment made to create the Business Development Organization was considerable and that the return on that investment was questionable.

At the same time, business developers were disgruntled and unhappy with support for their practice within the organization. Specifically, business developers were unsatisfied with the leadership, infrastructure, training, and investment being provided by Arthur Andersen for their growing business. There was a lack of direction and focus. It was not surprising, given this situation, that business developers expressed frustration with the level of respect and acceptance they were receiving from partners in the organization.

The Arthur Andersen Business Developer Initiative was created in 1989 and has been expanded as a result of pervasive changes within Arthur Andersen, including service line expansion and the desire for continued growth. Prior to the establishment of the Business Development Organization, Arthur Andersen did not have a central group specifically focused on business development. As a professional services organization, partners at various locations within the organization were expected to develop business, maintain existing business, and provide expert professional services. Partners and managers have always had primary responsibility for sales of Arthur Andersen services, yet they have received limited training on business development. There was concern within the organization that these goals could not be maximized within the current structure. Consequently, the Business Development Organization was created to assist partners and managers in these efforts. Business developers work with

176

partners and managers to identify, pursue, and obtain new business. The specific charge for the group was to identify potential business opportunities in various industries and service lines primarily in the United States. The group began with a staff of approximately five people. Between August 31, 1996, and August 31, 1997, the number of salespeople in the group increased from 40 to 80.

The primary client for this project was the managing partner of the Business Development Organization. Other key stakeholders were the business developers themselves and, indirectly, all Arthur Andersen partners. The primary client for the project met with Performance Consulting early in January 1997 to describe the situation and to discuss ways to increase the level of performance in the group. The needs he expressed at that time were to give business developers a forum in which to be heard, to have business developers and those they work with identify their needs, and to prioritize these needs and develop action plans.

The client's stated goal from the project was to create a successful business development group within three years, as measured by creation of a business developer career path, increased job satisfaction for business developers, and increased revenues for the parent organization. To achieve this, he wanted Performance Consulting to design and implement a process for determining business developer needs and for identifying and implementing an action plan for addressing those needs. He believed it was necessary to create a solution that integrated the needs of all stakeholders to the project.

Performance Consulting is an internal group of consultants with expertise in all areas of performance enhancement, including assessment and measurement; organizational design and development; team development; leadership development; and instructional design. The mission of the group is to provide clients with solutions integrating the full scope of performance enhancement services. The group was created in 1995 through a combination of three previously separate groups specializing in program evaluation, instructional design, and management development services. Performance Consulting includes individuals with deep academic and practical experience in each of these areas. Individuals within Performance Consulting work as part of the client team in designing and implementing appropriate solutions. They use a variety of methods and approaches in designing these solutions depending on what is most appropriate for the specific client situation.

Process and Activities Used to Accomplish Results

The core team for this project included the managing partner, a performance and learning manager working to directly support the Business Development Organization, and a performance consultant with a background in evaluation and measurement. Specifically, the performance consultant assigned to the project has deep expertise in program evaluation and in both quantitative and qualitative evaluation.

Based on the client's needs and goals, successful measures of impact were both quantitative and qualitative. Qualitative methods to gather input from stakeholders would be key to generating stakeholder buy-in. The development of a business developer career path and the increase in job satisfaction for individuals in the Business Development Organization were key goals for the client and were, therefore, an expected qualitative result of this project. Quantitative measures include the generation of increased revenues, which was also a desired result of the project. The generation of increased revenue is a lag indicator of successfully integrating the Business Development Organization into the firm. It will be monitored on a quarterly basis going forward. The client had expectations that all measures—the development of a business developer career path, increase in job satisfaction, increased respect within the organization, and the generation of increased revenues—would be used as indicators of a successful project. Assessing the importance of these goals from a business perspective was the first step in the performance evaluation process. This is consistent with Brinkerhoff's Phase 1 evaluation.

At this point in the project, the job of the performance consultant was to identify an appropriate strategy for analyzing performance needs and objectives for the project. As described in Phase 2 of Brinkerhoff's model, the purpose was to identify critical performance roles and factors to be improved in order to achieve the business goal. The performance consultant on the project, working as part of the team, suggested that to achieve the stated goals for the project, an evaluation strategy drawing on both qualitative and quantitative methods would be most appropriate. In this situation, the performance consultant recommended concept mapping as an appropriate technique.

The client had previous positive experiences and results on prior projects using concept mapping and pattern matching methods. The methods have been used in a wide range of settings, and are described in detail by W. Trochim in "Concept Mapping for Planning and Evaluation" (*Evaluation and Program Planning, 12,* 1). Performance Consulting has been applying and adapting the methods in a business setting. Concept mapping is a conceptualization technique that enables a group to articulate and assign meaning to ideas, the results of which are represented in the form of a physical map. This method, driven by a software program called The Concept System® developed by Concept Systems, Inc., produces a concept map that portrays the group's thinking (or conceptual layout) about a specific topic. Pattern matching techniques allow comparisons among measures; for example, a comparison of the importance and current performance ratings for each item on the map (see figure 1).

The concept mapping method was appropriate for assessing the current situation within the Business Development Organization, for clarifying future direction, and for measuring progress toward that direction over time. In this way, it is an example of what Brinkerhoff describes as "a strategic tool for leveraging continuously improved value." Performance Consulting has extensive experience using concept mapping and pattern matching as an evaluation tool within the Arthur Andersen organization. Its most effective applications have been in defining key issues and producing a conceptual picture of the issues that can then be used to drive action planning and measurement of progress toward goals.

The key benefit of the map is a three-dimensional picture that enables the client to better visualize and thus conceptualize the complexities, needs (current and desired state), and opportunities of their organization. Concept mapping and pattern matching is based on a five-step process as follows:

1. Generate ideas about the topic.

2. Identify how the ideas relate to one another by grouping them.

3. Prioritize the ideas by rating the importance of each.

4. Interpret the relationships and priorities to develop action plans through a group process.

5. Use the result as a framework to measure progress toward desired goals.

Performance Consulting had overall responsibility for all steps in the process. Specifically, Performance Consulting was responsible for assisting the client in organizing the process, determining the right focused questions to ask, and using the method to accomplish stated goals. Each phase of the process was managed by Performance Consulting as was the interpretation of data and the creation of maps and pattern matches.

The primary client agreed to key responsibility for identifying individuals to participate in the process. Individuals were chosen based on how critical they were to the creation of an effective integrated solution for the Business Development Organization. The primary client also agreed to work closely with Performance Consulting throughout the project, to prioritize results, and to actively encourage the implementation of action plans for sustainable results.

All business developers in the Business Development Organization and a group of Arthur Andersen partners and managers with whom they work were asked to participate in three data collection activities as part of the process. First, they individually brainstormed to develop a list of critical skills, knowledge, and behaviors for successful business development sales professionals. A master list of their ideas was compiled in which each item expressed a single idea. Each group member was then asked to indicate how items on that master list related to one another by grouping them "in a way that made sense" to the individual. Finally, they individually rated the importance of each item for a successful business development program as well as the business developer's current ability to perform each item.

The grouping data was analyzed, using multidimensional scaling and cluster analysis techniques, and interpreted in a facilitated meeting of the key stakeholder group. This activity produced a concept map, which is shown in figure 1. The individual items from the participants' brainstormed master list were grouped into 10 clusters on the map. Each cluster represents a key area for performance improvement. The distances between the clusters are meaningful; distances reflect how often participants grouped items together. Items (and clusters) closer on the map were seen as more similar to more people than items (or clusters) that are farther away from one another on the map. The map portrays the group's thinking about the relationship or similarity between each performance improvement area.

Clusters were next grouped into four categories. These categories were generated by the group of business developers and given names to represent components of success for the Business Development Organization. As can be seen in the map, World Class Selling, Skills for Sales Success, Business Development Process, and a Foundation for Sales Success in the Firm were seen as key to success for the Business Developer Organization. The importance of each category is represented by the height (the number of layers) of the clusters (that is, higher equals more important).

This three-dimensional map was also used to identify priorities for action items. Participant ratings of importance and performance ability were averaged for each item and for items within each performance improvement area. The resulting "gap" between importance and performance was used to determine immediate and long-term priorities. For example, an area rated as highly important and as low in current ability to perform indicates a priority. As a result, the project team was able to agree on the high-priority needs within the organization. The team was able to link other initiatives that were underway to these priorities, and to create a plan for addressing each need. As part of their involvement in the process, they also agreed to assist in taking action on items identified to be of high priority.

Finally, the map became the communication vehicle to report progress and impacts of actions in each of the identified performance improvement areas. It has also been a major input for developing a strategic business plan for the Business Development Organization.

Results

Consistent with Phase 3 of Brinkerhoff's model, five initiatives were identified as interventions for the Business Development Organization.

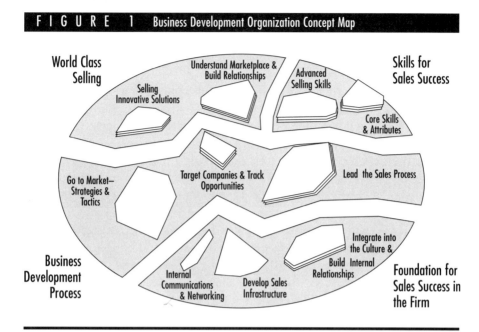

FIGURE 1 Business Development Organization Concept Map

Note: The concept map was generated with The Concept System Software®, Concept Systems, Inc.

These five initiatives, having been established in the past year, come as a direct result of the concept map. A two-day, highly interactive business development orientation program for newly hired business developers has been piloted. Evaluations of the program indicate that business developers show an increased understanding of the Business Development Organization and more confidence in knowing how to successfully integrate into the firm. They specifically mention the focus on strengthening their networking skills and increasing their understanding of the firm culture.

A two-and-one-half-day national sales meeting to be held quarterly has also been planned and conducted. The focus of this program is on providing opportunities for networking; sharing knowledge; increasing sales skills through advanced sales training offerings/presentations; recognition of sales efforts and successful integration into the firm through an awards program; and an increased awareness of products and services across the firm. A Business Development Organization communications plan and work plan has been developed. In addition, a common sales methodology within the firm has been developed and is currently being implemented. Finally, performance and learning needs have been identified within the Business Development Organization. Those needs include a career path, a recruitment and hiring process, various specific training workshops, and the establishment of objectives for next year.

Each planned intervention was scrutinized by asking, "To what extent does senior management agree with and support this intervention?" The project team also continued to review concept map results to ensure that sufficient interventions had been identified to address business goals. As a result of these initiatives and their successful implementation, the generally held view among other partners within Arthur Andersen is that the Business Development Organization is well organized, focused, and has mechanisms in place to address any issues that may arise.

The Business Development Organization has realized both operational and performance goals as a result of this project and is very satisfied with the outcome. Specifically, the project did meet the client's goal of identifying issues that led to designing and implementing interventions for performance improvement. In so doing, this project demonstrated what Brinkerhoff describes as implementation evaluation in Phase 4 of his model.

Using Phase 5 of Brinkerhoff's model, the project assessed its impact and found the interventions to have been successful. Results from this project are seen at the individual level and at the organizational level. At the organizational level, one year after completion of the initial concept map, the Business Development Organization is viewed as highly successful and results oriented. This is measured by the continued demand for business developer services, which has increased by 25 percent during the year. There also have been changes at the individual business developer level. They too are very satisfied with the results of the project. Business developers report that they now feel their concerns have been heard and are being addressed. Further, they believe they are becoming more respected within the organization and feel a greater sense of belonging. There are additional opportunities for growth and development individually as a result of the increase in employees within the group.

Perhaps most important to the client, the Arthur Andersen organization has become more focused on the sales needs of the organization and on the role of the Business Development Organization as a key driver in this process. Arthur Andersen continues to receive increasingly high marks from stakeholders for the work done by business developers.

The primary client for the project is extraordinarily satisfied with the outcomes of the project. He reports there is virtually "no noise" in the system one year after completion of the concept mapping process. He believes that all high-priority needs have been identified and are being systematically addressed. He believes that concept mapping is an exceptional tool for addressing issues within a major program. This is especially true where the outcome or desired state is not clear, and it is necessary to build consensus and obtain input from a variety of stakeholders. The process is sound, logical, and easy to explain. This makes it possible to gain buy-in from all participants as to the priority actions. One indication of the client's satisfaction has been his continued use and recommendation of Performance Consulting and concept mapping.

Brinkerhoff defines evaluation as *systematic reflection* in that it requires stakeholders in performance projects to pause occasionally to ask how things are going. Critical to its value is the systematic process of planning for the evaluation and the commitment of time, money, and resources to accomplish its goals. Performance Consulting defines evaluation broadly as information to inform decision making. In ideal situations, it is an ongoing process of systematic data collection, analysis, and interpretation that begins early and continues through completion of a project. The information gathered is used to steer direction and optimize performance improvement. The focus of this case study was on setting a direction and designing and implementing performance improvement interventions to improve performance in the Business Development Organization. To do this, Performance Consulting used the concept mapping and pattern matching method. This method is consistent with Brinkerhoff's five-phase evaluation approach. Brinkerhoff's delineation of evaluation phases and the questions to be asked at each phase are useful in designing a comprehensive evaluation focused on performance improvement.

Lessons Learned

• A key learning was confirmation that the concept map method is a powerful and effective method for enhancing performance. It allows the team to ask the right questions and to identify issues and actions that will have impact on performance at both individual and organizational levels.

• It is critical that performance consultants provide expertise that can add value to their clients. In this case, Performance Consulting was able to add value beyond our cost by facilitating a process for identifying focus and direction for the Business Development Organization, for identifying critical issues for which most required action, and for measuring the ongoing implementation of these actions.

• To improve the process, other stakeholders, such as key marketing personnel, should be asked to participate in the initial creation of the map. This would include input from another stakeholder group and would help to gain their overall support of the resulting actions.

• The objectives and processes used in concept mapping could have been better explained to the Business Development Organization if done at a meeting prior to the actual start of the project. This would increase initial understanding and have a favorable impact on participation and response rates.

The Authors

Constance Filling is director of Performance Consulting, which provides broad organizational development services to Andersen Worldwide. These services include leadership development, team development, organizational development, measurement and assessment, and the design and development of learning solutions.

Filling has primary responsibility for the strategic and tactical management of the group and is involved in the full range of services from client service planning to day-to-day operational management. Her prior positions at Andersen Worldwide include director of human resources at the Center for Professional Education, where she was responsible for recruiting, developing, and retaining personnel to meet the business needs of the center, and manager in the Evaluation Services group, where she was responsible for directing program evaluation projects. Before joining the organization, Filling was an assistant professor at the University of Illinois, Chicago.

Filling earned a B.S.S. in sociology, psychology, and education from Cornell College. She received an M.A. in educational psychology from the University of Chicago, where she is near completion of a Ph.D. in educational sociology. She has authored papers in professional journals including, *Development Psychology, Urban Education Evaluation Planning and Evaluation,* and *Health Professions*. In addition, she has made presentations at the annual meetings of the American Education Research Association, the American Evaluation Association, the American Anthropological Association, and the National Society for Performance and Instruction.

Rose Setze is an evaluation specialist with the Performance Consulting group in Andersen Worldwide. Since joining the organization in 1995, she has been responsible for managing projects reflecting the unit's primary service lines including training and program evaluation, survey research, and measurement testing. Setze has made numerous presentations focused on systematic assessment of training effectiveness. Prior to joining Andersen Worldwide, she worked as an independent evaluation consultant and as an assistant director of a psychosocial rehabilitation research institute. She is experienced in the concept mapping, pattern matching, and measurement methodologies.

Setze received her B.S. in psychology from DePaul University, her M.A. in social sciences from the University of Chicago, and her Ph.D. in sociology program evaluation and planning from Cornell University.

Section Three Overview

The Organization Level of Alignment

This section provides insight into how a department structures itself for the transition from training to performance. Clearly, roles and responsibilities change; therefore, the organization of the department must also modify. In this section, there is a chapter describing how a large department made the transition as well as a chapter that focuses on the experience of a much smaller function.

In chapter 7, Robert Blalock describes how the transition occurred in a very large organization—SBC Communications, Inc. Key learnings include the need to separate the role of performance consultant from the role of those who design and deliver the learning services. Blalock also illustrates the power of having a governing board, composed of senior executive officers, to help provide direction to the performance department.

In chapter 8, Carman Nemecek shares the experience of her department, one that is much smaller in size. Her journey to a performance focus is compared with that of a business or product moving through the life cycle of start-up, growth, and maturity. In each stage of development, the department's structure was modified. Once again the need to adapt and be flexible, while keeping focus on the ultimate goal, is illustrated.

7

Organizing for a Performance Focus: A Large Department's Perspective

by Robert Blalock

QUICK READ

● A large department (approximately 700 employees) in a large corporation (120,000 employees) made the transition to a performance focus over a period of two years. There were three significant actions taken to support this transition, which are described in this chapter.

—Organize for a focus on performance. This requires the selection of a good model that is skills and practice based. It also requires the creation of a performance consultant position that is separate from the learning and instructional side of the department.

—Establish a shared standard as to what constitutes quality instructional performance objectives, and seek alternative methods, including use of technology, for delivering learning services.

—Build a governing board composed of senior executive officers of the organization who will take an active role in directing the success of the new performance organization.

● Allocating resources and time to measurement of impact is critical to success. Being able to demonstrate results increases the opportunities to work with management only as they come to realize the value of this type of service. Having a plan for communicating successes is also vital. Without a plan, no one will ever know!

SBC Communications, Inc., (SBC) is an international leader in the telecommunications industry, with more than 31 million access lines and four million wireless customers across the United States, as well as investments in telecommunications businesses in eight foreign countries. The company completed a merger with the Pacific Telesis Group in April 1997. Under the Southwestern Bell, Pacific Bell, Nevada Bell, and Cellular One brands, the company through its subsidiaries offers a wide range of innovative services including local and long distance telephone service, wireless communications, paging, Internet access, cable TV, and messaging, as well as telecommunications equipment and directory advertising and publishing. SBC has nearly 120,000 employees. SBC reported combined 1997 revenues of $25 billion.

Prior to January 1996, all the various training groups within Southwestern Bell and other SBC Communications, Inc., organizations would have readily admitted to the importance of performance improvement as a primary goal. Like most corporate training organizations, however, they would also readily admit to shortcomings in the strategies, processes, and day-to-day execution of tasks designed to achieve that goal. Time and resource pressure rarely if ever allowed for the ideal instructional design model to be followed. Training programs could and *would* be created quickly at the client's request, and the instructional materials, self-study manuals, job aids, and classroom instructors usually received high ratings on the end-of-class evaluations. People were *trained,* and the delivery of significant amounts of "students days" was reported each year (190,000 in 1995). But it was painfully obvious to many in these training organizations that the tyranny of the urgent would routinely take precedence over focused, measurable performance improvement—a common state of affairs among similar corporate training groups at that time.

Although many of these training professionals were aware of the gaps, the traditional telephone company regulated environment, and its attendant organizational momentum had for years favored status quo methodologies, being very cautious in their approach to new ideas in the training arena. Dramatic change would require a new direction from the top of the organizational chart. In January 1996, that launch order was given.

The shift of the SBC Center for Learning to a true performance-focused organization is, to a great extent, the product of a new "take a risk and make it happen!" leader who came with a new vision coupled with a personal passion for results—business results measured by performance improvement.

This is the story of that change, the establishing of a group of approximately 50 staff, functioning full time in a performance consultant role, and its impact on the new performance-focused organization.

THE JOURNEY—MOVING TOWARD A PERFORMANCE-FOCUSED ORGANIZATION

In late 1995, SBC's senior vice president for human resources named a new president of the newly formed subsidiary, the SBC Center for Learning. Her charge from SBC's top leadership was to create a state-of-the-art, centralized training group that would effectively and efficiently lead the development of SBC's human capital as the "new day" of competition rocked the telecommunications industry. At that time, there were approximately 60,000 employees in SBC, Southwestern Bell, and SBC affiliate organizations. To expedite the process, the Center for Learning president started an aggressive personal learning program to discover what industry leaders were saying about the future of training and what would be the key components required to produce such an organization. Very quickly the president formed some strategic conclusions:

● Most successful corporate universities have an actively involved governing board consisting of senior-level corporate officers.

● Accelerating investments in instructional technology and alternative media delivery could enable more *efficient* learning across the enterprise. These initiatives would not only be a wise investment but would also send a culture change message: "It's a new day, new ways, let's get with it!"

● *Successful* (efficient *and* effective) alternative instructional media initiatives would also position the Center for Learning as a model of sound risk taking.

● Although alternative media courseware would be key enablers of creating a skilled workforce, they were incremental (very valuable, but nonetheless incremental) improvements on existing systems and processes. The new president came to the conclusion that in order for SBC's *people* to truly be its competitive advantage, the focus had to shift to *performance*. The Center for Learning had to paradigm shift from "We are in the training business" to "We are in the *performance* business" and measure its success by its impact on clients' bottom-line business results!

These conclusions framed the beginning of the Center for Learning's shift to a performance-focused organization. Three significant actions were agreed upon: (1) There would be a shift in paradigm to one that focused on performance; (2) there would be increased use of alternative media; and (3) a governing board would be established.

Paradigm Shift to Performance

The organizational structure of the training department that preceded the Center for Learning had needs analysis, design, and delivery (instructors) within each major content area (for example, leadership) or responsibility group (focusing on a certain client or group of clients, such as network/technical training). In early 1996, the president reorganized to cluster staff in their functional area of specialty (for example, design or delivery). The Center for Learning had approximately 300 staff at this time. See table 1 for a chart of the resultant organization.

This reorganization was accomplished by letting everyone "bid" and interview for a job they would like to do. Those selected as performance consultants came from all across the organization, but primarily they were individuals who had been doing some form of needs analysis, design, or delivery.

The establishing of a separate group with full-time responsibilities for performance consulting was a clear signal to the organization that there was a

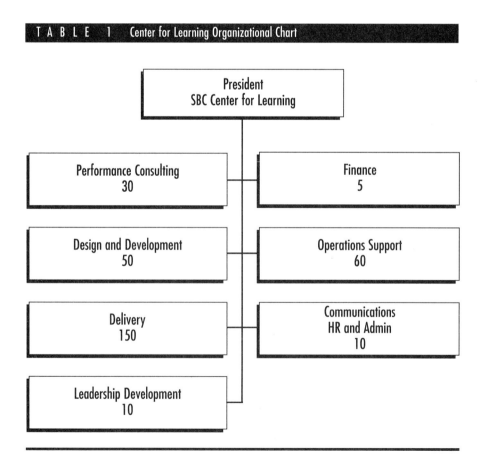

T A B L E   1   Center for Learning Organizational Chart

President
SBC Center for Learning

Performance Consulting
30

Finance
5

Design and Development
50

Operations Support
60

Delivery
150

Communications
HR and Admin
10

Leadership Development
10

new focus within the Center for Learning. Performance Consulting was, in turn, organized into three groups: one to focus on the wireline sales and call centers client organizations; one to focus on the wireline network/technical clients; and one to focus on the wireless client organization. That structure has remained unchanged to the present, the only difference being that each area has grown in size (number of consultants) and scope (each group is now responsible for client organizations spanning the new SBC territory of California, Nevada, Texas, Missouri, Kansas, Oklahoma, and distinct geographical areas in Illinois, New York, Massachusetts, and Maryland).

From research done by others, we learned there are organizations that are incorporating the performance consulting role as a part-time responsibility for individuals in design or delivery. A key factor in the success of performance consulting at the SBC Center for Learning was the organizational segregation and the mandate to focus exclusively on that role. It is interesting to note that this organizational structure and focus came primarily from the vision of the new president of the Center for Learning. Even though all the management team agreed with and fully supported this new structure, some expressed the view: "Sure, this is fine. It's one way to do it. There are probably many other ways that could be just as effective." A year later, that perspective had dramatically changed (as noted in the final paragraph of this chapter).

Instructional Technology/Alternative Media

A shift in focus to performance had many implications for the learning solutions that would be utilized. Recognizing the benefits of alternative media, the Center for Learning began to accelerate its investment in instructional technology. This had an indirect, positive effect on the shift to performance in two ways: clearer instructional objectives in training materials and an expanded knowledge of the range of training solutions that could be used to close a skill or knowledge gap.

The Center for Learning's 1997–1999 strategic plan established goals to staff the design and development team with the "best and the brightest." This was further detailed that by the end of 1999, 40 percent of the positions would be staffed by a person holding a graduate degree in instructional design or instructional technology; 30 percent of the positions would be staffed by a person with two-plus years' experience in focused instructional design work; and 30 percent of the positions would be staffed with subject matter experts (SMEs). These SMEs would bridge the relationship between requisite skill or job knowledge and instructional design. As these positions began to be filled with degreed and well-experienced designers, course objectives began to be much more behaviorally focused. When performance consultants indicated that their research suggested that a training solution was warranted, they were required to list preliminary instructional objectives in their report to the design and development group. All involved in this process began to focus on writing good objectives.

In mid-1997, the Center for Learning created a full-time position entitled "performance consultant—measurement and evaluation." This person serves as a specialized resource to the performance consultants, assisting them with research strategies, data analysis and interpretation, and the design of appropriate measurements to evaluate learning gains, skills transfer/retention, and translation of improved performance into business results numbers. By September, this specialist designed and began to deliver a one-day class on writing performance objectives to everyone in the design, performance consulting, and delivery (instructors) groups. The result is that everyone in those groups now has a shared understanding (standard) for what constitutes a well-constructed performance-based objective. The confidence of performance consultants to write and recognize quality performance objectives has greatly increased.

As the Center for Learning began to develop and use more computer-based training (CBT), multimedia Web-based training, Infomedia CDs, and a virtual reality program, performance consultants and designers alike benefited from an expanded knowledge of the range of training solutions that could be used to close a skill or knowledge gap. And since most of these alternative media examples included embedded knowledge and skill assessments, they also began to be more creative with the construction of learning assessments. The result was increased confidence in their abilities to be very creative about training solutions targeted at performance improvement.

The Board

The Center for Learning's 12-member board of directors was formed early in 1997 with the senior vice president for human resources assuming the role of chairperson. The board meets once a quarter. Board members are senior-level officers such as SBC's senior vice president, treasurer/chief financial officer, the president of Southwestern Bell Operations, the president/CEO of Southwestern Bell Mobile Systems, president/CEO of Southwestern Bell Telephone Company, the executive vice president of strategic marketing, and so forth. In October 1997, the board was restructured and welcomed to its membership the president/CEO of Pacific Bell, the president/CEO of SBC Directory Operations, and SBC's vice president/chief information officer. Clearly the involvement of these leaders is evidence of strong support for the Center for Learning.

The composition of the board was very important, as these senior executives would, at least four times a year, provide composite, high-level, strategic direction to the Center for Learning. This board ensures alignment of Center for Learning initiatives and the strategic business objectives and goals of SBC. An additional advantage was that board members would also provide in-depth information on the organization's budget, structure, management team, and capital needs—no end-of-year surprises. A second and equally critical aspect of this board was that they acknowledged and agreed to play an *active* role in championing new initiatives across the enterprise, to be engaged, strategic partners in the truest sense. This has proved over and over again to be a key factor in the Center for Learning's shift to a performance-focused organization.

When what used to be a known quantity (that is, a "training" organization that would simply react and fill clients' requests for traditional classes) begins to talk about a major shift in focus—away from its old, known role—the environment is ripe for misunderstandings. For many operations people, the training organization is somewhat of a "black box" (little understood as to its real benefit, merely a requisite stop for many technical, proprietary systems and marketing assignments). With that very tenuous link to corporate "value contribution," and without a clear, shared understanding and commitment at high levels for the long haul, an attempt to shift to a performance-focused organization may easily fail.

Road Map for a Performance-Focused Organization— Putting the Pieces Together

At this point (March/April 1996) the Center for Learning had begun the shift to a performance focus, but there were some key elements missing. Performance consultants lacked a cohesive model and skills to be able to do their jobs; roles and responsibilities were vague; linkages (handoffs) between the functional groups were unclear; and there was no tool to automate parts of the process and facilitate linkages. The coming together of these elements would be the next stage in the evolution to a performance-focused organization.

In mid-1996, the president of the SBC Center for Learning sensed that the organization needed an additional resource who could lead the performance consulting groups as they acquired the necessary skills and worked through role clarification and identification of the handoffs, particularly between the consulting and course design groups. In addition, the area of measurement and evaluation needed focused attention if it was to be an effective part of the center's success. In July 1996, the president recruited the author to serve in these roles.

Skill Building

An external supplier was selected as the resource for the model and training of performance consultants. The first class was held at the Irving, Texas, campus location in August 1996. Since then subsequent classes have been held so that all performance consultants have completed the training. We selected this supplier because his model and process emphasized partnering, contracting, and a thorough and easy-to-follow plan.

In our initial selection process to retain performance consultants, our criteria were sketchy; they are much more concrete now. We decided that since this was a new role with some fairly unique responsibilities, it would be best to just let the process work itself out on its own. If we felt candidates were somewhere in the ballpark (skills- and aptitude-wise) and they were definitely interested, we would both learn by letting them try on the role and give it their best shot. If they later decided it was not right for them, we could fairly easily find them a spot in some other area of the Center for Learning (another advantage of a large organization).

We also positioned the training in the same vein. At every class, we have announced that the class in itself will help people decide if the job of performance consulting is for them. If, at the end of class, they want to self-select out of the position, we'll gladly accommodate as quickly as that can be arranged. Good performance consultants must really like what they do. It is a unique function that involves frequent interaction with key SBC management, which means it is best to have people doing the job who are fully committed.

How many out of the 50 have self-selected out of the role? Two so far. Did we waste money sending them through the training? Absolutely not! In their current roles as instructors, they now have a very good understanding of the performance consultant job, and that really helps with the collaboration needed between the functional groups. In fact, our director of instructional design and technologies is lobbying to have *all* his staff go through the training not only for the insight and understanding of the process but also as career preparation, so they will be ready to step into any performance consultant slot that might become available.

Assessment and Measurement

Another key part of the road map to a performance-focused organization is getting the performance consultants reasonably comfortable with data collection, interpretation, and evaluation of results. This does not require them to obtain a doctorate in statistics. For the Center for Learning, our Ph.D. expert (performance consultant-measurement and evaluation) is working fine. The key skills he brings to the organization are his knowledge plus his ability to serve as a consultant to the other consultants.

Why is measurement so important? It is the proof of results, or, conversely, it is the insight as to why a certain behavior is not a gap or a cause. Without valid data, we are all just sharing opinions. An excellent example of the power of measurement happened at our October 1997 board meeting. The meeting went from 10:00 a.m. to 3:00 p.m. After we covered the usual financials, the operations report consisted of a string of 15 presentations by individual performance consultants discussing the results of analyses and interventions used to assess and close performance gaps. Every board member was thoroughly engaged throughout the entire day, even the one who had not been able to attend in person but was linking in via teleconference from San Ramon, California. Throughout the meeting and in subsequent conversations, there were statements of praise from the board members—all concerning the data and measurements presented.

Many training organizations are now doing some measurements and reporting results especially of the "training days saved by using alternative media" type. Those are fine and valid, but there is a world of reportable data on performance that should also be explored. Good data and measurements are powerful. When the data are clear and you understand and know how to present the information, the whole client engagement/contracting process goes a lot more smoothly.

Roles and Responsibilities

The SBC Center for Learning organization now has approximately 700 staff with about 50 of those in the three performance consulting groups shown in table 2. Each director (over each performance consultant group) is responsible for managing his or her team and their assignments with clients. We have found that some individuals can handle more clients than others, plus each client needs to be evaluated on criteria that help to prioritize the time required to be spent with clients (based on their importance). All of the Center for Learning's SBC clients are apportioned into one of the three areas of responsibility shown in table 2.

At the SBC Center for Learning, we have both performance consultants and consultants. They perform very similar jobs, the primary difference being one of supervision: The performance consultant supervises consultants. Performance consultants serve in two roles: account manager and client advocate.

● **Account manager.** Based on an understanding of both the Center for Learning's *mission* and business plan and SBC's overall corporate strategies, the performance consultant proactively assists clients with the identification, analysis, and resolution of their human performance/business needs. In many respects, performance consultants are using "consultative selling" as they bring the Center for Learning's expertise, products, and services to address real business needs and thus deliver value (improved performance) back to the corporation. In this role, performance consultants are strategically partnering with clients to identify needs and bring the Center for Learning's resources to them.

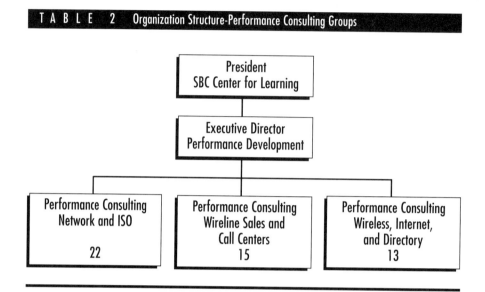

T A B L E   2   Organization Structure-Performance Consulting Groups

President
SBC Center for Learning

Executive Director
Performance Development

Performance Consulting Network and ISO	Performance Consulting Wireline Sales and Call Centers	Performance Consulting Wireless, Internet, and Directory
22	15	13

● **Client advocate.** Based on a constantly increasing understanding of *the client's* business plan and goals, the performance consultant is also bringing back to the Center for Learning client needs or requests so a resolution occurs that represents *the client's* best interests. As an effective *client advocate*, the performance consultant *manages the Center for Learning* on behalf of the client.

These two roles are not contradictory. They do require that a performance consultant be able to skillfully balance and represent the needs of both parties at the same time and work them through to a creative win-win for both. The performance consultant's two major roles involve related and different activities that drive to "success." Table 3 illustrates some examples.

The performance consultant's responsibilities related to the above roles fall into four categories: client relationships, assessment, measurement, and project management.

1. Client Relationships

● Gains access to decision makers, being viewed as a credible and valued business partner

● Proposes appropriate interventions(s) based upon client needs

● Is the overall account manager for the client(s) and the Center for Learning

2. Assessment

● Obtains client business goals information and determines how the Center for Learning can help the client achieve these business goals

T A B L E   3   Performance Consultant Roles

Account Manager Role	Client Advocate Role
Center for Learning ➡ Client	Client ➡ Center for Learning
Look at business needs, goals, and results and identify performance issues in order to engage or contract for services.	Understand the client's business.
Identify the goal (performance model).	Be the "primary point of contact."
Identify performance gaps and causes of gaps. Help the client understand the implications of those gaps on achievement of business results.	Manage the interface. Identify clients' business issues that have implications for the Center for Learning and the Center for Learning's processes, and manage a successful construction of that interface that satisfies the client and appropriately utilizes the Center for Learning's resources.

- Communicates client needs

- Guides and coaches consultants to analyze client needs using a performance analysis process

3. **Measurement**

- Oversees ongoing measurement and evaluation plan

4. **Project Management**

- Formulates and reviews overall performance objectives for each client intervention

- Orchestrates and leads teams as appropriate

- Determines and gains agreement on project scope including analysis, funding, measurement, interventions, processes, and milestones

- Mobilizes resources both internally and externally to meet client needs

- Assists in project prioritization of the clients' entire portfolio by consulting with clients, cross-functional team members, or decision makers as appropriate

Measures of Performance Consultant Success

We are working on specific measures to evaluate the performance of a performance consultant. This is a work in progress. Currently we want to evaluate the following areas:

- Whether or not the client interface is happening.

- A quality measure of the interface itself—Is the performance consultant seen as a "consultant" by the client, providing strategic assistance and custom solutions? Or, is the performance consultant clearly a "member of the client's team," embedded in the client's key meetings and conversations, missed when absent, assumed to be present (no invitation necessary).

- Some form of customer satisfaction (how the client perceives the performance consultant).

- Number and quality of Level 3 and 4 measures/reports completed on any learning interventions for which the performance consultant is the sponsor.

- Business results value delivered to the client's organization as a direct result of the performance consultant's work.

- Endorsement and use of the Center for Learning by the client.

Linkages, Collaboration, and the Tool

We know that a performance focus requires collaboration across functional areas. We know that key processes should have collaboration embedded in them. For the past three months we have been involved in an intense process improvement initiative focusing on the key processes at the Center for Learning. Two of those processes that have the most direct impact on performance and performance consulting are labeled "the product/project management process" and the "performance consulting process."

Work is in progress to ensure all the key aspects and linkages of those processes are in place, effective, and efficient. Figure 1 captures the key flows of the process in use at the Center for Learning.

While the above work is ongoing, we have customized a tool so it can serve as a shared tool across performance consulting and the instructional design team. Some phases of the tool reflect the key processes in our performance consultant process; the remaining phases reflect the customized approach to courseware development used in our instructional design and

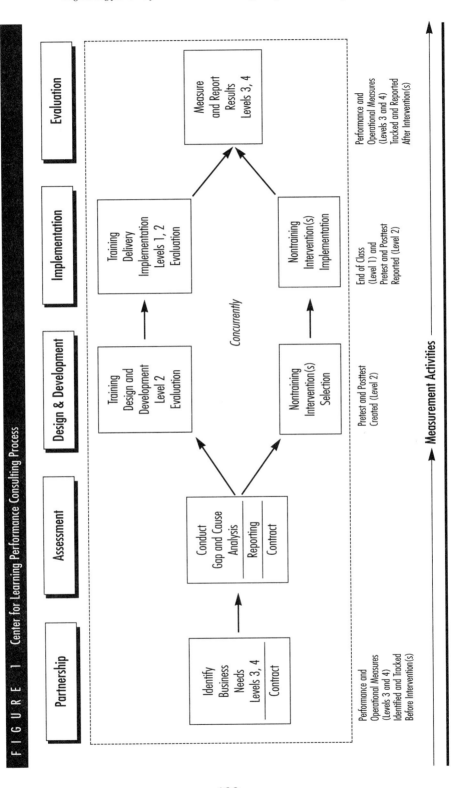

F I G U R E 1 Center for Learning Performance Consulting Process

Partnership	Assessment	Design & Development	Implementation	Evaluation

Identify Business Needs
Levels 3, 4
Contract

Conduct Gap and Cause Analysis
Reporting
Contract

Training Design and Development
Level 2
Evaluation

Nontraining Intervention(s) Selection

Concurrently

Training Delivery Implementation
Levels 1, 2
Evaluation

Nontraining Intervention(s) Implementation

Measure and Report Results
Levels 3, 4

Performance and Operational Measures (Levels 3 and 4) Identified and Tracked Before Intervention(s)

Pretest and Posttest Created (Level 2)

End of Class (Level 1) and Pretest and Posttest Reported (Level 2)

Performance and Operational Measures (Levels 3 and 4) Tracked and Reported After Intervention(s)

Measurement Activities

technologies group. This tool was deployed in December 1997. Preliminary reports indicate that it will serve well as a guide to automate many of the performance consulting steps; then, if a training solution is identified, the data and documents can be handed off to the design group.

A Vision and Mission statement for a Performance-Focused Organization

The SBC Center for Learning *is* a performance-focused organization. We are on the road, learning as we go. We also want to continually get better at this business of performance. A key indicator of the central drivers of any organization are the words reflected in its mission and vision statement. The mission of the Center for Learning is to leverage learning to *maximize performance through consulting* and the development of leadership, business, and functional skills to enable SBC and its affiliates to win in the global marketplace. Its vision is to be a *strategic business partner* by creating innovative, *measurable performance solutions* that unleash SBC's competitive prowess.

We know we are on target with our efforts when we consider the following incident. In June 1997, the Center for Learning management team met in Phoenix for an intense week of strategic planning to structure the newly merged training groups (the Pacific Bell merger was signed in April 1997). The SBC Center for Learning now consisted of approximately 700 employees with responsibility for the training and performance improvement initiatives for 120,000 employees across the SBC enterprise. One of the planning exercises during that week was to categorize the Center for Learning's offerings in terms of their strategic importance to SBC and whether or not they were a "differentiating," "core," or "other" product or service. *Differentiating* was defined as "critical to the success of the organization; even though it could possibly be outsourced, it must remain internal and must be given priority/lead status." Can you guess what jumped out as the premier differentiating service for the Center for Learning? That's right—performance consulting. And there was a clear consensus that it needed to be a separate unit, able to focus exclusively on the key roles of partnering and assessment.

The Author

Robert Blalock is the executive director-performance development for the SBC Center for Learning. He is responsible for linking learning strategy to performance improvement throughout SBC with direct management responsibilities for the Center for Learning's Instructional

Design/Instructional Technologies, Performance Consulting, and Learning Measurement and Evaluation Groups.

The Center for Learning is SBC's corporate university with primary facilities in Irving, Texas, and San Ramon, California. The Center for Learning provides state-of-the-art learning and performance improvement initiatives to the approximately 120,000 employees in its Southwestern Bell, Pacific Bell, Nevada Bell, and Cellular One businesses and in SBC international subsidiaries and interests around the world.

Prior to joining SBC, Blalock served as director of learning technologies for the AMR Training & Consulting Group at the American Airlines Learning Center. He holds a Ph.D. in instructional/organizational communication plus degrees in education/instructional design and accounting.

8

Organizing for a Performance Focus: A Small Department's Perspective

by Carman Nemecek

QUICK READ

● In this chapter, a small department of 13 employees successfully transitioned from training to performance by passing through stages similar to those of a business or product moving through its life cycle: start-up, growth, and maturity. Each stage is characterized by different goals, roles, accountabilities, organization structure, and infrastructure.

● The goals for start-up are to determine the approach to take in beginning the transition and to build credibility within the business for the new performance department. It is also vital to respond to the many questions that are asked by the department's employees and by the organization—all those who will be affected by the change.

● During the growth stage, the infrastructure (systems and processes) must be developed to support the increased demand for performance services.

● Finally, the maturity stage requires continued refinement of the infrastructure necessary to run the department, and a revised organizational structure is required to manage the performance improvement effort at this time.

Consolidated Communications, Inc., is a telecommunications company providing local, long distance, Internet, and directory services, with annual sales totaling $250 million. At the time this transition to performance took place, the company had 1500 employees; a recent merger has swelled the company size to 4500. The Performance Improvement Group, a department composed of 13 people, undertook the transition described here.

In June of 1995, Consolidated Communications, Inc. (CCI), a 1500-person telecommunications company, combined the Consolidated Communications Training and Development Department and the Continuous Quality Improvement Department into a new organization. The logic for bringing nine trainers and eight quality facilitators together was that both groups were doing training and facilitation of some kind for one or more of the six divisions of the company, called business units. A new director had been brought into the company, and there was a belief that there were synergies that would come from the two departments working as one. Both departments had been successful in the past, but the way their success was measured was starting to be questioned. The telecommunications industry was undergoing dramatic change, and leaders of the business were questioning whether the traditional approach to training and quality improvement would be adequate to keep pace with the rapidly changing requirements of the business.

There were several indications that change was needed. Attendance in training classes was starting to wane. People were enrolling in courses and then either canceling at the last minute or not showing up at all. There were dozens of quality teams spending inordinate amounts of time producing results that either no one cared about or that could not be sustained 30 days after the teams disbanded. Tens of thousands of dollars were being spent each year on training and quality initiatives, but it was difficult to determine the return that the business was getting for that investment. It was time to change the focus from delivering programs to managing performance and getting business results.

The mission of the newly combined group was to find a way to enhance the way people do things, to make them and the business more efficient and effective. The new group wanted to have a positive effect on business results and be part of creating a work environment that enabled people to do their best. The ability to improve performance was a sustainable competitive advantage, both for the new combined department and for the business at large.

THE MOVE TO PERFORMANCE

Many challenges were encountered in the move from a training and quality focus to a performance focus. This was truly uncharted territory. The incumbents in the training and quality groups knew that they needed to change, but they did not know what to do or how to do it. People understood the need to move away from a qualitative system that measured success primarily on how people felt about the experiences they were having, to a quantitative system that was more concerned with performance, productivity, and contribution to the bottom line. The way they felt about actually doing that was a different story. Roles were being redefined. The skills, competencies, expertise, and paradigms necessary to be successful in this new role were not the same as those that had made the incumbents successful in the past. People were going to be expected to be much more proactive and strategic. Positioning within the organization would be different. The expectation that relationships and partnerships would be established with clients in positions at the top of the organization made some of the incumbents uncomfortable. The concept of contracting with clients to complete projects that had strategic significance and could be tied to business results was not well understood. All of these unknowns changed a relatively stable environment to one filled with ambiguity, uncertainty, and fear.

The transition from training to performance at CCI passed through stages similar to those of a business or product moving through its life cycle. Proactive management of the life cycle was, and continues to be, an important role for the leader of the initiative. Each stage has been characterized by different goals, roles, accountabilities, organization structure, and infrastructure. The following sections describe the start-up, growth, and maturity stages of the experience at CCI.

Start-Up Stage

There were two primary goals in start-up. The first was to determine what the new approach to performance was going to be. The second was to build credibility within the business units for the process. Enrolling the incumbents in the definition of the new performance organization was very important. They needed to understand that the changes to be made were not incremental. Breakthrough or transformational change was required.

A key challenge for the new group was organizational perception. The reality was that these were the same people who had been performing staff functions prior to the departments being combined. The top leaders of the business supported the new direction and the director was positioned at an executive level, reporting to the president of the company, but a name change alone was not going to be enough to suddenly change the way the group was regarded. If the new group wanted to be positioned at higher levels in the organization, be invited to be planning partners with the business unit heads, and be seen not as a staff function but as operational members of the line organization with valued areas of expertise and competence, there was work to be done. This was a painful and frustrating stage of development for all involved.

The team had many questions. What were the new product/service offerings? How would the new concept be positioned within the company? What were the new roles and accountabilities? What process would be used? What structure would be required to support the effort? What competencies would be needed, and how would those skills be developed? What about incentives and pay? And last, but not least, what would the new department be called?

Some of the reactions to the proposed changes were surprising. These were people who claimed to be change agents for the organization. That appeared to be true, if someone else was expected to change. It did not seem as applicable when the tables were turned and they were the ones being asked to make changes. The incumbents had a significant investment and strong loyalties to their individual departments. They were not anxious to change that.

The company also had its share of questions. Would management training still be offered? Where should they call when they needed training classes? Did this mean that they did not have to be concerned with quality anymore? Could they still start quality teams? At this point, there were not many clearly defined answers to the questions.

A start was made to try to identify the products and services that would be offered by the new department. The first attempt resulted in repackaging the things currently being done. The initial product/service offering is shown in table 1. It was the best that could be done at this point in the transformation. There were too many unknowns early in the change process for people to be more creative about product/service offerings. There was only capacity to offer new and improved versions of the things that were already being delivered. Even though it was not a revolutionary new product/service list, it was enough impetus to get the initiative started.

Next, agreement was reached that internal business partnerships had to be formed and that this group had to have a new way to add value to the business. Internal clients were identified, and a strategy was formulated on how to begin to establish new kinds of relationships with them. But the group got stuck once again. There were too many personal unknowns and fears for people to be able to get by the most pressing question, "What is going to happen to me?"

| **T A B L E   1**   Initial Product/Service Offering of Department |

Personal Effectiveness Training	Team Effectiveness Training	Organizational Effectiveness Training
Sales	Team Building Exercises	Consultation
Leadership	Team Training	Strategic Planning
Software	Benchmarks and	Goals and Measurements
Technical	Measurements	Baldrige Assessment
Quality	Team Development	Training Needs
Customer Service	Strategy	Assessment
Administration	Facilitation	Surveys
Training Effectiveness	Team Assessment	System Reviews
Assessment	Team Curriculum	Employee Programs
Training Needs	Development and	"New Thought"
Assessment	Delivery	Development
	Facilitation Curriculum	Organizational Perform-
	Development	ance Assessment

So in the true spirit of transformation, two working teams were established to write new job descriptions and define a new organization structure. The job descriptions were never completed for this phase, but a new organization structure was created. It is shown in figure 1. It was decided that the best way to begin to establish relationships higher in the organization was to align specific incumbents with specific business units. The director positioned this concept with the business unit heads, and agreement was reached to proceed with the new structure. In hindsight it was premature to try to establish the organization structure at this point. Louis Sullivan made the statement, "Form ever follows function." Trying to create an organization structure before clearly understanding the roles and accountabilities for this work violated that premise. As a result, the initial organization structure was more reflective of the needs of the new performance department than it was of the needs of the business.

Determining which people would support which business units was another difficult task. Because two fairly diverse groups had been combined, people were at very different pay and skill levels. There was significant cognizance of who should be reporting to whom and those at the highest salary levels were not necessarily those with the requisite new skills. There were also different titles in the two departments, and those titles had hierarchical significance in CCI's culture. The most senior person in the group was

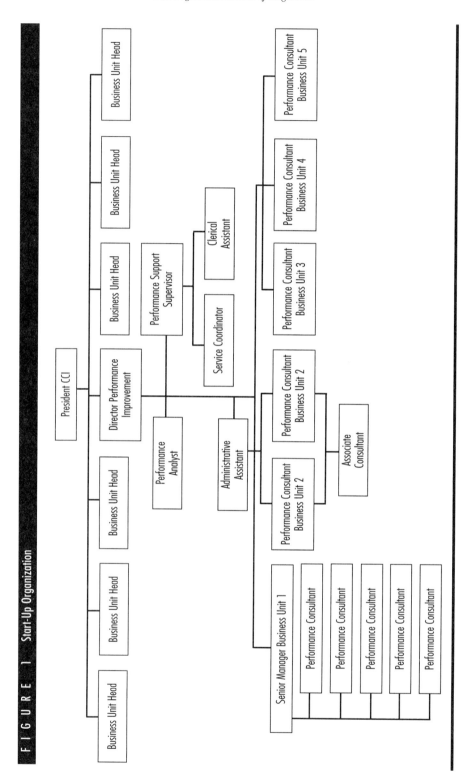

F I G U R E   1   Start-Up Organization

unsupportive of the new direction, which added additional complexities to an already complex situation. The business unit leaders were partners in deciding who would be assigned to support their business. In some cases, candidates had prior experience with the business unit, so those arrangements were relatively easy to make. In other cases, they had to go through an interview process and "sell" the potential client on their value. All incumbents found places on the new organization chart, but it was apparent that one of the key roles of the director would be to find more suitable jobs for those incumbents who would probably not be able to make the transition to this new role. An arbitrary decision was made on titles, and people in the new department were called performance consultants. At the end of this stage, of the 17 people who began the transition, six were placed into other jobs in the organization, one left the business, and one new person was hired.

Once names were associated with business units, the performance consultants began making appointments to conduct interest interviews with executive-level functional leaders. The primary objective of the interviews was to begin to understand the strategic objectives of the functional heads. It was soon discovered that not all of the business units had strategic initiatives. It was a great opportunity for the director of the performance effort to offer service facilitating the establishment of strategic objectives. It was a way to demonstrate the new kinds of services that would be offered by the newly formed organization. This was a significant event for acceptance of the new concept, but it was a double-edged sword. The director became incredibly busy facilitating strategic sessions. That meant that time was not being spent on the important infrastructure and personnel development work that needed to be completed to make this a truly viable initiative. The people in the new performance consulting roles did the best they could, but it was not the optimum way to manage this change.

Headway was being made, but there continued to be struggles. People were again reminded that this was going to be different kind of work. It required different skills and a different mindset. People were going to need to be proactive and work on their own without a great deal of support and supervision. It was not going to be a function with direct control of work outcomes. Authority in the new world was going to come from the ability to influence others, not from having direct responsibility and control of the work being done or the decisions being made. There was the realization that some very worthy and beneficial things might be uncovered but not implemented because of the new accountability structure. Lack of control also could mean that things got implemented differently than they would if direct authority was available. In the training and quality environment, there were specific things to do. Quality teams got started or training classes were delivered. There were questions about how credit would be earned in this new world. If the new authority came from the ability to influence, there was a chance that efforts made by performance consultants could be invisible. It was also difficult to understand how a job could be made out of conducting interest interviews. Lack of clarity continued to be a significant issue.

At the beginning of this change to performance, the director negotiated an agreement with the president of the company for this initiative to be funded for a period of time with unknown return to the business. This was a very important negotiation. There continued to be worry about the perception the company had of the department, and some of the performance consultants wondered how long the organization would tolerate the cost of performing what some felt was not very meaningful work. There was a tremendous amount of ambiguity involved with this new role. It was not a comfortable time for people who were used to being in the business of making people feel good about training and quality experiences.

To add to the concern, there was no longer a clear understanding of what people were to be told when they called to request training. Almost all of the classes that had been provided were programs that had been purchased off the shelf. There had been some top-notch instructors in the group prior to the change in focus, but many of them were not comfortable with the new direction, and they were seeking other work. The old approach was not producing long-term return-on-investment to the business. Yet the department could not just suddenly stop responding to requests. As a short-term solution, a brief questionnaire was developed. When people called to request a training class, they were asked what they would like people to do differently as a result of training. There was resistance from the requesters to answering even this simple question. For a period of time, training programs were still conducted that did not provide a great deal of value to the individual or the organization over the long term. Until a better alternative could be provided and the consultants could understand more clearly what the needs of the business were, it was the only viable alternative.

The next challenge came from not really knowing how to establish a new process for doing this kind of work. Telephone calls were made to colleagues to try to find someone who was trying to make the same changes. Inquiries were coming up empty. After months of working on this new approach, it still was not clear exactly what "it" was. Job descriptions were incomplete, and a new name for the department had not been determined.

Then four opportune things happened. First was the discovery of the book *Performance Consulting: Moving Beyond Training,* by James and Dana Robinson. It gave legitimacy, a framework, and a name to the work that was being attempted. Arrangements were made for a consultant to conduct a skill development session, and major progress was made toward establishing the process that would be used to implement this initiative.

See figure 2 for a copy of the CCI Performance Improvement Process Work Flow Diagram.

Second, a résumé was received from a senior-level person who had been trained as a management consultant and who had been working for several years as an internal consultant. She was interested in making a career change. It became obvious during the interview process that she had the skills, expertise, and experience that could become the basis for further defining the new roles and responsibilities. She decided to accept a position in this start-up department, and another significant step forward was made. A consulting firm was contacted to determine if they could help develop a competency model to define the requisite skills necessary for the performance consulting role. The results of that work are discussed later in the chapter.

Third, one of the business unit leaders agreed to use the new process, and the first performance contract was developed. One of the departments in his business unit was experiencing high levels of turnover. Using the performance improvement process work flow diagram, an analysis was completed and improvement opportunities were identified, including work environment changes and skill development needs. The recommendations were successfully implemented, and turnover was reduced. The performance consultant on the project was invited to be a regular attendee at the business unit leader's staff meetings. The consultant then had an opportunity to learn, firsthand, the issues and concerns facing the business unit. It provided the means to begin to proactively identify areas of the business in need of improvement. As a result of the successful completion of this project, the performance department had its first referable client.

Fourth, after much discussion, debate, and consternation, the group established themselves as the Performance Improvement Group, fondly known as the PIGs. A logo was designed for the department, so that any work completed by the group would be easily recognized. This was a significant, unifying event that soundly established the department's new identity.

Several other projects were successfully completed, and reports of the valuable contributions being made by the PIGs began to spread through the company. This was a good news/bad news situation. The demand for the services provided by the department began to rise rapidly, and there were not enough qualified people available to meet the demand. That moved the initiative into the next stage of development—growth.

Growth

As with start-up, there were two goals for the growth stage. The first was to develop infrastructure systems to support the increased demand. The

| F I G U R E 2 | CCI Performance Improvement Process Work Flow Diagram |

| **Process** | **Outputs** |

Partner with Clients
  – Proactively
  – Reactively

• Understand primary initiatives

Collect Information

Identify Need(s)
  – Process
  – Skill
  – Work Environment

• One/several business needs
• Business needs data
• Prioritized needs
• One selected

Who Should Be Involved?

• Team may be formed
• Ad hoc group
• Proceed "as is"

Determine Current State
  – Process
  – Skill
  – Work Environment

• WHAT are people doing? (performance)
• HOW are they doing it? (process)
• Operational Results (Is)

Who Should Be Involved?

• Team may be formed
• Ad hoc group
• Priced "as is"

Describe Future State

• What do people need to be able to do? (performance)
• How will they do it? (process)
• Problem statement
• Target for improvement

Identify and Validate Gaps

• Validated performance and process issues

212

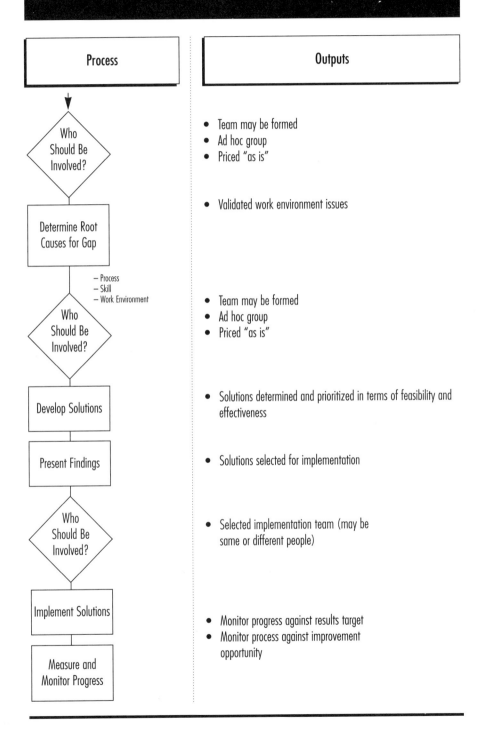

FIGURE 2 CCI Performance Improvement Process Work Flow Diagram *(continued)*

Process	Outputs
Who Should Be Involved?	• Team may be formed • Ad hoc group • Priced "as is"
Determine Root Causes for Gap	• Validated work environment issues
— Process — Skill — Work Environment	
Who Should Be Involved?	• Team may be formed • Ad hoc group • Priced "as is"
Develop Solutions	• Solutions determined and prioritized in terms of feasibility and effectiveness
Present Findings	• Solutions selected for implementation
Who Should Be Involved?	• Selected implementation team (may be same or different people)
Implement Solutions	• Monitor progress against results target • Monitor process against improvement opportunity
Measure and Monitor Progress	

second was to define the competencies for the performance consulting role and, as quickly as possible, enhance the skills of the performance consultants. There were enough people in the department to do the work, if their skills were honed quickly and the infrastructure was developed to support the heavier workload.

In start-up, time had been spent refining the original performance consulting process (figure 2), but nothing had been done to put an infrastructure in place to get the actual work completed. An early selling point for this initiative was that the work the performance consultants did for the business units would be tied to the strategic initiatives of the business. As the demand for consulting services increased, the rigor applied to determining the link between the work and the strategy began to diminish. In the zeal to serve, it was forgotten that the performance consultants were to be working as strategic partners with clients to ensure that meaningful work was being done. A large number of projects had been opened with clients. Some were tied to strategic initiatives; others were not. Work was being agreed to on an ad hoc basis, and complaints were beginning to be lodged by clients. There were many projects under way that they had not sponsored. The inevitable questions began to be asked: "Why were so many performance consultants meddling in their business?" "How much was this costing them?" "Why weren't classes being taught and quality teams started, like they used to be?" This was a wake-up call that some serious issues and concerns still needed to be addressed.

The ability to manage projects was nonexistent. Nothing had been put in place to determine who was working on what for whom. This caused several problems. People in the business units had become familiar with the consultants, the work, and where they sat in the business unit location, and they were becoming, in Peter Block's words, "a pair of hands." A structured process for managing projects had to be devised to get the work back under control. A project proposal form was developed to help address the project management problems. It became the basis for the work done with clients, and once completed and agreed upon, it served as a contract between the performance consultant and the client. It addressed many of the concerns being expressed. The purposes for the project proposal form were the following:

- define the scope of the project

- identify all project team members, and outline their roles and responsibilities

- describe major steps, activities, deliverables, and time frames for the project

- ensure that project assumptions and constraints were discussed and agreed upon

- ensure that the client agreed to the work being done by requiring a signature

- lend a degree of formality to the work being contracted

- provide a tracking mechanism for effective time and resource management

- provide a mechanism for project status updates against agreed-upon milestones.

Implementation of the project proposal form helped get the work process back under control. It did not address the concerns about the number of performance consultants working on business unit issues.

The organization structure that was in place aligned performance consultants with specific business units. Because there were different expectations and requirements from business unit to business unit, the workload between consultants was not balanced. Some business units were fully utilizing all the consulting resources assigned to them. Others saw people who were underutilized. A method for sharing work between business units had to be developed to balance the workload.

The first attempt at workload management was not successful. Time estimates were completed for projects being worked. Those estimates were entered into a department-wide spreadsheet that showed the total number of work hours available for the month. For several reasons, it was not a workable solution. It was very difficult to do the estimates, and administration of the spreadsheet was impossible. Some of the business unit heads did not want the consultants who were assigned to them working on other business unit projects. Several issues had to be addressed, including the current organization structure. It appeared that the start-up structure might have outlived its usefulness.

While trying to solve this dilemma, the year-end budgeting process began. The financial experts in the business decided it was time for the business units to begin paying for their performance consulting resources. It was the expectation of the budgeting team that head count, operating, and capital expenses for the performance consultants assigned to a particular business unit would be the responsibility of that business unit's budget. Suddenly many of the strongest advocates of this valuable work were beginning to question what they could afford. Their concern took an interesting turn. None of them wanted to lose the support, but many did not want to begin paying for it. This was a sobering moment for the Performance Improvement Group. There was more business than it could handle. More value was being returned to the business than it was costing, but the group still found itself in a position of having to justify its existence. It was another frustrating moment for the newly focused group.

The resolve to calculate the amount of time spent on client-sponsored projects immediately became stronger. Within a matter of days, the consultants had devised a time-reporting system that could be used for cost allocations. They also proposed that the organization structure be revisited, and they presented out-of-the-box ideas on how new services could be positioned to ensure that value was being perceived by the business unit. Time was spent with high-level clients to ensure that they still believed in the value of the group. The value was confirmed, and, working together they reached an agreement on a cost-allocation method that made everyone comfortable. The time-reporting system that had been developed was used to validate the allocations that were charged back to the business units.

The underlying concern of cost justification was really a concern about workforce utilization. Because of the way the department was organized, it was becoming difficult to ensure that all resources were fully utilized. The work in the business units was becoming more diverse, as the concept of performance improvement continued to mature. The product/services list had been expanded (see table 2), and it was becoming increasingly difficult to ensure that the particular performance consultants assigned to the business unit would have all the requisite skills to handle the different types of projects. Keeping the workload balanced using the start-up organization structure was not easy.

At the same time that these issues were being addressed, work was being done with a consulting firm to develop a competency-based performance system. The performance consultant role did not fit into the classic job description and pay model used by CCI. The traditional criteria used to evaluate a position's value to the organization were not easily applied to this role. These internal consultants were professional, individual contributors, with few or no direct reports. Their power came from their ability to influence without direct authority and responsibility. Performance consultants were responsible for three primary outputs: (1) to form strong partnerships with key clients in the organization; (2) to identify and contract for performance and process improvement initiatives; and (3) to design and complete performance assessments, facilitating decisions regarding actions to be taken. When learning actions were identified, performance consultants assisted in identifying what needed to be learned and the most appropriate methodology for learning; the actual implementation of the learning solutions was accomplished by employees with the business unit or was brokered to external suppliers.

Once again, the business unit leaders were called upon for help. Nine senior-level people were taken through a process to identify the characteristics they believed were important for the performance consultants to demonstrate. Interviews of exemplary performers were conducted to better understand the job and the role, and the database of the consulting firm

T A B L E   2   Expanded Product/Service Offering

Service Category	Specific Skill
Performance Improvement	Process Review Problem Solving Data Analysis Measurement Development Gap Identification Skill Assessment and Development Work Environment Analysis Implementation Support Best Practices Research—Internal and External
Project Planning	Project Management
Surveys	Survey Assessment and Analysis Survey Development and Implementation Survey Results Reporting
Training	Training Support: Development and Design Outsourcing Referral Consulting
Facilitation	Strategic and Tactical Facilitation
Team Building	Activities Exercises Off-Site Experiences Videos Team Dynamics
Orientation	New Employee Orientation
Focus Groups	Development Facilitation

retained to assist was used to compare the performance consultant position with like positions in a variety of external organizations. After the analysis was completed, a competency model was constructed that consisted of 15 competencies. Each competency was defined and had a baseline or minimum expected level identified. The competencies and proficiencies identified for the performance consulting role at CCI are as follows:

Five Core Competencies (baseline competencies identified at time of selection)

1. Information seeking: an underlying curiosity and desire to know more about things, people, or issues

2. Analytical thinking: understanding a situation by breaking it apart into smaller pieces, or tracing the implications of a situation in a step-by-step way

3. Conceptual thinking: the ability to identify patterns or connections between situations that are not obviously related, and to identify key or underlying issues in complex situations

4. Interpersonal understanding: the ability to accurately hear and understand the unspoken or partly expressed thoughts, feelings, and concerns of others

5. Impact and influence: an intention to persuade, convince, influence, or impress others in order to get them to go along with or to support the speaker's agenda.

Four Distinguishing Competencies (developed to elevate performance of consultant to a "best-in-class" level)

1. Focus on client needs: focusing one's efforts on discovering client business issues or needs, agreeing on a plan of action, and reaching consensus on desired outcomes

2. Results orientation: a dedication to reaching the desired project outcomes or business results, even when it means overcoming obstacles or problems that may arise

3. Project leadership: the willingness to assume the role of leader of a project team

4. Self-confidence: a belief in one's own ability to accomplish an assignment and select an effective approach to a task or problem.

Six Technical Skills

1. Industry knowledge: understanding the vision, strategy, goals, and culture of an industry

2. Business knowledge: awareness of how business functions

3. Presentation skills: ability to organize, prepare, and present information in a format suited to the audience

4. Communication skills: ability to communicate clearly and specifically, both verbally and in writing

5. Personal computing: ability to use different types of software proficiently

6. Project management: understanding of and ability to apply project management skills, tools, and techniques.

Competency assessments were completed for each of the consultants. They received feedback from several sources, including their clients. Once the assessments were complete, feedback was provided and personal development plans were created for each person in a consulting role. Ten consultants were now in the organization: one senior consultant, three consultant IIs, four consultant Is, and two associate consultants. The four levels carried different demonstrated competence and different pay ranges.

This model allows people to build a career performing this kind of professional work. They can continue to earn additional pay and gain more responsibility without having to transfer into a management or line job. Movement up the career ladder is dependent on demonstration of higher-order competence and the needs of the business.

It was now apparent that the existing organization structure no longer made sense. Aligning resources with the business units was a good strategy when the department was in the start-up stage, but the functions that were being performed had changed significantly. It was time to update the organization chart. The new organization structure is shown in figure 3. All the consultants would report directly to the director of performance improvement. Skills and competencies had been identified, so it was easier to match required skills to project requirements. It was a more practical organization for maximizing workforce utilization, and it eliminated the parochialism that had begun to develop under the old structure.

After making the structure changes, an unexpected lesson was learned. The business unit alignment worked well when the objective was to develop new relationships and learn the business of the business. Over time, however, the consultants began to be perceived as "insiders." One of the values that was brought to the equation early on was the consultant's ability to provide an external perspective and play a neutral role. Initially, they were seen as impartial players, less likely to be influenced by the company politics that often surrounded projects. After living in the business for several months, both the perception and the reality of the ability to remain neutral began to diminish. When the organization structure changed, the consultants moved back to a central location and no longer had an office or

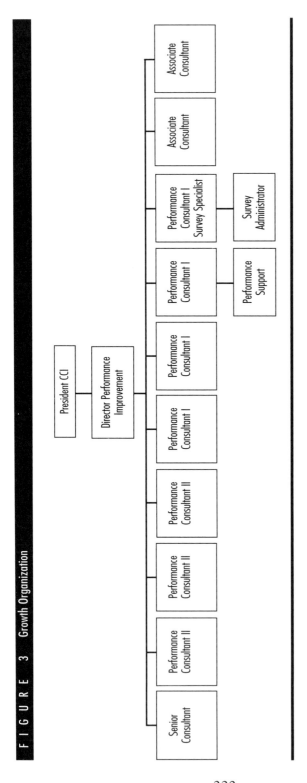

FIGURE 3 Growth Organization

a business telephone extension on the business unit premises. Even though many hours and days of the week were still spent on site, work space and telephones were found in an ad hoc manner, just as they were for external consultants coming in to complete projects. Within a very short period of time, the neutral position was reinstated, and the requests to be a "pair of hands" or surrogate managers virtually disappeared. This was an unanticipated benefit of the new organization structure.

Things were progressing nicely. Business was good. People in the company were beginning to understand that training classes, with no ties to business needs, were not producing the desired changes in behavior on the job. Legitimate skill development needs were being uncovered through performance projects, and the consultants were able to use new models to meet the needs of their clients. A couple of strong external partnerships had been formed with like-minded training companies. These partnerships have continued to grow, and outsourcing at least the design and development work for skill development needs has been a win-win solution. Several extensive skill development initiatives have been implemented with some large performer groups in the company. By using a model that ties the performance of people to the needs of the business, the results have been exceptional. Demand for performance consulting was continuing to increase, but at a decreasing rate. This signaled the move into the next stage of the life cycle—maturity.

Maturity

The most pressing concern in the maturity stage continued to be refinement of the infrastructure and processes used to run the performance business. The process still had the ability to cause confusion and misunderstanding. Despite the efforts that had been made, project assignment was still somewhat ad hoc and was causing frustration to consultants who were now almost always fully utilized. It was time to review roles and responsibilities, processes, and the organization structure once again.

The conclusion was drawn that additional changes needed to be made. The consultants treated the Performance Improvement Group as a client and used the performance process to analyze the current situation and make recommendations for improvements. Recommendations were made that were the most dramatic since the initial decision to combine the training and quality departments. The recommendations included changes to roles and responsibilities and to the performance process.

The director of the department was promoted to vice president. The expanded responsibilities made it difficult to continue the direct reporting relationship of all the consultants. There were still some problems with ensuring that the projects contracted were strategic. There was still some inequity in work assignments, with some consultants having higher utilization rates than others. Our goal was to have each consultant utilized for client work a minimum of 75 percent of available time. There was again work to be done, and the vice president of performance improvement was not going to be able to get the things done that needed to be done.

Two new roles were introduced. Both would report directly to the vice president of performance improvement. The first role was that of the consultant manager. This person would have business, management, and consulting experience and be responsible for day-to-day management of the performance operation. He or she would manage the pool of performance consultants, establish project priorities, match skills required for the project to the available resources, and make project assignments. The role of coach, developer, and mentor for the performance consultants would also be part of the duties of this role. The second new role was that of the performance consultant coordinator. This role would be responsible for developing and maintaining policies, methods, and procedures for the department. The key responsibility of this position would be to establish a project-tracking, monitoring, and feedback process. There was not a good system for cataloging completed projects for future reference. It would be the responsibility of this function to determine a method for creating an internal best practices database. As projects were assigned, the coordinator would conduct a search to find like projects. That data would be provided to the consultant along with the project assignment documents. This role would also complete external best practices work for the consultants. Figure 4 shows the organization structure for the maturity stage of life-cycle development.

A new process for completing performance work also was developed. That flow is shown in figure 5. It shows the key role that the consultant manager plays in the redesigned process.

The changes were in progress when CCI merged with another organization. Six months into the merger, it appears that the department is moving into the next iterated curve of development. The company with whom CCI merged has not moved from training to performance, so many new challenges and opportunities lie ahead. The department is once again faced with establishing new relationships and partnerships. Some of the new executives do not know what performance improvement is or what their role will be in the initiative. New training colleagues have heard about this concept, but they do not know what needs to be done to make the move to performance.

Roles are again being redefined. Skills, competencies, expertise, and paradigms will shift once more. The environment is again filled with ambiguity, uncertainty, and fear. As with the first round, probably not all of the members of the performance group will be able to adapt or be willing to make the necessary changes. But unlike the first time, the department now

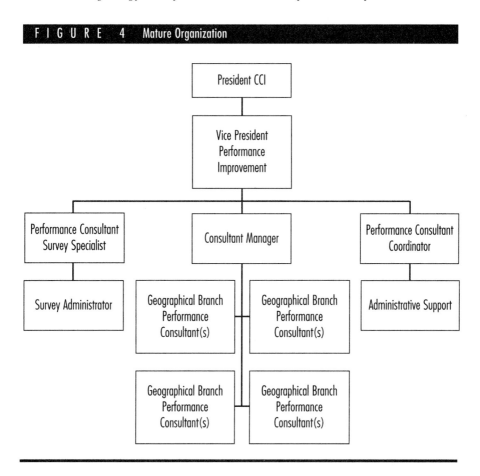

F I G U R E 4 Mature Organization

has experience. They know what they are doing, and they have been successful in moving one organization from training to performance. The model is sound, and there is confidence that progress and success will continue in the new environment. It appears that the only thing constant about this move to performance is the continuing need to deal with change. As CCI merges with another company, it is possible that the Performance Improvement Group will find itself at the start-up stage for yet another cycle of growth.

The last stage in a business or product's life cycle is decline. Departments faced with downsizing and possible extinction are experiencing the final stage. Gratefully, the Performance Improvement Group at Consolidated Communications, Inc. has not moved into decline. We have many colleagues who have not been as fortunate.

F I G U R E 5 Updated Work Flow Diagram

Process

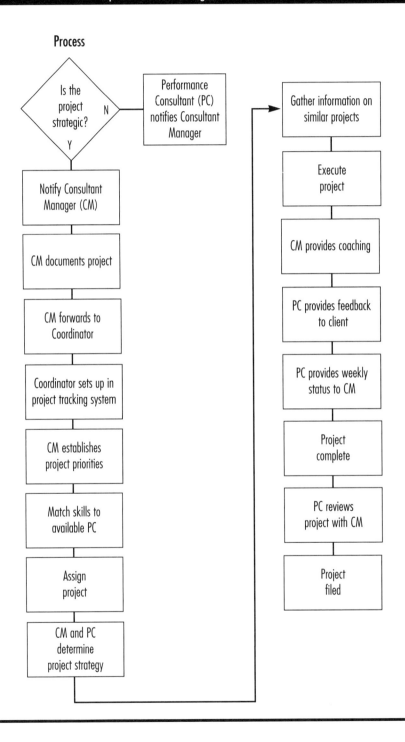

The Author

Carman Nemecek began her business career in 1972 in the retail industry, where she held positions in purchasing, retail store management, and small business ownership. In 1986 she joined Ameritech Corporation, where her positions included management of sales, marketing, project management, customer service, and quality. She has been involved in directing, managing, and implementing major start-up initiatives throughout her career. In 1995 she joined Consolidated Communications, Inc., as the vice president of performance improvement, to develop their performance group.

In her current position, she heads a team of performance consultants responsible for forming business unit partnerships to improve workplace performance. She and her team work with the presidents of Consolidated business units, addressing process and people performance issues. The performance improvement group provides many consulting services to the organization, including process review, work environment analysis, project planning, survey development and implementation, and skill development.

Nemecek has a B.S. and an M.B.A. from Michigan State University. She is the author of *The Owners Manual: Internal Consulting to Improve Performance*. She is also a frequent guest speaker at conferences throughout the country.

Section Four Overview

The Performer Level
of Alignment

This section focuses on the job of the performance consultant. In chapter 9, Judith Robb describes the job outputs that a performance consultant must produce for each phase of the performance improvement process. She also provides in-depth information about the on-the-job behavior and enabling skills and knowledge of effective performance consultants.

Chapter 9 is followed by two case studies that describe how internal performance consultants apply the concepts and techniques in the real world. These case studies, each in a different setting, demonstrate the universality of the human performance improvement process.

In chapter 10, Tom LaBonte focuses on how to develop performance consultants through both learning and work environment actions. This chapter provides step-by-step information about establishing a competency-based assessment system whereby developmental needs are identified. It also describes various learning, work environment, and leader actions that were used to create an environment that supports the development and encouragement of successful performance consultants.

9

The Job of a Performance Consultant

by Judith Robb

QUICK READ

- The performance consulting process focuses on three phases:

    —Partnering with the client

    —Assessing performance

    —Implementing interventions.

- The key outputs of the performance consultant in each phase include:

    In phase 1—Partnering

    —Client partnerships that have been identified, developed, and maintained

    —Client's agreement to gather missing data.

    In phase 2—Assessing

    —A written contract with the client to assess performance (gather missing data)

    —Identification of, and the client's agreement to, the desired performance needed to produce business results

    —Assessment to identify the strengths and gaps in desired performance and the causes for such gaps

    —Reporting of assessment results so that the client will see the logical patterns and interconnection of gaps and causes and will want to take appropriate actions.

In phase 3—Interventions

  —Contracts to implement actions that were identified

  —Internal and external business partnerships to expedite the implementation of interventions

  —Implementation of interventions to improve performance and processes

  —Measuring and reporting results to the client.

● Regardless of a performance consultant's role, responsibility, or outputs throughout the process, a performance consultant must never lose sight of the goal: to improve the processes and human performance in support of the client's business goals.

Imagine that you have spent the past five years of your professional career as a trainer. You have just received word that your job is changing from trainer to performance consultant. The message may have been, "We are converting the training organization into a performance department." If you are lucky enough to have received this message, embrace the challenge.

Consider the following facts offered during the "Performance Consultant: The Job" session at the 1997 ASTD Conference in Washington, D.C. Almost 60 percent of large U.S. corporations indicate they have downsized their human resource development (HRD) departments; in some instances, the staff has decreased by 50 percent. Outsourcing of traditional jobs associated with training and development continues to increase. Alternative delivery is growing. New jobs are entering the HRD profession, jobs such as performance consultant or performance technologist. These facts indicate a significant paradigm shift: Business now places a reduced relative value on the historical position of HRD.

Being results oriented is intrinsic to business. If a problem exists, a solution is sought. Until now, HRD professionals have offered a standard solution: Better-trained personnel produce better results. Performance consulting diverges from this position. A performance consultant seeks first to identify the underlying and interactive causes of a problem. Then a solution is sought. By applying performance-consulting disciplines to arrive at a more comprehensive solution, a performance consultant can respond to a client's business needs in another way.

If you are in transition from training to performance consulting, you are probably asking questions of yourself (your boss, peers, or others), such as the following:

- What does a performance consultant do?

- How will my job change?

- What will be expected from me?

- What do I need to know to be successful?

- How will I know if I have been successful?

- What kind of support will I need as a performance consultant?

If you are asking similar questions, congratulations. You are practicing a key skill of a performance consultant: questioning. This chapter will explore these questions and more as it focuses on the job of a performance consultant. We will begin with the question, "What does a performance consultant do?" The answer to this question will incorporate concepts from the author's studies and experiential observations as an internal and external performance consultant as well as concepts from *Performance Consulting: Moving Beyond Training* by Robinson and Robinson (1995).

Next, we will delve into the first phase of the human performance improvement (HPI) process: partnering with the client. This section will begin building the foundation for success as a performance consultant by creating strong business partnerships. It will explore what performance consultants do to create these partnerships and to secure agreements to gather missing data—data needed to make sound business decisions.

Moving through the HPI process, we will explore phase 2: assessing performance. The purpose of this stage is to identify the performance strengths, gaps, and causes affecting business results. In phase 2, performance consultants secure performance assessment contracts, gather missing data, analyze the data, and report results. In reporting the results, a performance consultant works with the client to reach conclusions, identify implications, and agree on actions to be taken.

Finally, the chapter will look at phase 3: implementing interventions. This phase will touch on the role of performance consultants in the implementation phase of the HPI process.

WHAT DOES A PERFORMANCE CONSULTANT DO?

In response to the question, "What does a performance consultant do?" the best perspective was offered at the 1997 ASTD conference: "Performance consultants define and align the client's business, performance, learning, and work environment needs." These needs are embedded in one another forming a hierarchy. Figure 1 portrays this hierarchy of needs as they are defined and aligned below.

Business needs are the operational (perhaps strategic) goals for a unit, department, or organization. Business needs are expressed in operational terms, which are the hard data measures used to monitor the "health" of the organization. *Performance needs* are the behavioral requirements of people as they perform a specific job. Performance needs describe what people need to do to meet the operational goals. *Learning needs* are the skills and knowledge people must acquire if they are to perform successfully. *Work environment needs* are the systems, tools, and processes required if the performance needs are to be achieved.

The needs, when defined and aligned, provide a framework for seeing what people in an organization must do, know, and possess to achieve busi-

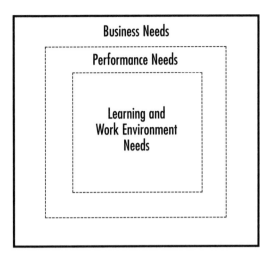

FIGURE 1 Hierarchy of Needs

Business Needs

Performance Needs

Learning and
Work Environment
Needs

ness results. This framework applies to companies as a whole as well as to individuals, such as performance consultants.

The description of the job of a performance consultant will focus on the performance needs as summarized in figure 2 and how these on-the-job behaviors produce job outputs, shown in figure 2. This figure is a graphic model of "The Job of a Performance Consultant." It presents the relationship of the four needs to the three phases of the HPI process and to a performance consultant's ultimate objective—to produce results that have a positive effect on a client's business goals.

Before beginning the exploration of the HPI process, let's focus on the results shown on the far right of figure 2. We start here because the client's business goals should be part of every decision and considered at every juncture. The results may just be words on paper. Or they may mirror exactly what the performance consultant is doing. In either event, an improvement in performance or processes that affects a client's business goals is far and away the most important measure of success for a performance consultant. Let this measure of success guide you in making daily decisions. Success is not about what you say you have done for clients. Rather, success is what clients say you have done to help them achieve their desired business results.

Now let's examine the core work process of a performance consultant and the needs as shown in figure 2. The purpose of each phase of the process is the following:

F I G U R E   2   The Job of the Performance Consultant

NEEDS

PROCESS

RESULTS

Improved Performance in Support of the Client's Business Goals

1. Partnering with the Client
2. Assessing Performance
3. Implementing Interventions

JOB OUTPUTS (Performance Results)
- Client Partnerships
- Client Agreements

- Contracts
- Desired Performance
- Assessments
- Agreement for Actions

- Contracts
- Partnerships
- Interventions
- Results

PERFORMANCE (On-the-Job Behaviors)
- Establishing a Partnership
- Providing Proactive Support
- Responding to Requests for Assistance
- Securing the Client's Agreement to Gather Missing Data

- Contracting for an Assessment
- Identifying Desired Performance
- Developing a Performance Model
- Identifying Performance Strengths, Gaps, and Causes
- Reporting Results and Agreeing on Actions

- Securing Contracts for Performance Improvement Actions
- Brokering for Resources Through Internal and External Partnerships
- Managing HPI Projects
- Measuring and Reporting Results

LEARNING (Skills and Knowledge)
- Analysis Skill
- Business Knowledge
- Change Management Skill

- Facilitation Skill
- Human Performance Technology Understanding

- Influencing Skill
- Model Building Skill
- Project Management Skill

- Questioning Skill
- Listening Skill
- Relationship Building Skill

WORK ENVIRONMENT (Factors)
- Systems: Selection, Promotion, Compensation, Feedback
- Tools: Models, Computer Hardware/Software, Procedures, Documentation
- Processes: Human Performance Improvement, Change Management, Project Management

Source: Adapted from the work of Dana Gaines Robinson and James C. Robinson

- *Partnering with the client*—to identify, build, and maintain a strong business relationship

- *Assessing performance*—to gather data, analyze the data for patterns and connections, collaborate with the client to identify the impact on business goals, and secure agreement for actions to be taken and measures of success

- *Implementing interventions*—to manage and facilitate performance improvement efforts through internal and external partnerships, and to measure and report results.

In addition, the job of the performance consultant is defined for the following:

- *Job outputs*—the performance results you strive to achieve in each phase in the HPI process

- *Performance needs*—the on-the-job behaviors needed to produce results for clients

- *Learning needs*—the skills and knowledge needed to perform successfully throughout the HPI process

- *Work environment needs*—the systems, tools, and processes needed to perform successfully.

Phase 1: Partnering with the Client

The purpose of phase 1 is to develop client partnerships. When you communicate knowledgeably with clients about their business goals, measures of success, performance and learning needs, and work environment issues, you are establishing yourself as a strong business partner. If you are a strong proactive partner, the client is more likely to accept you as a member of his or her leadership team. As we begin to explore phase 1 of the HPI process, let's look at the job outputs as shown in figure 2.

- *Client partnerships*—strong ongoing business relationships that focus on the client's business success and that are not project specific

- *Client agreements*—the client's agreement for you to gather missing information and confirm existing performance data

Now, let's see how performance consultants achieve these phase 1 outputs by exploring the on-the-job behaviors as shown in the performance needs of figure 2.

Establishing a Partnership

When asked, "Who is your client?" many performance consultants who are new to the field have responses such as customer service, marketing, sales, branch offices, and so on. Please focus on this premise. Although a department name provides a reference to the client's organization, the client is a person. To identify the person, ask, "Who owns the business and performance needs of the business group?" Ownership means that the person has the most to lose if the business and performance needs of the department are not met. Keep in mind that successful performance consultants are on a first-name basis with the person who is their client.

Now, determine if the person identified has the authority and funds to address the business needs. Keep in mind that funding is really about investing—making sound business decisions to achieve favorable business results—not just about who has the budget dollars for actual expenditures. Thus another perspective on the client is gained if you identify who has the most to lose if sound business investments are not made.

If the person identified does not meet the ownership, authority, and funding filters, do not stop. As you function in the role of performance consultant, you will naturally and inevitably be led to the desired individual. At some point, only that person can address your questions and interventions. When you are finally communicating with that individual—and in some cases it may be a group of people—you are communicating with the client.

How does the client see you? Some clients may view you as a source for course offerings, the person who delivers the training classes they have requested. They may view you as someone who will solve all their problems. Yet some clients may not even know you exist. One reason for this may be your lack of visibility in that you rarely "drop in" and visit people in the client's organization. For those of you functioning as internal performance consultants, another reason may be that you are at a different organizational level than the client. You may be in a company where the client is much higher in the company hierarchy.

This company hierarchical structure raises the issue of who in the performance department partners with the client. This issue must be resolved. For example, in some performance departments there are client liaisons that establish and maintain the client partnerships. A client liaison keeps the others in the performance department abreast of developments and responsive to the client's needs. Regardless of the client's current perception or position, you or others in the performance department will need to identify the client, determine who will be responsible for partnering with the client, and agree on how this relationship will be nurtured and maintained.

In supporting clients, the performance consultant may sometimes be proactive and at other times reactive. The difference between being proactive and simply responding to a client's request for assistance is framing and reframing. Proactive performance consultants frame initial client interactions in performance and business language. Business language focuses on the client's operational goals at an organizational level and how a client measures success. Performance language focuses on the behaviors needed to achieve these successful operational results.

When responding to a client's request, a performance consultant may need to reframe the request into business and performance language, especially if it is a training request. As you work to establish and maintain a strong business partnership, consider a number of variables that will affect your success. Review the following list, and assess the strengths and gaps that may exist for you:

- *Role*—the role and responsibilities of a performance consultant—as seen by you, the client, and others in the performance department

- *Time*—the time to plan and prepare, the client's time to meet and discuss needs and requests, and the time needed to assess the performance and processes affecting the client's business goals before implementing interventions

- *Knowledge*—about the client's business, organization, and industry

- *Skills*—in facilitating meetings, influencing others, questioning to obtain missing information, listening actively to ensure effective communication, and building a strong business relationship with the client

- *Understanding*—of human performance technology and change management

- *Flexibility*—in interacting with clients while maintaining objective, bias-free approaches to situations and people

- *Self-confidence*—in managing your own performance when placed in new and challenging situations

- *Tolerance for ambiguity*—your comfort level where it is unclear and difficult to examine goals, processes, and performance needed to achieve business results

Are there any gaps for you? If so, take the initiative—create and implement your own development plan—to close the gaps.

Providing Proactive Support

Let's take a look at your role as a proactive partner. In providing proactive support, gather as much information as possible to gain an insight into the client's needs. Proactive performance consultants ascertain their clients' business goals, how clients measure success, what they do to achieve success, what their status is in achieving success, and what may be affecting success.

Business goal data are of different kinds: drivers, strategies, measures, and challenges. Drivers indicate why the goals are important. Strategies describe the methods that are or will be employed to achieve the goals. Measures are the quantifiable operational data used to determine success. Challenges are the potential barriers that come from within and outside the client's organization. This information can usually be found in readily accessible documents from the client's organization and industry publications. Below is an example of a typical situation encountered by a performance consultant. The performers are customer service representatives (CSRs). The business goal is to resolve customer inquiries in a timely and effective manner.

● *Driver*—Customer survey feedback indicates customers do not like to make multiple calls to resolve an issue.

● *Strategies*—Resolve customer inquiries on the first call. Ask customers how successful we have been in responding to their inquiries. Track customer responses from the monthly customer survey. Report results to everyone who has an impact in achieving the goal.

● *Measures*—Resolve 97 percent of customer inquiries on the first call.

● *Challenges*—Internally, approximately 40 percent of the workforce has been on the job for less than six months, and computer equipment and software are antiquated. Externally, a lack of a qualified labor pool exists, and rapid industry growth is resulting in increased competition for market share, resources, and people.

Now identify the client and the performer group(s) that will have the greatest impact in achieving the goal:

● *Client*—director of customer service

● *Performers*—customer service representatives who respond to customer inquiries, customer service supervisors who support CSRs, and service technicians who respond on site to customer problems.

The proactive performance consultant should delve into what is known and unknown about the client's business goal(s). As you begin gathering data you will need a method, model, or map to organize and document data. The Performance Relationship Map is just such a tool and is described in detail in *Performance Consulting: Moving Beyond Training* by Robinson and Robinson. The map displays the complex interrelationships of components of a given business goal for a specific performer group and provides a way to organize the results of research, identify missing information, develop questions to gather missing information, and document a client's responses. Let's continue our earlier example:

- *Results*—Desired: annually resolve 97 percent of customer inquiries on the first call as measured by the monthly customer survey. Current: as of March, 93 percent of the customer inquiries were resolved on the first call. The previous year-end customer survey result was 94 percent.

- *Performance*—Desired: what should CSRs do to resolve customer inquiries on the first call? Current: what are CSRs currently doing to achieve operational results?

- *Barriers*—Workforce is relatively new. Computer equipment and programs are antiquated.

You have identified and documented the client's goal, along with what is known and unknown about this goal. Now, meet with the client. Your own goal in this kind of meeting is to establish yourself as a business partner—a person who is committed to the client's business success. Here is what you should do during this meeting:

- Identify or confirm the client's highest-priority business goal(s).

- Confirm what is known and unknown about the performance, learning, and work environment needs that may affect the business goal(s).

- Determine if the need is for learning or performance improvement.

- Secure an agreement to gather missing data.

The missing information is almost always multifaceted and interrelated, thus adding to the complexity of client interactions. In the initial meeting with the client, start from the client's point of view. Confirm what you know. Then ask questions to gain insight into what you do not know. To accomplish this, develop a mental framework of the interrelationship of needs, outcomes, performance, and environmental factors that have an effect on performance.

Before the meeting, develop and organize a set of questions based on need. Incorporate the client's business knowledge and language into your questions. Organize the questions so that they link the client's frame of reference to the associated need. Your objective in asking questions is to move from the client's frame of reference through the needs found in the hierarchy of needs, shown in figure 1.

Once you orient the client's data to one of the levels, you have started the process of defining and aligning needs. Next, continue the client interaction so as to move outward through the various needs. Define each need until you arrive at the client's business need. At this point, continue asking questions to make certain the four needs are fully defined and aligned. The questions you develop and ask are key to your ability to readily define and align the needs and to obtain missing data. Therefore, until you "own" these questions, keep a copy of the questions next to your phone, in your date-book, or someplace where you can access them quickly and easily.

As you interact with the client, remember to remain focused on framing your discussion in business and performance language. Confirm what you know about the client's business goals and the performance needed to achieve the goals; identify what you do not know; gain access to the people who have the most credible data; and obtain an agreement to gather the missing data from the relevant people.

Responding to Requests for Assistance

A client partnership may begin with a call from a new client. How are you going to respond, especially if the client is requesting training or is describing a work environment issue? Remember, the goal of a performance consultant is to reframe the request into performance and business language. All of the variables affecting success that were described earlier are important, but two variables—your role and time—can be significant as you reframe the client's request.

Your role as a performance consultant and the client's view of it may differ greatly, especially if your previous role focused solely on training. If the client needs to change his or her perception of you, first you will need to change your own perspective and behaviors. Time is an elusive variable, especially when the client's perception of time does not include the time needed to reframe requests into business and performance language, or the time needed to assess the performance needs of the organization before implementing solutions. When your time frame and the client's time frame do not match, call on your flexibility, objectivity, self-confidence, and tolerance for ambiguity to reframe requests and gather missing data.

What does a successful client meeting look like when you are responding to a client's request for a training class? Because the goal is to reframe the request into performance and business-need language and to determine the behavior changes needed, you manage the meeting in the following manner:

- Confirm the purpose of the meeting.

- Identify any new issues since the original request was made.

- Secure agreement that the original goal is still a priority item.

- Confirm the client's commitment to the time allocated for the meeting.

- Summarize what you know and do not know about the request by using performance and business language to reframe the request.

Let's explore an example of how to reframe a client's request into business and performance language. In this example, the client wants a team-building class for his work group. The client has identified a solution and wants it implemented. To reframe the request, you will need to ask questions. If you have not yet developed the facility to spontaneously ask a question that will obtain the right information, prepare your questions in advance.

Now, let's analyze several of the questions you might ask and how the client could respond. Your goal is to determine what kind of behavior change the client expects and how that behavior change will affect business results. As you think about the request, determine where you would place the client's request in the hierarchy of needs (figure 1). The client's request for a class implies a lack of skills and knowledge—a learning need. To define and align the learning need with the performance need, you might ask, "What do your employees need to be doing differently?" This question links the client's perceived skill deficiency to on-the-job behaviors expected from the people in the performer group. The client may respond, "Because of the latest personnel cuts in our department, we need to work as a team to meet our customers' needs." What did you hear in this response? What needs did the client identify? How will you capture and organize the response? What questions will you ask to frame the client's response?

Let's take a closer look at the response to determine what needs are being expressed and what to ask next. The client's response provides general information for three of the four needs, as shown in table 1. *Meet customers' needs* alludes to a business need (an operational goal). *Work as a team* opens the door to explore performance needs. *Department cuts* provides an insight into possible performance barriers in the work environment.

Because the client has not fully defined the performance need, begin reframing the request by asking a performance question using the client's language. For example, you could ask: "If the people on your team were meeting the customers' needs, what would they be doing? What behaviors would be seen? Is anyone on the team an effective team member? If so, what does he or she do on the job?" If the client does not have any effective team members, or if the behaviors are new to the team, you might ask: "Do you know of any people in the company who are demonstrating the behaviors you expect of effective team members? If so, is it possible for me to talk with them?"

After aligning the learning request with the performance needed, you are ready to align the performance with the business need. For example, "How do you know if your team has successfully met the customers' needs?" Or, "How do you measure your team's success in meeting the customers' needs?"

Once the business need is confirmed and the measure of success identified, you are ready to identify the work environment barriers having an impact on performance. For example: "Have they demonstrated effective team behaviors in the past? If so, what is keeping them from demonstrating these behaviors?" For additional work environment questions, refer to table 1. If the client describes what people need to be doing on the job, secure confirmation from the people who are demonstrating these behaviors. In

T A B L E 1	Defining and Aligning Needs

Client's initial request:	A team-building workshop
Consultant's initial question:	What do your employees need to be doing differently?
Client's initial response:	Because of the latest cuts in our department, we need to work as a team to meet our customers' needs.

Excerpts from Initial Response	Need*	Questions to Define and Align Needs
Meet customers' needs	BN	(BN) How do you know if your team has successfully met the customers' needs? How do you measure success? (BN) What is the current status of your customer service goal? (PN) When your employees are successfully meeting the customers needs, what are they doing—what are their on-the-job behaviors?
Work as a team	PN	(BN) How do you know if your team has successfully met the customers' needs? How do you measure success? (PN) What are they not doing now that they need to be doing? (PN) Are there any employees who are demonstrating effective team behaviors on the job? If so, what are they doing? Who are they? Are they available as a resource to discuss what they do on the job? (WN) What is keeping your employees from performing as a team?
Department cuts	WN	(LN) What is the impact of department cuts to your "knowledge base?" Is there a knowledge deficiency since the cuts have taken place? If so, what are the deficiencies? What do people need to know? (PN) What is the impact of department cuts to your employees' performance on the job? (BN) How? (Focus on what they can no longer accomplish.) (WN) Why? (Focus on barriers created by cuts.)

* Organized by hierarchy of needs: (BN) Business Need, (PN) Performance Need, (LN) Learning Need, (WN) Work Environment Need

addition, substantiate their credibility by determining if they are currently performing the job, highly skilled and knowledgeable in areas relevant to the job, respected by their peers, and willing to speak openly and honestly.

As you ask questions, the client could provide a variety of responses. Your success in reframing the client's training request will be founded upon your ability to do the following:

● focus questions on identifying, defining, and aligning the client's highest priority business and performance need

● link the learning and work environment needs (frequently provided without being asked for) to the client's business and performance needs

● mentally identify the needs expressed in a client's responses

● continually reframe the responses into performance and business language.

Reframing the client's request may not be achieved easily. Until you have a track record of positive results as a performance consultant, the client may continue to ask questions about when the class will be given, related workshop delivery questions, or other training inquiries on his or her agenda. Prepare yourself to always start from the client's point of view. Ask questions that will define and align the four needs—business, performance, learning, and work environment. Push back on training requests that do not reflect clearly a lack of skills and knowledge. Use a method to organize the interconnections in the data you are gathering. The Performance Relationship Map discussed earlier is one method. Use active listening skills to confirm that you and the client agree on the reframed request.

Securing the Client's Agreement to Gather Missing Data

Your reframing questions serve two purposes: They enable you and the client to identify what is known and not known about the situation, and they increase the client's awareness about what additional information is needed if the problem is to be resolved. At this time, offer to gather the missing information. When the client has clearly defined the business need and agreed to let you gather missing performance data, you are ready to begin phase 2—the assessment phase.

Phase 2: Assessing Performance

The purpose of phase 2 is to obtain credible performance data that describes performance and identifies performance gaps and the causes of those gaps. This will provide the client with information needed to close performance gaps, which in turn will increase the probability that the client will take targeted, successful performance-improvement actions.

As we move to phase 2, let's look at the outputs as shown in the business needs of figure 2.

- *Contracts*—written agreements that recap the client's agreement for you to gather missing performance data

- *Desired performance*—on-the-job behaviors a specific work group demonstrates to achieve business results

- *Assessments*—the identification of the performance strengths, gaps, and causes for gaps

- *Agreement for actions*—the client's agreement to take action to close the gaps revealed in the assessment results

To ensure achievement of these deliverables, you will need to propose and employ a very systematic, efficient, and timely process. Keep in mind that phase 2 can range from a simple process that takes place over several days to complex processes encompassing extensive use of resources occurring over months, even years, for change management and performance improvement projects.

At this juncture, the goal is to gather, analyze, and present information from which the client can clearly identify the barriers and the interventions needed to improve performance. If you propose solutions before you present analyzed data, you will own the solutions, not the client. Now let's take a closer look at the on-the-job behaviors shown in the performance needs of figure 2.

Contracting for an Assessment

Once you and the client reach an agreement to gather the missing data, confirm the purpose of the performance assessment. Make sure you and the client are in agreement as to the decisions that will be made from the information collected. Once there is agreement, secure a contract that is a written agreement. Performance consultants sometimes overlook this important document, especially those who are new to the field, who work for the same company as their clients, or whose previous role and responsibilities did not include contracting with clients.

A contract is a document that recaps what you and the client discussed and agreed upon in your initial meeting. It may be a letter, an electronic memo, a short contract, a long contract, or whatever you and the client recognize as an agreement for work to be performed and results to be achieved. Regardless of the form, an assessment contract should include the following elements:

- *Scope of work*—a statement of the client's business need, performance need, and measure of success.

- *Milestones*—the major areas of work to be completed by the performance consultant or the project team or both. The work includes identifying desired performance, assessing typical performance, interpreting assessment data, and reporting the results.

- *Resources*—the project cost and manpower needs.

- *Schedule*—the start and finish dates for major project milestones.

Refer to table 2 for examples of how an assessment agreement can address the above issues.

Identifying Desired Performance

Once you have a contract, you are ready to identify the desired performance. Desired performance (the behaviors needed to achieve business results) provides a baseline to assess the behaviors of typical performers in a performer group. Desired performance may also be referred to as *best practices*. People who demonstrate desired performance are known as *exemplary performers*. The processes to gather performance data include observation, interviews (one-on-one and focus groups), questionnaires, and documentation reviews. If the job is new, subject matter experts may be needed to establish the desired performance.

Let's take a closer look at these data-gathering processes. Observation and interviews provide the opportunity to collect qualitative data (stories and examples expressed in behavior language). These processes, however, are labor intensive, costly, and time consuming. If labor, cost, and time are critically scarce for the client, consider using telephone interviews, focus groups, or both, to gather qualitative data. Telephone interviews accommodate a large number of people in various locations during a short window of time. A focus group accommodates a large number of people in one location. If quantitative data will suffice, use questionnaires. They accommodate a large number of people and require fewer resources than observations and interviews. Although documentation reviews provide quantitative and qualitative data and require fewer resources than other processes, you should determine if the content will provide credible on-the-job performance data.

To recommend the most effective and appropriate process, consider the characteristics of the various data-gathering processes, the source(s) of data, and the following variables:

- *Exemplary performers*. Who are they? Where are they? Are they credib with their peers? Are they willing to speak openly? Do they exist in ' client's organization? If not, where are they, and will you have acces them?

- *Subject matter experts*. Who are they? Where are they? Do they exist client's organization? If not, where are they, and will you have access t

| T A B L E 2 | Sample Terms of a Performance Assessment Contract |

Component	Term
Scope of Work	
CLIENT'S OBJECTIVE	To retain customers, customer service representatives need to resolve customer inquiries on the first telephone call to the Customer Service Department. The measure of success: Resolve 97 percent of all customer inquiries on the initial call.
DESIRED OUTCOMES	• Strengths, gaps, and causes for gaps in the performance or processes of customer service representatives in meeting the client's business and performance need stated above • Performance model for customer service representatives
ROLES AND RESPONSIBILITIES	Client agrees to: • Identify and provide access to exemplary performers, subject matter experts, and project team members • Provide access to client documents, reports, and materials • Communicate project scope of work, milestones, and schedule to appropriate parties • Resolve issues and remove barriers to project success • Meet with key project team members to review results • Identify impact of results and actions to close identified gaps Consultant agrees to: • Deliver desired outcomes on time and within budget • Identify and communicate to the client the issues and barriers to project success
FACTORS	• Internal: Forty percent of the targeted performer group has less than six months' experience on the job, and the computer equipment and software are antiquated. • External: Rapid industry growth has resulted in increased competition for market share, resources, and qualified people.

(cont'd. on page 247)

T A B L E   2   Sample Terms of a Performance Assessment Contract   *(continued)*

Component	Term
Milestones	
ASSESSMENT	Identify desired performance: • Facilitate one focus group with (10) exemplary performers. • Develop performance model for performer group. • Review performance model with subject matter experts. Identify typical performance: • Develop questionnaire (using performance model). • Send questionnaire to random sample of typical performers (800 performers) and supervisors of targeted group (50 supervisors).
RESULTS	Report results: • Interpret assessment results to identify strengths, gaps, and causes. • Meet with client to review assessment results, identify and confirm implications and actions needed to close gaps in performance or processes.
Resources	
COST	$xxxx
MANPOWER	(Number) of internal or external performance consultants (Number) of people from client's organization or company, for example, team members, exemplary performers, and subject matter experts
Schedule	
ASSESSMENT	Identify desired performance: Start—xxx x, Finish—xxx x Identify typical performance: Start—xxx x, Finish—xxx x Interpret data: Finish xxx x
RESULTS	Client meeting: xxx x, from xx to xx

- *Typical performers.* How many people are in the targeted performer group(s)? Where are they located? Will they respond openly and with credible information?

- *Project team members.* How many people will be needed? What will they need to do (on-the-team behaviors)? What will they need to know (skills and knowledge)? Are the needed resources available?

- *Schedule.* Is the manpower (performers, subject matter experts, and team members) available? What is the client's time frame for the project? What is the client's business cycle? How will the project affect the client's business cycle?

- *Cost.* What is the cost of the various data collection methods? Is funding available for the project? Most important, what is the cost and effect of poor performance and processes to business success?

- *Communication.* Will the client communicate project objectives, outcomes, agreements, processes, and schedules to the appropriate parties?

All of these facets must be integrated to achieve a workable guide. In gathering desired-performance data, you may be identifying the performance needed to achieve a specific business goal or, in other cases, broadening the collection of data to include the performance needs for all the business goals of a given performer group. In either case—specific or broad—the type of data will be the same. This data is the information used in a performance model. In *Performance Consulting: Moving Beyond Training*, Robinson and Robinson describe a performance model as a behavioral description of performance as it should be for the organization to achieve its business goals.

In some HRD departments, competency models are developed. Although performance models and competency models may contain the same information, the content is organized differently. Competency models profile the core skills and knowledge needed in a job cluster or job band, such as supervisors. Performance models identify performance results and behaviors of a specific work group, such as customer service supervisors.

Developing a Performance Model

To identify desired performance, let's explore the components, data-gathering process, and benefits of a performance model.

The components of a performance model. The model includes the business need, performance results, best practices, and quality criteria for a specific performer group. A model may, but not always, include competencies and the work environment factors that affect the achievement of results.

Performance results are the job outputs produced by people in a specific performer group. For an example of job outputs for a performance consultant, refer to the business needs in figure 2. As reflected in the assessing performance process (phase 2) of figure 2, the job outputs include contracts, desired performance, assessments, and agreement on actions to be taken. Best practices describe desired performance, the on-the-job behaviors of exemplary performers. For a summary of best practices for a performance consultant, refer to the performance needs in figure 2.

Quality criteria are the measures of success. Although figure 2 does not show the quality criteria, it does show the job outputs. These can be used to establish measures of success. For a performance consultant, the measures of success for a client partnership could include an increase in client referrals, the client's public acknowledgment of your support, your participation as a member of a client's management team, and the client's repeated requests for your assistance as a performance consultant. Again, success is what the client says about you, not what you say you are doing for the client.

Competencies are the skills, knowledge, and attributes needed to achieve desired performance. As discussed earlier, competencies provide a basis for identifying core competencies for similar positions across an organization and for designing training programs. For an example of competencies for a performance consultant, refer to the learning needs (skills and knowledge) in figure 2. Work environment needs focus on internal and external factors that have an effect on performance. Internal factors, which are within the control of the clients, are the systems, processes, and tools needed to achieve business results. External factors, which are outside the control of the clients, include industry trends, competition, and so on. Refer to figure 2 for an illustrative summary of the internal work environment factors for a performance consultant.

The process of gathering performance model data. When you met earlier with the client, you obtained information about the business needs, expected performance results, and measures of success for a specific work group. Now you are ready to gather best-practice data by observing people as they work, interviewing exemplary performers in specific performer groups or subject matter experts if the job is a new job, or conducting a focus group of exemplary performers, or using all these means to gather behavioral data. The skills and knowledge needed to gather performance model content include questioning, active listening, and recognizing the difference between competency language (what people know) and performance language (what people do).

How will you know if you are hearing competency language or performance language? For example, someone might say, "Everyone in our group needs to know how to work as a team." You might say to yourself, "I know what it means to be a team member." When you hear a statement with the words *understand* or *know*, you are hearing an assumed need for competency. Others might say, "We need to operate as a team." In this statement, the word *operate* may sound like performance language. The team behaviors are still unknown, however, because *operate* could mean controlling the functions of a machine, controlling the affairs of business, performing surgery, or even carrying on a military action.

To ensure that you have identified the behaviors, ask probing questions. In the examples above, use the reference to teamwork to ask a behavior question. If you are interacting with a client, the question might be: "Do any of the employees in the targeted work group demonstrate effective team behaviors on the job? If so, what are they doing?" If you are questioning a exemplary performer, you might say, "Please describe what you do as a team member to . . . (achieve the operational results identified by the client)?" Your questions are the primary source of information, so employ them wisely.

The benefits of a performance model. Performance models are used to improve the performance of an individual, a specific performer group, organizations, and companies. They are also used to ensure that performance needs and business needs are strategically aligned and to communicate, monitor, and measure the performance and results needed to achieve business goals. Variations on these uses are as follows:

● Supervisors and employees use models to improve performance. They use the models as a framework for coaching employees and to create developmental plans.

● Performance consultants use models to provide proactive support to their clients. A performance consultant uses consolidated, employee-development plans to identify performance strengths and gaps within and across work groups and organizations. A performance consultant collaborates with clients to identify actions needed to close gaps.

● Performance consultants use models to respond to clients' requests for assistance. The models become tools to use in reframing requests into business and performance language and identifying performance gaps, the lack of skills and knowledge, and the work environment factors that affect the achievement of performance results.

● Individuals interested in securing a position in a targeted performer group outside their own group use performance models to self-assess their level of performance and to create individual development plans.

● Clients use models as part of the strategic planning process. A model provides baseline information on how best practices affect business results in the current business climate.

Identifying Performance Strengths, Gaps, and Causes

You have identified the best practices of exemplary performers, and the client has agreed with this desired performance. You are ready to gather performance data from typical performers in the performer group and need to identify a data-gathering process and consider the variables described earlier.

The processes include observing typical performers at work; interviewing typical performers—one-on-one or in small groups; conducting a survey—face-to-face, by telephone, or by distributing a questionnaire; and reviewing data—reviewing records, documents, and reports from the organization. The variables include identifying the kinds of data needed—quantitative or qualitative; the size and location of the targeted performer group; the availability of resources such as time, labor, and funding; and what must be done to ensure confidentiality of individuals participating in the assessment.

When considering which data collection process to use, remember the need for confidentiality. A lack of confidentiality will diminish, and possibly destroy, your credibility and the credibility of the data collected. Consideration of the variables listed above will help you in proposing, discussing, and securing agreement from the client as to the most appropriate method to assess typical performance in the performer group.

Depending on the scope of the assessment process, you will need to identify a way to interpret results. You could, for example, summarize the interview notes from a small focus group, create spreadsheets to analyze quantifiable data, or develop and maintain a database to analyze, interpret, and report assessment results. In some performance departments, interpreting results is done by a performance analyst whose main function is to capture and code data, cluster data into logical data sets, and propose reasoned conclusions. Regardless of the method employed, the data must be pertinent, accurate, and communicated.

Reporting Results and Agreeing on Actions

In reporting the assessment results to the client, present the results in a way that the client can see the reasoned conclusions and identify the implications to his or her business success. Success means that you have secured the client's agreement to take the actions needed to close performance gaps. Plan carefully, and answer the following questions:

● What type of meeting for "reporting results" did you and the client discuss and agree upon in the initial client meeting?

● What kind of information does the client need in order to make sound business decisions? (For example, does he or she need quantitative or qualitative information?)

● How will you present the assessment results? (An executive summary, detailed report, slides, charts, graphics, video, or what?)

● How will you maintain the confidentiality of assessment participants?

As you continue preparing for a successful meeting with the client, you will need to anticipate some additional factors.

Set the stage. Communicate and secure the client's agreement to the purpose, expected outcomes, process, and time frame for the meeting.

Present the assessment results. First, provide a summary offering logical data patterns and interconnections (for example, performance strengths and gaps, plus processes to support business goals). Avoid solutions at this juncture. Present details as needed to support the summarized results.

Collaborate with the client to identify actions to be taken. If you have considerable knowledge about the client's business, change management, and human performance technology, he or she may look to you for guidance in identifying the most appropriate intervention. Take care to ensure that the client reviews and accepts the results of the performance assessment. This need for the client's review and acceptance is why you avoid offering solutions early in the HPI process. Your goal is not for the client to accept your solutions. Rather, you want the client to own the interventions needed because he or she has been extensively involved in reviewing the assessment results and formulating the solutions.

Secure the client's agreement for actions to be taken. Once the solutions are identified, secure the client's agreement to implement the solutions identified. In addition, identify your role in the implementation process, which may include functioning as a broker, facilitator, team member, or project manager.

Determine how the effect of each intervention will be measured. Examples of such measures are operational results, changes in on-the-job performance, modifications in the work environment, and cost avoidance. Many factors need to be considered when identifying the most appropriate measures. Such factors include the purpose, the specific change desired, work environment factors, sources of data, data collection methods, measurement design options, time frames, budget, who will perform the measurement, and last, but most important, whether the scope of the measurement effort is a sound business investment.

Phase 3: Implementing Interventions

This section will be more succinct because this is an area in which performance consultants generally are the most comfortable and competent. For example, if a client calls with a solution (a training class) and wants it implemented, it is very easy to provide the service. Be aware that if you skip or skim over the partnering and assessing phases in figure 2 and jump to the implementing phase, you run the risk of owning the results of a possibly ineffective solution.

The purpose of phase 3 is to close performance gaps using credible, client-identified and client-supported actions. When these actions are implemented, performance should improve. As a result, performance consultants will have reached their ultimate goal—improved performance in support of their client's business goals. The job outputs of phase 3 are shown in the business needs of figure 2.

● *Contracts*—written agreements to implement the interventions and projects the client identified in the assessment phase.

● *Partnerships*—the internal and external partnerships that are critical to the success of a performance consultant.

● *Interventions*—the HPI actions the client has agreed to take. In many cases, the actions require the services of other internal and external partners.

● *Results*—the expected outcomes or how success will be measured.

Now let's take a closer look at the on-the-job behaviors shown in the performance needs of figure 2.

Securing Contracts for Performance Improvement Actions

Once the client has agreed to the interventions needed, confirm the scope of work and your role in implementing the interventions. These factors will drive the number of internal and external contracts needed in this phase. If your role is project manager or facilitator, you could be responsible for securing and monitoring multiple contracts.

As discussed earlier in the assessment phase, the contract may be a letter, an electronic memo, a short contract, a long contract, or whatever the client recognizes as an agreement for work to be performed and results to be achieved. Regardless of the form, the purpose of a contract is to identify the scope of work, the milestones, the resources, and the schedule (refer to table 2 for the components of a contract). Note that milestones for HPI projects and interventions will differ from the assessment example.

Brokering for Resources through Internal and External Partnerships

Once you reach the implementation phase of the HPI process, the importance of partnerships is critical. Based on the scope of work and your role, you may need to broker for additional resources. Have you developed partnerships with key internal and external resources? As shown in the learning needs in figure 2, an important skill for a performance consultant is relationship building—the cornerstone of effective partnerships. Successful performance consultants practice relationship building as an ongoing, never-ending process with clients, internal contacts, and external resources.

As described throughout this chapter, the role of a performance consultant is to define and align the client's business and performance needs. In many cases, this alignment requires actions that can be addressed only by resources outside the performance consulting work group. Do not wait for a project to identify and develop relationships. Start today. Success as a performance consultant may depend upon your ability to successfully partner with others outside of your control.

Managing HPI Projects

At this juncture, if your role is to manage or facilitate HPI actions or projects, you need to utilize standard project management skills and techniques to plan, organize, and monitor the work of others. You may be called upon to communicate benefits at various stages in the life of a performance change project, for example, when securing project resources, recruiting project team members, and overcoming resistance to the change process from clients and other individuals and groups. In addition, you may be called upon to facilitate the removal of barriers and the resolution of issues affecting the performance change process or project team.

Measuring and Reporting Results

Based on the impact measures agreed to in the assessment phase, your role at this stage could be to measure the results of actions taken; broker for resources to measure the results; or manage a project to design, develop, and implement the measurement process. If your role includes managing the measurement process, you will need to utilize standard project management skills and techniques described earlier.

Once you complete the measurement process, report the results. As described earlier in this chapter, reporting results of any kind requires planning. What method did you and the client discuss and agree upon? What does the client expect from you? Plan carefully; this could be your opportunity to provide proactive support for the client.

Conclusion

The performance consultant may be a client liaison, interviewer, analyst, project team member, or project manager whose responsibilities may vary depending on the structure of the performance department and his or her level of performance, skill, and knowledge. Performance consultants may be involved in producing results in each phase of the HPI process. Never take partnerships for granted. Building and maintaining business relationships with clients, internal contacts, and external resources is a never-ending process, not a project-specific activity, and is critical to your success. To ensure success as a performance consultant, never lose sight of your goal: to improve the processes and human performance in support of the client's business goals.

References

Robinson, Dana Gaines. "Performance Consultant: The Job". Pittsburgh, PA: Partners in Change, 1997.

Robinson, Dana Gaines, and James C. Robinson. *Performance Consulting: Moving Beyond Training*. San Francisco: Berrett-Koehler, 1995.

The Author

Judith Robb began her career in 1968 as a customer service supervisor and training supervisor. In 1984 she joined the Pacific Gas and Electric Company where she worked as a trainer, training supervisor, internal consultant, director, and senior performance consultant. In 1994 she established her own performance consulting practice, the Robb Group of San Francisco, California. Currently, her primary focus is on working with clients to define and align their business, performance, learning, and work environment needs. Her consulting services include coaching clients in the performance consulting process, conducting performance and process assessments, developing performance models, and providing performance-consulting training. Robb is qualified to administer and interpret the Myers-Briggs Type Indicator® (MBTI). She designs and facilitates workshops using the MBTI and temperament for personal development, communication, teams, and leadership.

Robb has a B.S. from the University of San Francisco and is an M.B.A. candidate from St. Mary's College in California. She was a founding member of the performance consulting organization that won the 1997 American Society for Training & Development Best Practice Award for Performance Consulting. She is the coauthor of *Temperament and Type Dynamics: The Facilitator's Guide*, published by TRI of Huntington Beach, California.

Case Study

From Reengineering to Performance Consulting

by Cam Graham

COMPANY NAME: Petro-Canada

INDUSTRY TYPE: Integrated oil company

ORGANIZATION PROFILE

ORGANIZATION SIZE:

5,500 employees.

KEY PRODUCTS AND SERVICES:

Exploration, refining, and marketing of petroleum products.

ANNUAL SALES:

$5.6 billion (1996).

DEPARTMENT NAME:

Learning and Performance.

DEPARTMENT SIZE:

Seven local (approximately 50 related positions organization wide).

MISSION FOR DEPARTMENT:

In partnership with business leaders, predictably improve business results by supporting the creation of a Personal Best Performance Environment.*

---

*Personal Best Performance Environment, © Petro-Canada, 1997

PRIMARY REASONS FOR TRANSITION TO A PERFORMANCE FOCUS:

1. Self-initiated desire to have the function add measurable value to the business and secure a more strategic long-term role within the organization.

2 Many new business initiatives are identifying a need for employee training and improved people performance.

Initiatives Resulting from a Major Reengineering Project

The organization recently completed an 18-month reengineering project in its oil refining and crude supply processes. The purpose of the project was to improve profitability by streamlining and standardizing processes across the company's four refinery operations.

The final project report identified significant financial gains and numerous process, system, and structural changes. In support of these changes, the report identified a need for employee training in skill areas covering refinery operations, maintenance, and lab testing. Senior management believed the success of the reengineering initiative would depend greatly on employee training and were willing to allocate additional resources to ensure the reengineering recommendations were delivered. This case study involves implementation at one refinery location during an 18-month period.

Building Awareness and Business Credibility

Local refinery management appointed a person to oversee the training function to ensure it would meet its deliverables. This became the role of performance consultant being described. The performance consultant was asked to ensure that the identified training was implemented in an effective and timely manner. The performance consultant believed a traditional training approach would not deliver the desired results. The first major challenge in moving to a performance-based approach was answering the question, "Why change?" It was important to demonstrate a commitment to delivering the requested training while working with management to share the benefits of adopting a performance-based approach.

The significant investment budgeted for employee training provided a good reason to conduct several "training effectiveness" workshops with local management. The 60- to 90-minute awareness sessions, which shared training impact research, were followed by working sessions on overcoming typical barriers to on-the-job skill use. The goal was to sensitize management to the many factors outside the classroom that affect on-the-job skill use and to demonstrate the consultant's desire to generate measurable business results. Generally, management was appreciative of gaining these new insights, and ultimately it developed a number of actions to ensure training dollars would be invested wisely. This included more attention being paid to what happens before and after a training initiative.

As a result of the awareness sessions, management made two decisions:

1. Before training is delivered, people will be made aware of the expected business results and asked to identify the support they require to deliver the results.

2. After training, people will measure the specified business results and identify any barriers to delivering them.

Despite these insights, management was unwilling to delay the training schedule recommended in the reengineering report. Overcoming the resistance to any schedule delay required a new approach. An early lesson learned was to adopt an approach of helping business leaders make more informed business decisions rather than imposing a new training process. An "80/20 rule" was adopted as a tool to remind people that, typically, less than 20 percent of trainees will be successful if work environment factors are not considered; and more than 80 percent will be successful when they are considered.

This approach saw individual business leaders deciding how much effort would be expended before and after a training initiative. The question asked by the consultant became, "Are you sufficiently satisfied we can generate the results you require?" If so, let's move on; if not, what more needs to be done? Provided there is agreement to measure outcomes, the results ultimately speak for themselves.

A Request for Lab Testing Training

The reengineering report recommended upgraded skills for refinery operators to supplement the product quality testing done by dedicated lab technicians. Clients expressed the business need as "improved competitiveness through cost reductions and plant optimization." This would be achieved by operators making product quality adjustments 24 hours a day, seven days a week (the performance need). There was a request to develop and deliver training for 135 refinery operators in 10 new lab testing skills. The first challenge was to identify the specific business results expected and how they would be measured. Local management was eager to initiate training and believed sufficient analysis had been done during the reengineering project. It was important to minimize the time required and to position the assessment as establishing objectives for "trainees."

Members of operations and lab management were brought together for two, half-day working sessions (initial project meetings). The sessions resulted in a five-page document detailing the following:

- specifically how costs would be reduced

- general descriptions of required on-the-job performance

- eight business measures to be tracked

- seven work environment actions, 10 management actions, and six learning actions (see table 1).

Based on this more thorough performance discussion, line managers determined that only 20 percent of operators would actually perform lab tests. This meant it was unnecessary to train all 135 operators, as originally requested. The clients agreed that the identified actions would move the project forward significantly and that there was value in taking the time required. The consultant was asked to guide the overall project, and line managers were identified to lead teams in each of three areas: management actions, learning actions, and work environment actions.

In consultation with refinery operators and lab technicians, the "management actions" team was responsible for developing specific targets for each measure and the associated financial impact. The "learning actions" team prepared detailed performance descriptions and supporting procedures (job aids). The "work environment" team was responsible for answering and dealing with the question, "Once operators have the necessary skills, what else is required for them to perform as expected?"

The identified measures were tracked and reported monthly for eight months following project implementation. Ultimately, the measures became part of the annual business plan. All targets were achieved or exceeded.

A Request for Computer Skills Training

The reengineering report recommended upgraded computing skills for 450 refinery employees. The goal was to streamline communications and prepare employees for a new computerized business system being introduced as part of the reengineering recommendations. The business and performance needs were stated at an organization level but were not explicit at the local and department level.

Based on the insights gained during the lab testing project, management was more receptive to front-end assessment. Over a two-week period, a series of client interviews were conducted to describe their department business and performance needs and to establish the work environment needed to support desired performance. Clients were asked questions in three areas:

1. What are you expecting your people to do more, better, or differently after acquiring their new skills?

2. Once your people have the necessary computer skills, what might prevent them from using their skills as desired?

259

T A B L E   1   Lab Testing Project: Actions Identified During an Initial Project Meeting

Work Environment Actions	**Management Actions**	**Learning Actions**
Finalize installation and commissioning of new quality control center testing equipment.	*Initiate* an effective change management process.	*Designated operators* develop basic *knowledge* of:

Finalize installation and commissioning of new quality control center building.

Adjust operator responsibilities and priorities to incorporate sample testing responsibilities.

Adjust lab technician responsibilities to incorporate changes in sample testing responsibilities.

Develop measurement criteria and documenting system for sample testing.

Develop a process map for sample testing work process. (Cover the entire cycle from business need, through test completion, to the need being satisfied.)

Maintain a project schedule coordinating the activities and progress of all three action groups.

Sponsor **project teams** to accomplish work environment actions.

Sponsor an **implementation team** to accomplish learning actions.

Confirm whether lab personnel will be responsible for any emergency or "overflow" testing for the tests being transferred to operators.

Confirm the "times of day" when sample testing will be performed by operators.

Confirm which operators will be expected to perform sample testing.

Assign responsibility for maintaining the lab testing equipment.

Confirm who will deliver the required training.

Implement performance improvement plans with the operators involved.

Support the people logistics involved in delivering the learning actions.

- the testing process
- interpreting test data
- chemistry being used
- business impact of test data

Designated operators develop *skills* to:
- perform sample testing
- use testing equipment
- calibrate testing equipment
- respond to test results

Designated operators understand the role of the lab information management system database and possess the *skills* to properly enter and retrieve test results.

Designated trainers develop the technical *skills* and *knowledge* listed above.

Designated trainers develop *train-the-trainer* skills in basic instruction and evaluation.

Persons responsible for maintaining the lab testing equipment develop the *knowledge* and *skills* to adequately maintain the testing equipment.

3. What types of productivity or business result improvements might you see when people perform in this new way?

Simultaneously, a skills assessment survey tool was developed and delivered to determine the base-level skill of each employee and whether the necessary computer equipment was available. The interviews and skill assessments revealed the following:

- Business and performance needs varied by department.

- Existing skill levels varied within and across departments.

- Work environment barriers existed in all departments.

Armed with this data, a business case was prepared that included the following:

- the business and performance needs of each department

- skill gaps by department

- costs to close skill gaps by delivery option

- work environment barriers by department

- return-on-investment by delivery option (*based on the 80/20 probability of skills being used as desired*).

A data reporting meeting was facilitated with refinery management to share the results of the client interviews. Management found the business case format familiar and easy to understand, which facilitated easy decision making. This also reinforced the consultant's desire to focus on measurable business results. During the data reporting meeting, management decided to develop workers' computer skills in stages over a 12-month period. This approach supported just-in-time learning and provided time to overcome known work environment barriers. The Learning and Performance team was asked to be responsible for delivering the learning actions and for reporting measurement data. Department managers would be responsible for setting clear performance expectations and for ensuring work environment barriers were overcome.

Before attending a learning session, people received an electronic questionnaire covering the following points:

- How are you expecting your performance to change as a result of using your new computer skills?

- What specific skills do you need to develop during this session?

- How will you and your department benefit from your new computer skills?

- How do you plan to follow though and measure your progress?

Instructors, called "learning coaches," used this information to tailor learning sessions to individual needs and to ensure that practice sessions represented the learner's actual work environment. Thirty days following completion of a learning action, learners were sent electronic reminders to check in on their progress (see table 2). These "30-day check-ins" were intended to support learners in identifying and communicating barriers, and to reinforce their progress. The data would be summarized and trending reports would be provided to department managers.

During early stages of the project, less than 40 percent of learners carried through with their measurement commitment. There were two primary barriers to achieving the project's follow-through objectives: (1) People feared negative consequences from being measured; and (2) there was insufficient measurement and reporting capability within the Learning and Performance function. A number of corrective actions were undertaken, including the following:

T A B L E   2   Computer Skills Project: Sample 30-Day Check-in Questions

1. I am using my new skills to improve my on-the-job performance:
   - ☐ Not at all
   - ☐ Rarely and only with help
   - ☐ Rarely with some help
   - ☐ Occasionally
   - ☐ Frequently and with some help
   - ☐ Frequently and without help

2. I am using my new skills to do the following on the job:

3. By using my new skills, I have achieved the following benefits for myself and my department (be as specific as you can):

4. I am having to deal with the following barriers to using my new skills to the fullest:
   - ☐ Insufficient access to equipment (or facilities)
   - ☐ Insufficient access to appropriate support resources (people or materials)
   - ☐ Making time to practice the skills I've learned
   - ☐ The opportunity to use the skills I've learned in my work
   - ☐ Getting support from my leader/supervisor
   - ☐ Getting recognition and reinforcement for what I've learned
   - ☐ Other
   - ☐ I have experienced no barriers.

- placing more emphasis on self-measurement

- sensitizing supervisors to people's fear of punishment and embarrassment

- sacrificing some accuracy in the interest of measurement question clarity

- asking performers how to improve measurement questions and tools.

As the capability to collect and report measurement data increased, so did people's willingness to generate and act on the data. When department managers started to receive timely and actionable trending data, they were eager to take action. As the project neared completion, more than 75 percent of learners were measuring and acting on their follow-though commitments.

There were two key learnings during this project: (1) Sufficient measurement discussion up front is critical to conducting meaningful and constructive measurement after a learning initiative; and (2) measurement activity must be simple and easy to implement. Ask managers what type of evidence they will accept, and deliver that type of evidence. The evidence clients will accept is often less onerous and more anecdotal than might be expected.

Lessons Learned

There were many lessons learned during this 18-month period. The most important of them are detailed below.

Understand the Business of the Business

Learn the business language being used by clients and understand the pressures facing both managers and workers. This enables you to understand the implications of clients' requests and actions. When you can see, and acknowledge, the implications on business results, you can build credibility and trust with your clients.

Form Relationships

Seek out a variety of people who are willing and able to provide support. They may include progressive business leaders; others attempting a similar undertaking; colleagues in related functions; or seasoned practitioners willing to share their patience, experience, and wisdom. Make early allies of people in other support functions to avoid turf wars.

Start Small and Avoid Announcements

Look for initiatives with a high probability for success. These may include any situations involving significant upside gain; significant pain associated with the status quo; progressive business leaders; or manageable deliverables, time frames, and resources. Avoid making flashy announcements. Let measurable results do the advertising. Advertise by doing it. Don't make promises that may be difficult to keep. Adopt an approach of under promising and over delivering.

Don't Seek Perfection and Be Sure to Measure Results

Take what the situation will allow and choose carefully based on how much change the system and the client are likely to tolerate. Clients need to feel that your service is actually helping. Keep the end goal in mind and always push for the opportunity to measure. Measurable results are a license to future opportunities.

Be Bold

Change requires a strong personal commitment to lead the way, demonstrate confidence, and endure resistance. Don't fear the unknown. Avoid second-guessing choices that have been made. Learn from the situation and remain focused on the future. Balance the need to make tough choices with a willingness to nurture others through the initial sense of loss and anxiety associated with change.

The Author

Cam Graham is currently a senior advisor within Petro-Canada's organization effectiveness function. Petro-Canada is one of the largest Canadian oil and gas companies, operating in both the upstream and downstream sectors of the industry and employs more than 5,500 people.

Cam leads a field-based team of human resource development (HRD) professionals providing services in performance consulting, business reengineering, and learning interventions. With only three years of direct HRD experience, he is a relative newcomer to the field. During his 19-year oil industry career, Cam has held a variety of line management positions in sales, marketing, and planning. His unique business background has been instrumental in changing the face of HRD within Petro-Canada and is highly valued by his clients.

Case Study

Performance Models—A Key to Performance Improvement

by Kathleen O'Hara

COMPANY NAME: Prudential HealthCare

INDUSTRY TYPE: Health care

ORGANIZATION PROFILE

ORGANIZATION SIZE:

3,000 associates located in 15 Southeastern cities.

KEY PRODUCTS AND SERVICES:

Provider of employee benefits to local, regional, and national markets.

ANNUAL SALES/ASSETS:

Approximately $9 billion.

DEPARTMENT NAME:

Professional Development Division.

DEPARTMENT SIZE:

Seven associates.

MISSION FOR DEPARTMENT:

The Professional Development Division, working in partnership with customers, provides services, guidance, and resources that support associates in the continuous improvement of their performance in achieving business results.

PRIMARY REASONS FOR TRANSITION TO A PERFORMANCE FOCUS:

Senior management was open to focusing on development of associates, but there was a high level of dissatisfaction with training received to do the associates' current job. Also, senior management had no evidence of return-on-investment dollars for training.

Background Information

Our newly created Professional Development Division was christened as a separate unit under the human resources (HR) umbrella reporting to the vice president of HR. Our vice president, along with 13 other functional vice presidents, reported to the president of Southern Group Operations. The key clients for our first performance consulting assignment were the vice president of Medicare and the vice president of operations for our Florida cities (see figure 1). The vice president of Medicare was responsible for the introduction of our managed care product into three Florida cites that were the first to be approved by Medicare to enter this market. The vice president of Medicare reported directly to the president but had a dotted line to the vice president of operations for Florida. The executive directors of the three Florida cities reported to the vice president of operations. So buy-in from both vice presidents and the executive directors was essential. In our efforts to reengineer and move beyond training into the world of performance consulting, our team knew that we must partner with this senior management team and link our approach to critical business needs if we were to be successful.

Process and Activities Used to Accomplish the Results

This case study describes how we helped one of our internal clients accomplish a critical business goal. He needed to expand the revenue and customer base by entering the Medicare managed care market. This project spanned eight months and included front-end assessment, training and nontraining solutions, and measurement of impact. At this point, it may be helpful to include an overview of the performance consulting services provided to our clients:

● forming partnerships with clients and key stakeholders (for example, client team)

● creating performance models for sales, telemarketing (direct marketing), and member services positions

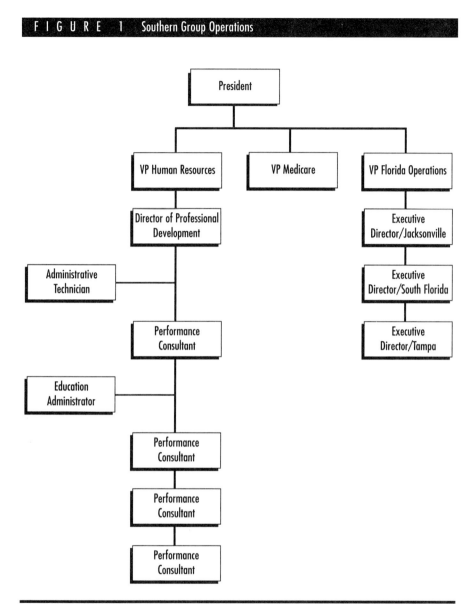

FIGURE 1 Southern Group Operations

- implementing a behavioral interviewing training program for all hiring managers and creating a selection tool for the sales representative based on the performance model

- providing assistance during design of training

- creating selection/interviewing tools and providing coaching for the individual hired to deliver training and support for the Medicare function

267

- designing evaluation and measurement systems to determine (a) learning and (b) impact from training programs and other interventions.

Now that we have described the big picture, let's walk through the major activities that our team took to provide these services.

Forming Partnerships

Our partnership with senior management started prior to a request for assistance from the vice president of Medicare. To lay the foundation regarding how we wanted to work with each business unit, we scheduled a meeting with each member of senior management to share our strategic plan and discuss the following:

- goals of the partnerships

- benefits to be derived from these partnerships (see table 1)

- what is required of performance consultants and managers if the partnerships are to be successful

- obstacles that need to be overcome so the partnerships are successfully forged.

Shortly after these meetings, the vice president of Medicare came to us with a request for sales training. Here was our first opportunity to conduct an initial project meeting to transform his request into a focus on performance and business results. We started by asking him questions regarding the performance he would see if the sales training were successful. He had difficulty answering, so we suggested that setting performance expectations for this new sales representative position would be important to the success of the business (our first step in moving the client from a training focus to a performance focus). We then asked him if they were performing as they *should*, how would this affect the operational results? We needed the client to identify the targets the company was setting for this new salesforce. We determined that each sales representative would be held accountable for a specified number of enrollments per month, a percentage of retained members after six months, and a specific closing ratio—that is, the percentage of people whom the sales representative called on who actually enrolled in the SeniorCare program. Then we asked him about some of the external obstacles to achieving those operational targets—the forces outside the company that could impact results. He mentioned that many new competitors were entering the market, causing pricing pressure, and that health-care reform and government regulations changing constantly presented a challenge for the salesforce.

Next we redirected the discussion to the kind of performance that the sales representative would need to exhibit to achieve the operational results. We asked about other potential causes of nonperformance: "Even if

T A B L E   1   Benefits From Partnerships

Benefits to Professional Development	Benefits to Southern Group Operations Management
• Increased learning about the business of the business • Opportunity to demonstrate value-added role in the organization, increasing credibility with the organization • Broadened career opportunities • Increased personal and job satisfaction	• Increased results obtained from educational and developmental investments • Improved work environment that fosters increased productivity • Decreased situations in which an investment in training is made that does not yield results • Increased knowledge about what is required to ensure performance excellence • Opportunity to draw upon an additional resource in support of their business goals • Demonstrates a model of partnerships that can serve as an example to others in their department

the representatives completed the sales training, what other factors in the work environment might make it difficult for them to perform?" He mentioned it might be difficult to develop a system to provide the representatives with qualified leads. We asked if it would be helpful to find out what other obstacles might get in the way of the representatives' performance. At this point, we summarized our conversation, and he agreed that it would be helpful to have additional data regarding the performance of very successful representatives as well as barriers to their performance and achievement of the business results he had identified. We used a similar pattern of questioning for all three positions for the Medicare market: sales representative, direct marketing representative, and member sales representative. This was our big break—our first contract for a performance assessment!

At this point, we needed to be sure the client was comfortable holding off his decision to begin work on the sales training. We explained that the skills and knowledge would be the underlying ingredient for the representatives to perform as required and that any design of learning needed to be linked to the performance we would be identifying in the performance model. He agreed to hold off on hiring an instructional designer until the model was built, and we agreed to find a designer who would link the model with the training design. Another small victory!

The next challenge was to build a coalition of key stakeholders in this project. Our strategy was to involve the decision makers early in the process, provide them an opportunity for input, and gain their support for implementation of these new tools. The client team was made up of the vice president of Medicare, the vice president of operations, the newly hired SeniorCare marketing directors, and the executive directors of the three cities in which we would launch our market entry. We needed to keep them involved and updated throughout the eight-month project if we wanted a successful implementation.

Forming Performance Models

Our biggest challenge in building the performance models for these three positions was learning the technical skills required for building a performance model. Each model contained business and performance results, best practices required to achieve the result, and quality criteria to measure how well the result was accomplished. We also gathered data on work environment obstacles and enhancers to achieving those results, as well as selection criteria for each job. The major components of a model are listed in table 2.

Being newcomers to the work of performance consulting, we contracted with an external consultant to coach us through the data collection process. Because two of the three jobs were new to Prudential HealthCare and we did not have access to exemplary performers, we decided to use three different data collection strategies. For the sales representative position, we conducted a focus group with the newly hired marketing directors, who had all managed exemplary sales representatives, and we used the external consultant to obtain benchmark data for this job. For the telemarketing (direct) model, we interviewed people who held that job with some of our competitors, and managers and performers in companies who do telemarketing for other corporations. The third model was the easiest, because we were able to collect data from exemplary performers in the commercial member service areas and then have subject matter experts in Medicare revise the best practices and measures to service the senior population.

During this process, we kept the client team involved and updated them regularly on our progress. We sent them periodic e-mails to show our progress against the action plan we had created. They were also involved in providing input to each of the training modules as it was designed, and the designer would contact them directly with any questions so they would

T A B L E 2	Components of a Performance Model			
Business and Performance Results	Best Practices	Quality Criteria	Work Environment Obstacles	Work Environment Enhancers
The operational (quantifiable) results of the business unit and the outcomes that a performer must achieve on the job if the organization's business goals are to be attained	What effective performers actually do on the job to achieve performance results	The criteria used to measure the performance result	Forces within and outside the organization that make accomplishments of performance results difficult	Forces within and outside the organization that make accomplishments of performance results easier

know their input was being addressed. It was the client team's job to ensure that the managers and performers they had selected to be interviewed were available to participate in the project. If there was a delay, we would call and ask for their help. We also called to thank them for recommending someone who had been an outstanding interviewee.

Building models to accurately reflect how a job is performed is an art and science with a steep learning curve. But as we progressed from our first model to our third, there were big leaps in our capabilities to collect and analyze data. Once the models were completed, we conducted a validation meeting for each and got the final approval to implement them. This meeting is a critical part of the partnership, because the decisions from this meeting will determine if there will be a contract for implementation. It is an opportunity for the client team to shape the final product and make it "theirs." The more input and edits the client team makes to the model, the more likely they are to invest in the actions necessary to implement it. The outcomes of this meeting may depend on how well you have maintained the client's level of interest and involvement during the entire assessment process.

To prepare for the validation, we designed the outcomes and agenda for the meeting and asked for the client's input. We also identified who, in addition to the client team, should be at the validation meeting. We agreed on a geographical representation of exemplary performers (when available) and a few managers of the position. The client was asked to invite them to the meeting. We asked the client to facilitate introductions and opening comments and to explain the purpose of the project: What were the business drivers as well as his or her expectations for today's meeting? In addition to the outcomes and agenda, we designed a cover letter for each participant that reviewed the project, the sources of the data, uses of the performance model, and the process for editing the model. These were sent to everyone a week ahead of the meeting. As a project team, we conducted a "dress rehearsal" for the meeting and decided how we would handle issues, concerns, and next steps. Since the validation was a very interactive process, we were able to gather all the client input to edit the model, discuss concerns and issues, and walk away with an action plan that consisted of shared responsibility for future actions to ensure the implementation of the model.

Implementing Behavioral Interviewing

One action to support performance change for SeniorCare was the introduction of a behavioral interviewing training program for all hiring managers. Following the client team's approval of the selection criteria for all new sales representatives, we set up a meeting with the vice president of Medicare to discuss the hiring process and how we could provide support.

We believed that the greatest risk to achieving the business results was on the front end. It was critical to select the appropriate candidates the first time. We shared research data with the client that indicated the cost of a hiring mistake was 30 percent of the annual salary for the position. We discussed the legal aspects of hiring errors and the cost implications if the hiring process was inconsistent. We asked if the current managers had the skills to select the best candidates. As a result of this discussion, the vice president influenced the team to attend a two-day behavioral interviewing training session.

We were able to locate the appropriate vendor and work with them prior to the session to be sure that the selection tool and process they would build in class was based on the performance model. We had to do a little arm-twisting to get all involved to take two full days out of their schedules, but the class and the tool they built were a big success. And as we all know, hiring managers are more committed to using a tool they have constructed themselves.

Linking Learning to Performance Model

Here our service was to broker the design work. The client also wanted our input during the design process. Being a part of this process allowed us to ensure the link between the performance and the learning design. We contracted with a sales training instructional designer who also shared our performance technology or systems-thinking approach to training. He worked in a collaborative fashion with our team and the client team. After completing each module, he would edit the curriculum based on our feedback. In that way, the client team became the true "owners" of the end product and were more willing to support it.

The client team also agreed to have sales managers conduct an orientation with the new sales representatives. As part of the orientation, the sales managers would explain the purposes of the performance model and review the performance expectations. Then they would reinforce that the sales training session the representative would attend was designed to support the performance defined in the model. As further reinforcement of this linkage, we had the sales training designer build an introduction to the performance model as part of the leader's guide. In this way, the instructor would link what the representatives were learning to the performance that was expected on the job.

Selecting and Developing a Medicare Sales Trainer

The client sponsor knew that ongoing sales and product training would be critical for the success of the Medicare product as we expanded into new markets. It would require a dedicated resource. We agreed, but we also wanted to be part of the selection process. Our team had a vested interest in helping them pick the right person to fill this role. We wanted a partner who was a systems thinker, not just a trainer. To facilitate that result we offered to create a list of the competencies we believed were critical to success. Once the client agreed to the competencies, we designed the selection process and built two behavioral interview guides: one for our team to use during the interview process and one for the vice president of Medicare. Table 3 illustrates the competencies critical to this role.

The deciding factor in the selection process was a training simulation we designed to be presented by each of the finalists. We invited key stakeholders (SeniorCare marketing directors) to the simulation and asked for their input since they would be working closely with the Medicare sales trainer in each local market. The vice president of Medicare relied on our feedback to guide the final selection, and he set the expectation that the new Medicare sales trainer would continue a collaborative relationship with our function. He truly had become a champion of our services.

Forming Evaluation and Measurement Systems

The vice president of operations, although impressed with our products and services, urged us to make sure that what we had provided for Medicare actually worked. The three cities selected as the most viable markets with the greatest probability of success were the pilot sites he wanted to measure. This was definitely counter to our corporate culture of constant activity and new initiatives with little or no analysis and measurement. What an opportunity

T A B L E   3   Medicare Sales Trainer Selection Process

Competencies to Assess by Interviewer

Competencies for Assessment by Professional Development	Competencies for Assessment by Vice President Medicare
• Performance observation and feedback skill	• Project management skill
• Human performance technology understanding	• Coaching skill
• Project management skill	• Collaborative skill
• Coaching skill	• Performance observation and feedback skill
• Collaborative skill	• Presentation skill
• Presentation skill	• Self-knowledge/job fit
• Self-knowledge/job fit	• Technical skills —Business understanding —Industry understanding —Sales skill
• Technical skills —Training material writing skill —Training evaluation skill —Instructor facilitation skill	

Note: Presentation skill will be assessed by both professional development and the vice president during the simulation.

for us to prove our value and be measured by not only the quality and quantity of our services but also by their impact on the business! If the pilot was successful, it would be considered a model for a national rollout.

Since measuring impact was not in high demand, we did not have the internal capability to do this, so once again we contracted with an external consultant. We needed a coach to guide us through our first Level 3 and Level 4 evaluation. Our first challenge was to fill in a measurement design document as a framework for the project. The design document included such things as what information we needed to know to determine if the pilot was successful, data sources, how to collect the data, and decisions that would be made by the client as a result of the evaluation.

When we completed the measurement document, we created a three-phase action plan: (1) planning, (2) data collection, and (3) report of findings. This plan spanned about three months. We started the planning phase early to ensure that the sales representatives would be in their jobs a minimum of six months before we started the data collection. That would give them time to transfer their learning to the job, and managers would have an opportunity to coach and use their new skills. To measure impact, we took the following steps:

- determined the operational results for each city

- gathered data about on-the-job behaviors of the representative and coaching by the sales managers

- compiled and analyzed results

- presented data to the client team.

This project had the steepest learning curve of all. Our consultant coached us through the content analysis to determine categories of data and frequency of response. Using an approach called the "data funnel" (see figure 2), we began to interpret the data starting at the top of the funnel with the data results—actual facts from the surveys and interview guides we used. We determined patterns that were evident in the data results. Next, we determined the conclusions—statements that summarize the patterns. And finally, near the bottom of the funnel, we determined implications. These led to actions that should be taken to achieve the business results. These actions included both training and nontraining actions required to achieve business results.

It is critical for the success of the data reporting meeting that the client be actively involved in the action planning to ensure maximum buy-in for implementation. With that in mind, we designed the data reporting meet-

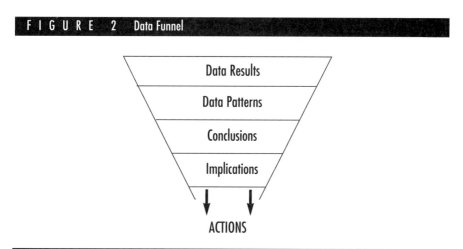

FIGURE 2   Data Funnel

Data Results

Data Patterns

Conclusions

Implications

ACTIONS

ing to be a facilitated discussion of the data and the conclusions we had reached. We asked the clients' reaction to each major conclusion and what the implications were to achieving their business results. We measured the success of the meeting by two things: (1) The clients came up with ideas and actions to be taken (we did not have to resort to the list of recommended actions we had created prior to the meeting); and (2) we created an action plan that the clients agreed to implement.

Results Obtained

Since the outcome of our partnership was to achieve operational targets, we can start with those measures. Overall, the enrollment results were higher than target in two cities and were lower than target in our two other sites (see figure 3).

In all cities that measured retention six months after enrollment, the retention rate was at or above target. The close ratio, defined as the percentage of prospects presented to those actually enrolled, was tracked in only Fort Lauderdale and Miami. In each of these cities, the actual close ratio was above target (see figure 4).

For performance change, we divided the data into areas of performance strength and areas of deficient performance to ensure we provided a balanced picture for the client. The major topics were: (1) obtaining and qualifying leads; (2) the on-site call; and (3) coaching and reinforcement. One of the significant findings, a real eye-opener for our clients, was that the plan with the highest quality and frequency of coaching and reinforcement also had the

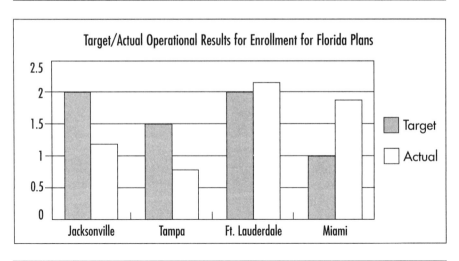

F I G U R E 3   Enrollments Per Representative Per Day

Target/Actual Operational Results for Enrollment for Florida Plans

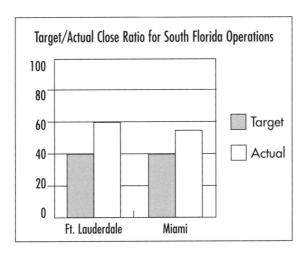

FIGURE 4   Close Ratio

Target/Actual Close Ratio for South Florida Operations

Target

Actual

highest operational results. When management saw the linkage, they decided to provide coaching training for all SeniorCare pilot sites. Since our corporate culture has not traditionally valued coaching as a management skill to improve performance, we saw this as a tremendous breakthrough.

Another significant outcome regarding our effectiveness as performance consultants was the strength of the partnership formed with the vice president of Medicare and the vice president of operations for the pilot sites. This was evidenced by invitations for a return engagement to reassess progress the following year, and to be on task teams to address work environment barriers identified in the report. Probably the biggest victory for the writer took place in a meeting with the national vice president of sales, when our client announced: "I used to think HR was just a function that provided some of those soft skills, but now I realize that Kathy is the only HR person who knows our business well enough to go out and sell a Medicare application!" That was the ultimate compliment—that we knew the business of the business.

Lessons Learned

With any project of this scope there are lessons to be learned. What we did well included building strong partnerships with key clients, collecting valid data, and influencing clients to take action in support of performance change and business results. What didn't go well, teaching us our biggest lesson, was our assumption that the vice president of Medicare could influence the executive directors to be accountable for actions to which they had agreed. We discovered too late that only the vice president of operations, to whom the executive directors reported, could provide the clout required to hold them accountable for coaching and reinforcing the performance of SeniorCare marketing directors. Also we needed the vice president of operations' direct involvement in addressing the work environment barriers identified in our impact evaluation.

Maintaining the partnership with clients requires constant attention. Even established clients can become preoccupied with other important issues. Often clients are promoted or moved into different positions, so a partnership needs to be established with a new person. Frequent communication is an effective way to maintain the partnership. This means eventually updating the established clients and clarifying with new clients how you and your function can help that person achieve his or her goals.

When beginning the journey to reengineering the training function, seek out a client with a critical business need. Don't wait for clients to knock on your door. They are not used to looking at you as a strategic business partner, so your challenge is to sell the benefits of a partnership and learn the business of their business. Then you must earn the right to "sit at the table" by providing value-added services that will have a positive impact on both performance and business results.

The Author

Kathleen O'Hara has been in the training and organizational development field since 1975. She began her human resource development (HRD) career as a trainer and account manager in customer support in a start-up software company. She moved from there to Wang Laboratories where she held various positions, including technical trainer, sales trainer, HRD specialist, and field HRD consultant. Prior to joining Prudential HealthCare, she was the manager of the training and development function for a software developer in the health care industry.

At Prudential HealthCare, she and a team of performance consultants were responsible for addressing the performance and development needs of all managers and associates in a region of more than 4,000 people as well as managing national projects that impact key positions across the company. She and her team provided many consulting services to the clients they supported, including the formation of performance models, identification of work environment barriers to performance, and determination of training needs. In May 1998 she accepted the position of director of performance consulting at BellSouth.

O'Hara has a B.S. in health education from Northeastern University, a certificate in human resource development from the University of Georgia, and an M.A. in adult education and human resource development/organization development from the University of Georgia.

10

Skills and Work Environment Required for Performance Consultants

by Thomas LaBonte

QUICK READ

● To successfully develop trainers as performance consultants, the performance improvement director must have—and communicate—a vision of the performance improvement process and expectations of the performance consultants.

● A four-step assessment process is used to develop the skill and knowledge of performance consultants:

—Identify and assign target levels for the competencies related to the position.

—Design the assessment process.

—Have each person take responsibility for self-assessment.

—Have each person complete a development plan with his or her manager.

● Skills and knowledge are developed in performance consultants through

—skill-building workshops

—continual learning activities

—coaches who help performance consultants apply the skills on the job.

● The role of the leader of the performance improvement department is to

—champion the process

—provide tools and people resources

—reward and recognize success

The Training and Development Department at PNC Bank received a wake-up call. The business needs of line managers were rapidly changing as competitive demands and customer expectations dramatically increased. The line was faced with the need to create and introduce new products and services, quickly implement new technologies, negotiate and successfully conclude strategic alliances, and efficiently integrate through mergers new markets, cultures, and thousands of new employees. How could training support the strategic and tactical business needs of the lines of business where the stakes included the future viability of the corporation? This was a daunting challenge facing a training department with a nearly empty tool box of deliverables. The staff were good performers but were largely skilled in stand-up classroom delivery. There were no competencies, no coherent curricula, no process for internal design, needs assessment, organizational development, or measurement. Training included a group of departments, largely operating in silos, with little true partnering with the line. Line managers were uneasy with the training capabilities available for their support.

Many training directors are facing similar challenges in how to maintain the nearly overwhelming pace of supporting the existing reality while transforming the skills and value of each trainer to the organization. There is one opportunity to do it right. The risks appear tremendous. So where to begin? How do you develop a highly competent staff capable of standing shoulder to shoulder with line managers in proactively supporting their business needs? How do you gain line manager and trainer support for what will be a long journey where change is constant?

THE VISION

It all starts with the vision of the training director on what the process, organization, and performer expectations of a high-performance training function will be, know, and do. It is a vision that must be easy to understand and yet convey a powerful message to the line and training organization of what will be different. The vision has as its foundation a process model that will translate the verbiage of the vision into practical actions supporting business needs.

The director of performance improvement and training at PNC Bank communicated a vision based on the critical business needs facing the corporation and the role of a "performance improvement and training" organization as a stakeholder in the company's future. The vision involved a radical change from a reactive, traditional training delivery function to a results enhancing, valued partner with the line. The vision was communicated not as a theoretical exercise but as a change in the value proposition of training as a revenue enhancing, service quality provider. Its mission was to support improvement of business results, increased employee skills, and productivity.

The director made several statements that set the tone for the vision and subsequent change process: Training collectively does not have the option to fail in making the transition to performance consulting. We must start this journey with every expectation of successfully gaining the skills and applying them intelligently for the maximum good of the corporation and its employees as well as for ourselves. We are all making this journey together. If we decide to stay as a team, then everyone will give 100 percent with no one having the option of selective participation. And finally, we are on a journey from which there is no return. The journey will never end. It will take three to five years to attain the minimum competencies needed to attain the vision, but the process will involve the whole of our professional lives.

The process introduced by the director of performance improvement and training is shown in figure 1. The process is an essential component for successfully achieving the vision and transforming the skills of trainers into performance consultants. The PNC Bank total performance improvement process was customized through a joint effort of the training organization and external partners. It is applicable for improving the performance of lines of business as well as serving as a blueprint for changing the skills of trainers. It is the responsibility of the training director to ensure the integration of the model into a systematic process supporting quality performance consulting implementation.

At what point does a trainer become a performance consultant? It is very important to understand that issuing a proclamation announcing a change in function with new titles but no deliverables to back it up is a death sentence to the transformation process. The director of performance improvement and training established several criteria at PNC Bank to ensure that the consulting verbiage and deliverables, when announced, would minimize client and trainer cynicism. To ensure that the transformation would be successful, the director of performance improvement and training took several actions to implement the vision, as outlined below.

COMPETENCY MODEL
AND ASSESSMENT PROCESS

The foundation for implementing the vision is answering the question, "What is the performance that should be expected of each trainer as a performance consultant?" The question requires analyzing client business

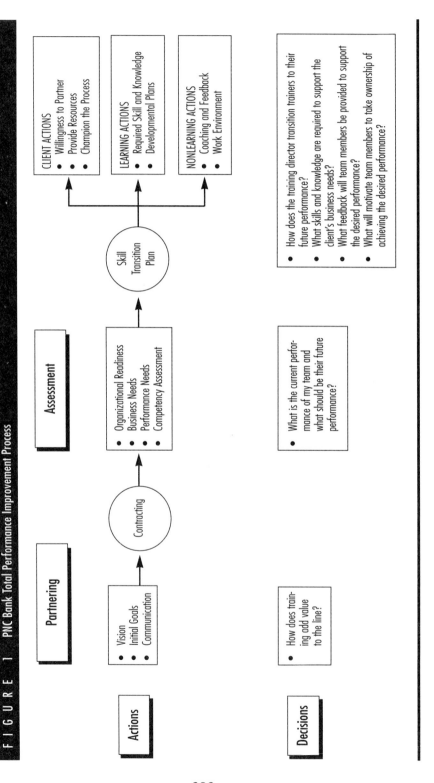

F I G U R E 1 PNC Bank Total Performance Improvement Process

Partnering

Assessment

Actions

- Vision
- Initial Goals
- Communication

Contracting

- Organizational Readiness
- Business Needs
- Performance Needs
- Competency Assessment

Skill Transition Plan

CLIENT ACTIONS
- Willingness to Partner
- Provide Resources
- Champion the Process

LEARNING ACTIONS
- Required Skill and Knowledge
- Developmental Plans

NONLEARNING ACTIONS
- Coaching and Feedback
- Work Environment

Decisions

- How does training add value to the line?

- What is the current performance of my team and what should be their future performance?

- How does the training director transition trainers to their future performance?
- What skills and knowledge are required to support the client's business needs?
- What feedback will team members be provided to support the desired performance?
- What will motivate team members to take ownership of achieving the desired performance?

needs, the current skills and knowledge of trainers—the "is"—and the future skills and knowledge needed to support the business—the "should." The should/is gap becomes the transition target that each manager and trainer focuses on for identifying learning and nonlearning needs.

These learning and nonlearning needs are supported by a competency model. The competency model answers the question of should/is performance. It is difficult for trainers to comprehend the journey to performance consulting without first understanding what they will be doing differently in the future from what they are doing today. It is the responsibility of the training director and each manager to clearly and repeatedly articulate the vision and the should/is scenario so that trainers understand the journey before them.

The creation of the competency model is started while the vision is being formed and communicated. The training director needs to determine what the outcomes or success measures are for a performance consultant. To do so, it is useful to put yourself in your client's shoes. What will be observable and valuable about the change in trainer performance? Seek line manager input to answer this question based on business needs. Use this as an opportunity to begin educating your clients about the value of the future performance consultant and the client's role in setting success measures as part of the consulting process. This partnering with the client will help in gathering data necessary to identify the skills, knowledge, and behaviors required for successful performance consultants. This data is essential for identifying competencies and performance results expected of internal consultants.

The director of performance improvement and training, the training managers, and an external partner created three competency clusters with 19 competencies to support the consulting skill transformation of PNC Bank trainers. The competencies serve as drivers of change and directly support the business needs of the lines of business. The following steps were used in the development of the competency model.

Step One

Identify target levels of competency and assign a target level for each competency to each position. The selection of target level to a position, not to a person, requires the manager to focus on client business needs and the trainer's performance needs. The target levels are based on three levels of performance expected of a position:

1. Knowledge and early application (K)—defined as being able to explain concepts, models, and definitions, and apply each at least once with a client.

2. Application (A)—defined as actually performing the competency at least four to five times proficiently with a client and meeting client expectations.

3. Innovation and Mentoring (I)—defined as mastery in coaching others on complex performance consulting skills and interventions, and the ability to innovate on the performance consulting process in solving client business needs.

PNC Bank created a matrix for each position, identifying the competencies, target levels, and target dates (see table 1).

Step Two

Build an assessment process (see table 2). Assessment focuses on determining the trainer's current skills and knowledge as evaluated against the competency target levels. The process is based on evaluating proficiency within each target level of competency. The final rating is reached through a consensus between the manager and trainer on the skills and knowledge he or she demonstrates on the job. Previous experience at other companies is included as long as the trainer presents evidence or talks through its application.

At PNC Bank, the training team and an external consultant built the assessment process. Several planning meetings were conducted with all training managers participating to create the steps in the process, determine how the assessment instrument would be developed, and prepare a communication and implementation plan. The training managers reviewed the process and solicited input from their team. The director of performance improvement and training then conducted face-to-face meetings with each training department to again outline and ensure understanding of the vision, discuss how we would accomplish the vision through the competency model and assessment process, and review the unique opportunity open to each trainer and the benefit to the company. While these meetings were under way, the competencies and the assessment instruments were being finalized.

With the final draft of the competency model and assessment process completed, the director of performance improvement and training conducted a planning and preparation session with the training managers. A checklist was used as a road map to standardize the assessment meeting (see table 3). A complete talk-through of the process was conducted, final revisions made, and dates set with the training managers for their assessment meetings.

All training managers prepared their self-assessments, gathered documentation, and annotated the assessment forms with evidence to support their ratings (see table 4 on page 288). The director of performance improvement and training scheduled an assessment meeting with each direct report. In addition to determining the manager's competency levels, this meeting also permitted the managers to experience the process so they could understand

TABLE 1   Competencies for Performance Improvement and Training

PNC Bank Sample Matrix

Name: _____   Job Title: Performance Improvement Consultant (Nonmanagerial)

Cluster	Competencies	Target Levels and Dates			
		9/16	10/17	11/18	12/19
Performance Consulting	Partnering and Relationship Building	A	A	A	A
	Assessment and Data Collection	A	A	A	A
	Performance Improvement Interventions	A	A	A	I
	Project Management	A	A	I	I
	Impact Evaluation	K	A	A	A
	Business Knowledge	A	A	A	A
	Systems Analysis	K	A	A	A
	Facilitation	A	A	A	A
	Coaching and Feedback	K	A	A	A
	Communication	A	A	A	A
	Problem Solving	K	A	A	A
Instructional Design	Instructional Analysis	A	A	A	A
	Instructional Design	A	A	A	I
	Instructional Development	A	A	A	A
	Application of Technology	K	K	A	A
	Instructional Product Implementation	K	K	A	A
	Learning Evaluation	A	A	A	A
Learning Facilitation	"Live" Facilitation	A	A	I	I
	Alternative Delivery Facilitation	K	A	A	A

285

TABLE 2   Competency Assessment Process

User Guidelines

Overview of the Process

The table below provides a brief overview of the competency assessment process and the tools that will be used.

Activity	Description	Tools
1. Determine competencies to be assessed in each wave.	The team member and manager will agree on the competencies to be assessed in each wave of assessment.	Competencies for Performance Improvement and Training
2. Assess current competencies.	The team member and manager will each independently assess the team member's current knowledge and skill in each of the competencies.	Competency Assessment
3. Reach consensus on ratings with manager.	The team member and manager will meet to compare and discuss their ratings. Based on the evidence provided by the team member, the team member and manager will mutually agree on the levels of proficiency achieved for each performance result.	Competency Assessment Rating Summary
4. Create individual development plan.	The team member and manager will jointly agree on development priorities for the team member and a development plan and timeline for reaching the target levels of proficiency within 18 months.	Development Guide Individual Development Plan
5. Review progress quarterly with manager.	The team member and manager will meet quarterly to review the team member's progress and to revise priorities and adjust methods and dates for reaching proficiency.	Individual Development Plan Competency Assessment Rating Summary

TABLE 3	Assessment Meeting Checklist for Managers

PNC Bank

Hold Team Meeting on Competency Assessment Process
• Distribute a competency assessment guide to each team member. • Explain purpose of the process and how it was developed and piloted. • Explain two waves of assessment and initial 18-month development phase. • Walk team members through the assessment materials. • Review scoring criteria.
Conduct Competency Assessment Session with Each Team Member
• Ask for examples and evidence to support team member's self-assessment. • Emphasize need to demonstrate skill and knowledge on the job. • Enter consensus ratings on assessment form.
Hold Team Meeting on Target Level Ratings and Development Planning
• Give each team member target competency levels for his or her position. • Review the development planning process and worksheet. • Schedule a development planning meeting with each team member.
Conduct Development Planning Session with Each Team Member
• Review ratings on assessment form and target competency levels. • Rank order development priorities. • Identify learning and nonlearning developmental actions. • Agree on developmental timeline for each competency. • Schedule first quarterly progress review meeting.

the perspective and anxiety of their team members. It also helped to finalize the managers' preparation and standardize the assessment approach, with the director serving as a role model. The assessment meeting was positioned by the director as a shared experience, a pilot, in which every manager would participate.

The assessment process was planned in two waves to make it less overwhelming and to focus on the high-priority competencies first. The competencies with the largest should/is gaps and critical to supporting client business needs were placed in the first wave. It still took the director of performance improvement and training an average of 2.5 hours to conduct each first-wave assessment.

T A B L E   4   Competency Model and Assessment Process Form

User Guidelines

Sample Form

For each behavior, circle the number that best represents your current level of knowledge or skill

PERFORMANCE RESULT #2: Plan assessment strategy and design tools.	Little or no opportunity to do it	Proficient, but need some coaching from time to time	Highly proficient, can handle situations without help
Knowledge/early application			
a. For a specific project in which you are involved, identify reliable sources and methods to use in obtaining assessment (SHOULD, IS, and CAUSE) data	1	2	③
b. Describe the advantages and disadvantages of various data collection methods that you have used with clients.	1	2	③
c. Identify and document specific business goals and initiatives to which a specific performance assessment is to be linked.	1	②	3
Application			
d. Develop a plan to form and involve the performance team in the assessment process.	1	②	3
e. Develop a strategy for collecting the assessment data.	①	2	3
f. Design, or manage others who design, the data collection instruments.	①	2	3

T A B L E 4 Competency Model and Assessment Process Form *(continued)*

Innovation/Mentoring			
g. Judge the appropriateness and comprehensiveness of a given assessment strategy and recommend alternatives/improvements.	①	2	3
h. Coach and mentor others on the development of assessment strategies and tools.	①	2	3
i. Negotiate trade-offs with the client when time or budget parameters are inadequate or additional resources are required.	①	2	3

Examples/Supporting Evidence:
a. For branch manager project, identified data sources and data collection methods
b. Described advantages and disadvantages of interviews, focus groups, observation, and questionnaires for branch manager project
c. Clarified six business goals for branch manager project
d. For branch manager project, developed plan to select and involve team members in assessment; client approved

Step Three

Each trainer takes responsibility for conducting a self-assessment of the competencies and for being prepared for the assessment meeting. During the session, trainers are asked a number of questions by their managers. If someone is watching you perform this competency, what outcomes and behaviors would they see? What results do you need to bring to the table to demonstrate proficiency?

Answering these and other questions objectively becomes the focus for the manager and trainer during the assessment meeting. After reviewing the approach and desired outcomes of the meeting, the manager and trainer place their ratings for each competency side by side to quickly identify gaps or areas of disagreement. Both work through the gaps by the manager asking a series of open- and closed-ended questions on how these skills or knowledge were learned and applied, and the results that were achieved. As the assessment progresses it becomes easier, since preceding agreements on skills and knowledge can be applied to a number of competencies. At the end of the meeting, the ratings from each competency assessment sheet are listed on a summary form and agreed to by both parties. The consensus from managers and trainers at the end of the assessment was that the principles and steps outlined and agreed upon by all at the beginning of the process were adhered to. Participants reported that it was a valuable opportunity for self-reflection and a clear indication of strengths and developmental needs. It centered the entire team on competencies as the common denominator of all that we would be, know, and do as performance consultants.

Several best practices and lessons learned from the manager pilot sessions were integrated into the final assessment plan. A critical success factor in the assessment process is the belief of each participant that the process is fair and credible. The manager and department meetings, the over-communication, requests for trainer input and active involvement of each team member, and the assistance of a respected external partner all helped to support belief in the process and reduce anxiety during its implementation.

Another best practice was the careful setting of expectations by the director, in person as well as through various media, to the training team. The director and managers expressed absolute trust in the integrity of the team and each team member's ability to objectively self-assess. Trust was demonstrated on both sides during the assessment meeting whenever a manager and trainer disagreed on a rating. Usually a compromise was reached. But if there was an impasse, the manager, after discussion, would agree with the trainer's rating. It was stated by the manager and agreed to by the trainer that he or she must be able to demonstrate proficiency to the standard with a client in order to validate the rating. If the trainer was unable to perform the competency to standard, then the manager's rating would prevail. Each trainer must be able to document, provide evidence, or give behavioral examples of skill, knowledge, and application to support a rating. Everyone in training, including the director, was expected to go through the process as a way of determining how they individually and collectively improve their capabilities and support provided to the client. Participation in this process was not an option. All trainers are accountable for their own competency development.

A final best practice took the form of a ground rule that, should the manager and trainer agree on a rating, then in the interest of time that rating would not be discussed. This would allow sufficient time to focus on those ratings where a gap was evident.

Step Four

Each trainer completes a development plan. The last step is to set a meeting date for the development planning discussion. This meeting is scheduled at least two weeks after the assessment session to allow time for the manager and trainer to reflect on the assessment ratings and possible development options. Creating a development plan is a negotiated discussion between the manager and trainer. This approach is essential if the trainer is to be expected to own the development plan and consulting skills transition.

The competencies to be developed are prioritized based on the severity of the gap between position target level, the trainer's proficiency, and client business needs. The top five competencies become the focus of the first 18-month development window. The manager guides and recommends, but the trainer decides development actions. Consensus is reached on timelines within the 18-month window. One nonnegotiable is that every trainer must be involved in consulting initiatives as an effective method of developing virtually all of the competencies.

Actions to Develop Competencies

Learning and nonlearning or work environment actions are specifically identified in the development planning meeting as the methods necessary to become a performance consultant. Learning and nonlearning actions must be planned as mutually supporting activities to be effective. Why? Because skills learned must have a receptive work environment for their application, or the skills are lost through lack of use. This is often seen in companies where training is considered the answer to performance problems. The paradox is that, although training is often part of the solution, it is rarely if ever the total solution to a client's business needs. Yet training is almost always requested by the client as their preferred solution. It is similar to a patient (client) going to the doctor (trainer) with a pain (business need) and asking for the orange pill (training) without allowing the doctor to diagnose the cause of the pain. The training director must take the position with the client and trainer that diagnosing the root cause of a performance problem and identifying actions to solve the problem the first time is one of the greatest contributions a performance consultant can offer. It is important that the training director early in the planning process focus on both learning and nonlearning actions to provide each trainer with the greatest opportunity for success in gaining consulting skills.

Learning Actions: Workshops

To be successful in the future, the trainer must transition to a performance consultant by achieving proficiency in consulting, instructional design, distance learning technologies, and measurement, as well as understanding the business of the business. Yet the most cherished skills of many of today's trainers are often the least valued or taken for granted by clients. Many trainers still define their value in terms of stand-up classroom delivery. The director of performance improvement and training at PNC Bank supported both formal learning and nonlearning actions as mutually supporting development opportunities. This involved each trainer's required attendance at an internal consulting workshop and informal learning actions through the application of skills on the job, with coaching and the sharing of best practices.

PNC Bank has adopted a series of workshops that build the necessary baseline of consulting competency needed for a beginning capability as a performance consultant. All new hires attend the Total Performance Consulting Process workshop offered in two three-day sessions. This workshop introduces a PNC-specific approach to performance consulting and integrates instructional design, alternative delivery, and measurement under a consulting umbrella. This workshop is ideally scheduled between three and six months after initial hiring to allow enough time for the newly hired trainer to get acclimated to the company.

A three-day instructional design workshop is required for positions requiring a high degree of proficiency in design and development. There is also a measurement workshop on the four levels of the Kirkpatrick model and balanced scorecard for those with appropriate target levels of competency in measurement and evaluation. The design and delivery of all of these workshops follows the same basic methodology.

The consulting workshop provides the process and skills umbrella for determining how the process model will be applied in supporting the client's business needs. The workshop is customized to the vision, values, strategic direction, and business-unique needs and terminology of PNC Bank. Each phase of the process is taught through the case study method.

Internal coaches provide guidance and feedback on the case study scenarios and, with a four-to-one ratio, provide each participant with an in-depth skill-building opportunity. Prework includes the trainers updating their competency assessment and development plans and bringing both to the workshop. A skills log maintained by the coach is used throughout the workshop to document skills learned by the trainer. Each trainer is also expected to come to the workshop with a performance consulting opportunity in mind that can be worked through as the workshop progresses.

At the end of the workshop, an action plan is created on next steps in starting the consulting intervention. The coach meets with each new performance consultant to debrief the skills log and the trainer's development planning worksheet. The performance consultants revise their development planning worksheets, noting competency improvements and additional development opportunities recommended by the coach. The performance consultants are expected to meet with their managers back on the job and review skills gained and lessons learned from the workshop. This is an important opportunity for the manager and trainer to talk through the expectations of consulting skills application with a client.

The director of performance improvement and training clarified his expectations at the beginning of the workshop on the implementation of consulting skills. The purpose of the workshop is not to make each trainer an expert consultant. This is unrealistic. All consultants, however, are accountable for using consulting skills based on the target levels of competency for their positions. The workshop provides a starting capability for achieving those target levels. Working as part of a consulting team and gaining experience over time will lead to competency attainment. A few positions will be designated as full-time performance consultants and will be responsible for leading consulting teams or working on performance models one-on-one with clients.

On-the-job development of consulting competencies needs to occur soon after returning from the workshop. More senior, experienced consultants may begin the process of working individually with a client on a consulting intervention. Most consultants, however, will be better served by becoming part of a consulting team. This affords the recent workshop graduate the opportunity to pair up with a seasoned consultant and learn through mentoring. It is critical that this first assignment be appropriately sized based on trainer readiness so that an early success is gained soon after workshop completion.

Mistakes are common during this early stage of development. Mistakes must be positioned and reinforced as learning opportunities. The skill transition process is a calculated risk that needs to be managed as such. The manager needs to provide positive coaching of the trainer when mistakes occur. The manager also needs to communicate frequently with clients to ensure they understand that honest mistakes may occur early in the skills transition process.

Continued Learning Actions: The Showcase

The director of performance improvement and training needed to sustain the momentum of trainer skill development gained through workshop attendance. Consulting skills, knowledge, and the integration concepts on instructional technology and measurement gained in the workshops needed ongoing emphasis. For a number of trainers, the new competencies were overwhelming, and concepts critical to their successful implementation were difficult to retain and apply. So the sustainment method needed to combine further opportunities for skill building with reinforcement of lessons learned from approximately 50 consulting interventions being conducted within the company. The solution was to pull all 165 performance consultants of PNC Bank together at corporate headquarters for a consulting best practices showcase. The objectives of the two-day showcase were threefold: first, to celebrate success; second, to share lessons learned and best practices; and third, to develop further the competencies of every consultant and administrator (nonexempt) in performance improvement and training.

The first evening involved dinner and the presentation of performance consulting awards to celebrate success. The presentations were interspersed with creative and humorous department skits to introduce each department and team member. The director of performance improvement and training set the tone for the showcase that first evening in reviewing the objectives and emphasizing the ups and downs the team had experienced in making the consulting journey to date. The vision that had been articulated more than a year earlier was now becoming a reality. High standards had been set, a great deal of resources dedicated to development, and the team had accepted the challenge and were making the journey to performance consulting together. It was now time to celebrate, while recognizing that a lot of work remained to be done. The agenda for the following two days included general sessions with all in attendance to address generic concepts and knowledge needed by the total training organization. Breakout sessions were conducted and attended at the discretion of trainers based on their competency needs and development plan.

While costly, the benefits of the showcase far outweighed the dollar expense. The showcase demonstrated tangible commitment by PNC Bank to the performance consulting process and each consultant's competency development. It was the first time in the history of the company that every consultant had come together under one roof. A great deal of team building and networking took place. The presentations by consultants on their consulting successes had a tremendous impact on those still hesitant about the process. The showcase was energizing yet provided a time to reflect on how far the group had come as an organization. Additional skills and techniques were learned through the sharing of best practices and attendance at the breakout sessions. There was a feeling of accomplishment and pride that transcended the showcase and carried forward when the participants returned to the office.

Nonlearning Actions

At PNC Bank, the director of performance improvement and training used a variety of approaches—including the role of the coach; strong leadership and communication; resources to support the desired performance; and incentives to motivate trainers to change behavior—and the education of line managers to support nonlearning skills application.

Coaching. After bearing the expense and time of having consultants attend one to three workshops and a showcase to learn consulting skills, the performance improvement director faced a critical dilemma. How do you support the effective application of newly learned skills on the job? The answers to this question must be carefully weighed, since nonlearning actions applied in the work environment fly in the face of strongly held client and trainer beliefs about training as the only solution for performance problems.

The role of coach was formalized as a mentor for guidance and support upon request. Newly prepared consultants often need a peer rather than a manager to think through the issues and bounce ideas back and forth. Credibility and a close working relationship already existed between the coach and consultant from the workshop(s). Creating additional opportunities to continue the learning exchange would strengthen the implementation of performance consulting skills. These coaches eventually formed the nucleus of a small but highly influential full-time consulting team available to support the most complex performance improvement initiatives while mentoring the next generation of consultants.

It is strongly recommended that internal coaches be selected as a primary source of performance consulting feedback. The coaches need to be carefully selected based on level of competency attainment and credibility, gained as an exemplary performer, risk taker, and business knowledge resource. The coach needs to be an excellent communicator and a passionate advocate for performance consulting. The coach must be recognized by the director as the best of the best, and the role of coach must be reinforced as one of great honor. The coaches at PNC Bank were selected by the director of performance improvement and training using these criteria: (1) Coach candidates were initially identified as outstanding performers in the performance consulting workshop and then attended special preparation sessions with an external consultant. (2) Each coach candidate then served an apprenticeship as an assistant coach and was assigned a seasoned mentor in one or more workshops. (3) The candidate was then formally recognized by the director as a coach.

It is important to note that the coaches do not replace the manager's developmental role. The coaches are technical specialists with a depth of consulting expertise to share. The managers are consulting generalists and as such bear responsibility for conducting progress reviews and spot coaching as opportunities make themselves available.

Leaders as process champions. The role of the director as the champion of the consulting process—the transformational leader with the vision to drive the change in trainer skills, knowledge, and behaviors—cannot be understated. Whether it is providing hands-on process support, resources, coaching, or celebrating success, the role of the director and managers is a fundamental prerequisite to the trainer's skill transformation. When the leadership of the performance improvement and training function serves the team as role models and practitioners of consulting competencies, then consultants are empowered to learn and perform.

The manager and coach are both faced with determining what feedback will be provided to sustain the consultant's skill transfer and desired performance. Timely and targeted feedback is essential to reinforcing the change in consultant skills and behaviors. It must be planned so that feedback is provided from several different but mutually reinforcing sources. Feedback can be provided from peers, clients, external consultants, and, of course, from the consultant's manager and coach. Establishing a formalized feedback process is the director's responsibility. Its implementation is the responsibility of each manager and coach to ensure that the process works.

The director of performance improvement and training set the expectation that all consultants would receive informal coaching at least monthly and formal progress reviews quarterly from their managers. This expectation was modeled by the director with his managers. The informal coaching may be a brief inquiry about the status of an intervention, praise or words of encouragement, or alternatives to consider as next steps. The quarterly progress review is a formal meeting at which the development plan is discussed in detail, and progress and new developmental actions are noted on the development planning worksheet. Both the consultant and manager are expected to come to this meeting prepared to share information on progress made toward attainment of competency target levels. The annual performance appraisal meeting holds no surprises, because the data for the meeting is taken from the quarterly progress reviews. The development planning worksheets are attached to the performance appraisal form and, along with evidence of results achieved, become the basis for a rating and appropriate reward and recognition.

Feedback also needs to be provided through the performance improvement and training communication channel. A performance improvement newsletter is an important nonlearning action in providing a forum for recognition and feedback on the implementation of consulting skills. Articles are written by trainers on lessons learned, promotions are listed, and congratulatory messages are made on consulting achievements. The newsletter also provides a forum for the director and managers to reinforce the vision, motivate the team through peer success stories, and inform line managers of the new capabilities of the performance improvement and training organization.

Coaching and recognition were further institutionalized at PNC Bank through monthly video conferences and quarterly face-to-face manager meetings. A portion of each video conference is devoted to spotlighting managers and their teams who are making progress in performance consulting. During the spotlight, managers are given the opportunity to share lessons learned and provide their peers with examples of consulting products and services.

Tools and people resources. What tools and resources will the performance improvement director need to provide in support of nonlearning actions and desired consulting performance? At PNC Bank, a valuable tool for the performance consulting transformation was the creation of the consulting tool kit. The tool kit is a 400-page binder that serves as a consulting process road map with a series of job aids, checklists, and templates of best practices designed to guide the consultant on how to apply the process with a client. The tool kit is given to consultants as they start the consulting workshop. It is used as a reference in the workshop and is fully integrated into the case studies. At least semiannually, the tool kit is updated as the consulting process becomes more institutionalized and new best practices are discovered.

Another nonlearning action resource is the ability to identify and retrieve consulting best practices on demand. Software, such as Lotus Notes, either standing alone or linked to a performance consulting Web site on the company intranet, provides excellent tools for capturing and disseminating knowledge to others pursuing similar consulting interventions. This also allows for timely communication on new consulting interventions, team assignments, and benchmarking best practices. A less technology-dependent solution to capturing best practices is to use the performance improvement newsletter as a monthly compilation of lessons learned.

The director of performance improvement and training created the role of the relationship manager as a resource in supporting the nonlearning actions for the consulting transformation. Some performance consultants are assigned the role of relationship manager based on their business knowledge, partnering and relationship building, and consulting competencies expertise. The relationship manager provides the communication and coordination interface between performance improvement and training departments as well as between performance improvement and training and the client. A relationship manager is assigned to each training department and to at least one line of business client. The relationship manager is expected to partner with and learn the client's business, identify and sell consulting opportunities to the client, and share that information with other consultants and clients. This role becomes a critical resource for performance improvement and training in providing timely response and improved service quality for the client's business needs.

In addition to the relationship managers and coaches, people resources also include informal networks of internal consultants supporting one another in sharing successes, mistakes, and best practices. The networks involve strong alliances with external partners who can bring tested processes and expertise to the organization. A vital people resource are line managers who will help champion performance consulting by providing consulting opportunities, subject matter experts to serve on consulting teams, and financial assistance.

Organizational resources. To support the consulting process, the performance manager considers other resources, such as organizational flexibility and adequate financial resources as essential to the transformation process. Organizational flexibility is a resource enabler that benefits both the client and performance improvement and training. Close alignment of the performance department to the business unit is essential to effective partnering. The priorities of the line must be the priorities of performance improvement and training.

The ability of performance improvement to effectively support client priorities dictates being able to quickly pull together cross-functional teams with the competencies and experience necessary for quality client support. These cross-functional teams exercise a multitude of competencies and are excellent sources of nonlearning skill development. An example is the absolutely critical requirement that consultants know the business of the business. Cross-functional teams allow consultants to quickly immerse themselves and confront a variety of new business issues that are mastered on the job.

Organizational resources also extend to partnering with staff areas such as human resources, marketing, and public relations. Often we fail to consider the support that can be provided by internal corporate departments to performance consulting initiatives. Maximizing the services of these staff partners in supporting consulting interventions is a requirement for success in an environment of constrained resources.

Core human resources functions such as recruiting, compensation, employee relations, and succession planning provide expertise in an integrated approach to resolving work environment barriers to performance improvement. At PNC Bank, a cross-functional team on turnover and retention used recruiters to refine behavioral selection techniques; employee relations specialists to conduct employee exit interviews; compensation specialists to ensure that the incentive program reinforced appropriate behaviors and supported retention; and consultants to develop a career planning process that effectively supported employee retention.

Market research conducts data collection surveys and focus groups, which provide a rich resource of assessment data of value to the consultant. Using this data or partnering with marketing for assistance in data collection saves the consultant many hours and a great deal of expense. Marketing was also part of the retention cross-functional team and conducted employee focus groups and compiled benchmarking data from peer companies. Close interface with corporate public relations on a marketing strategy for selling performance consulting to the line and to trainers is a tremendous benefit for the training director. Performance consulting needs to be marketed the same as any other product or service offered by the corporation. Getting quality coverage in the internal company media and scripting for presentations to line manager senior meetings on consulting benefits and in setting expectations is a critical success factor.

Mastering competing demands. The resource of time is very difficult for the manager and team members to reconcile early in the consulting transformation. The day-to-day demands of supporting the current business reality appear overwhelming when trying to also carve out the time required to learn and apply new skills with line managers. Performance consulting interventions must be planned to be as nonadditive to consultant workloads as possible. Much of the integration is handled by consultants realizing, with the support of their coach or manager, that a number of activities they already perform support the performance improvement process. Integrating the new demands into the mainstream of daily activities must be the rule not the exception.

Time is also created through economies gained in eliminating training that is not supported by needs assessment results and championed by a line manager. Much training conducted is based on trainer perception of need or a tradition of content delivery rather than on an analysis of business needs. Eliminating this training creates opportunity for higher value-added use of trainer time as well as tremendous savings in classroom training expense. Other sources of time savers for the trainer in transition are the use of instructional technology, such as computer-based training, and job aids. The moral to this story is that the training director and the trainers must be ruthless in managing their time to support the consulting transition, while always being attentive to the needs of clients and service partners.

Reward and recognition. What motivates team members to achieve the desired consulting performance? Pride in the achievement of new skills, recognition by their manager and line client, and the opportunity for financial rewards all motivate trainers to become performance consultants. It is the combination of well-planned and carefully implemented nonfinancial and cash incentives that are the most effective drivers of change.

The nonfinancial incentives are often least understood by managers. Yet they are effective, low-cost enhancers of behavior change. As previously mentioned, the director of performance improvement and training created performance awards at the showcase. Informal awards also included frequent presentations of PNC Bank gold pen and pencil sets for excellent results in consulting interventions. A recognition corner in the performance improvement newsletter is a low-cost but highly effective motivator. These types of recognition can be institutionalized as an ongoing tradition of inspiring and recognizing excellence in competency attainment.

The financial aspects of motivating change in trainer skills and performance deal with promotional opportunities based on demonstrating increased competency attainment and results valued by line clients. Through partnering with human resources, the director of performance improvement and training revised job descriptions to reflect consulting job titles and competency target levels to develop assignment of grades to positions. This enabled trainers to receive promotions to higher levels as they demonstrated that they had reached a target level of competency and achieved appropriate results.

The issue here is that if the consultant's company does not provide for the financial reward of those who gain the competencies and demonstrate increased value, then another company will. The performance director needs to carefully think through his or her consultant retention strategy. Otherwise, the company becomes an excellent provider of talent for the world at large.

Conclusion

The performance director by necessity must be willing to stake his or her personal credibility on leading the transformation skills process necessary for implementing performance consulting. The verbiage and actions of performance improvement leaders must be aligned if their consultants are to be expected to take the first risky and anxiety-producing steps in changing skills and behavior. This is the responsibility of leaders and the price for ultimate success.

The role of the leader is that of an integrator of process, as a visionary thinker and communicator, with the capability of translating the process into implementation actions for team members. Championing the transformation of trainer skills requires the leader to be the first in recognizing that his or her own skills must change and then to be the first to do something about it. The process champion must be part strategist, part tactician, and a member of the team in experiencing the transformation to performance consultant firsthand. Through experience, the consultant learns that approximately 80 percent of the barriers to improving performance are in the work environment. Understanding that learning actions cannot be easily sustained in a nonsupportive work environment is essential to the success of the trainer's transformation to performance consultant. Thus learning and nonlearning actions in developing consulting skills are planned and implemented in unison.

The consultants, not their managers or the company, own the competency development process. The directors must understand the power of this ownership, demand that the consultants accept ownership for their development, and trust in their people and that the process will work. It is critical that leaders not underestimate the ability of their team members to rise to the challenge.

The Author

Thomas LaBonte is a performance consulting and training professional with more than 20 years in academia, government, and business. Upon completion of undergraduate and graduate degrees in education, he accepted a joint faculty and administrative position as assistant to the dean of career programs at Anne Arundel Community College and was promoted two years later to director of institutional research and planning.

After seven years in higher education, LaBonte managed training departments in the U.S. Army with responsibility for leadership development programs and innovative delivery using interactive video. Ten years later, he transitioned into financial services as retail training manager at Barnett Banks, Inc. In February 1994, he accepted the position of vice president and manager of retail training at PNC Bank Corp. and was promoted to director of training and development in January 1995. In January 1997, LaBonte was appointed senior vice president and director of performance improvement and training. At PNC Bank, he transformed a traditional training organization into a valued service partner with line management by implementing performance consulting, alternative delivery of training, sales, and service leadership initiatives, and measurement and evaluation processes. In March 1998, LaBonte accepted the position of director of human resources for Centura Banks, Inc., in Rocky Mount, North Carolina.

LaBonte is a frequent speaker at national conferences on such topics as partnering with line management to support achievement of business needs; developing actions that will change employee performance; instructional technology innovations; and measuring the impact of performance improvement initiatives. He also serves on the board of directors of the American Society for Training & Development.

Putting It All Together

In this section, the big picture is described for both the transition process and the future of human performance improvement. In chapter 11, Jim Fuller provides an in-depth look at the many short- and long-term tactics required to successfully transition from training to performance. There is work to be done before taking on the first performance project. In addition, there is work required during start-up and over the duration of the transition process, which frequently can take years.

In chapter 12, James and Dana Robinson provide their predictions for what the future will bring as the HRD profession continues its journey from a training to a performance focus. The implications this focus has for the organizational and process relationship of HR, training, and OD departments are described.

11

Making the Transition to a Focus on Performance

by Jim Fuller

QUICK READ

● Planning is critical to the successful transition to a focus on performance improvement. Both short-term and long-term strategies need to be developed.

● Some of the work that must be completed, even before the first performance improvement project is initiated, includes

—forming a clear description of what is meant by a focus on performance

—selecting a single model of human performance improvement to use

—identifying potential performance consultants and analysts, developing them to fill their new roles.

● It is vital to get some wins early; so implement small projects and demonstrate the value of the performance approach. Continue to build awareness of the impact that this approach is having.

● Plan for the inevitable implementation barriers such as resistance, confusion over the role of the "training" department, staffing issues, turf wars, and funding.

The field of human performance technology (HPT) has received significant attention over the past few years. Many professionals in training organizations have sought to transform their group from a training focus to one with a broader performance improvement focus. Seeking to achieve radical organizational transformation, they create their presentation materials and march off to the boardroom to pitch the concept. Little do they know that they have just embarked on the fastest route to failure. Experienced sales professionals would consider it the worst possible scenario—selling a product with no brand-name recognition to a skeptical customer who is not aware of what the product is, or that they even have a use for it.

Others have been given permission, or even a mandate, to transform their organizations from those that supply training courses to those that focus on performance improvement. There have been very few resources available to aid in the transition process, and many have struggled in the process to become an HPT-driven organization. A training manager at a large corporation shared that he was now managing a performance consulting organization, but the only change that had occurred in the 12-month transition project was a change to new business cards that read "performance consultant" rather than "training developer." They were still in the business of fulfilling unsubstantiated training requests.

The successful transition to a focus on human performance requires a well-planned approach. The first step is not to announce that the training department is disbanded, for training is an important tool for improving performance. Nor is it wise to sell the management team on business results that you are not yet ready to deliver. Rather, the organization that wants to transition to performance improvement needs to begin planning and working quietly in back rooms of the organization. (See table 1.)

PREPARING FOR HUMAN PERFORMANCE IMPROVEMENT (HPI)

Few things are more frustrating than deciding on a solution and finding that you have to wait a long time for delivery. Before pitching HPI to the executive council, you might want to ensure that you are ready to deliver results. Significant preparation is required for a successful transition to a focus on performance improvement. This work cannot be skipped. Not doing the work early simply means that you will have to do it later, when time is short, resources are scarce, and tempers are hot. Take the time to do the appropriate prework.

Determine Who Needs to Be Involved as Advisers

First, determine who within the organization needs to be involved in the early work. Involving strategically interested parties early can turn them into allies. Leaving them out usually results in opposition and turf wars. Nobody likes surprises, particularly if those surprises appear to be assaults on their charter. Organizations or individuals involved in human resource development (HRD), process improvement, and organization development (OD) should all be considered. Identify about six of the most critical and influential parties on the list. Do not create a formal committee or task force; just get their agreement to review work and make recommendations regarding how their organizations can help with this transition. You'll be building buy-in and support, while reducing opposition and charter conflict.

Form Definition of Human Performance Improvement (HPI)

With the advisers in place, it is time to begin the backroom work. The first backroom task is to generate a simple and understandable definition of HPI to be used in the organization. Managers and potential sponsors will become confused and disenfranchised if the definition of what you are proposing changes weekly, or if there are multiple definitions floating around. This is a common early mistake—to promote HPI within the organization without being able to explain to a senior manager exactly what it is. A fumbled answer will leave the manager completely unimpressed and confused.

T A B L E 1	Preparation Steps
1.	Determine who needs to be involved as advisers.
2.	Form definition of HPI.
3.	Select a single HPI model to use.
4.	Identify specific people who will perform the HPI work.
5.	Position HPI into the organization, illustrating its benefits.

307

The definition of HPI should be short and snappy. You should be able to share it with somebody during a 30-second elevator ride and not need flipcharts or diagrams to explain it. Test the definition with people who are not involved with the profession. The definition is ready when it meets the 30-second time frame, and your parents can finally understand what it is you do for a living. The day after I worked out a concise definition, I had the opportunity to share it with a senior manager during (can you believe it) an elevator ride. Here is what I said:

> HPI is a careful and systematic approach to identifying the barriers that prevent people from achieving performance that contributes to the success of the organization. We then create solutions that quickly and effectively remove the barriers so people can improve their performance and achieve their full potential at work.

This definition resulted in an invitation to present at the manager's next staff meeting. Send a copy of your definition to your advisers to keep them informed about what you are proposing to do within the organization.

Select a Single HPI Model to Use

The second backroom task is to select a single HPI model that will work well within your organization. You could build a model from the ground up, but that activity has low return-on-investment (ROI). Most models share the same basic components: Start with the business need, identify the necessary performance, implement the gap analysis, determine root causes for the gaps, and identify solutions that will remove the root causes. Find a model that is simple and understandable. Customize it for your organization if necessary. Show the model to your advisers to get their input and support. By obtaining an agreed-upon model, you will defuse the "model battle" problem. When confronted with conflicting models, management will typically send the model owners back to do battle until a single recommendation emerges. Several organizations have spent more than a year in task force meetings attempting to get different parts of the organization to agree to a single HPI model for the organization. Meanwhile, no HPI is going on.

Identify Specific People to Perform the HPI Work

So far, the backroom efforts have defined what you are going to do (the definition) and how you are going to do it (the model). The third backroom question is who will do it. This is a dangerous question, because there are multiple answers. In the long run, you might envision all the training, OD, and HRD professionals taking an HPI approach to their efforts. It would be rare for an organization to be successful starting with an implementation this large. The transition to performance improvement requires some coaching and hand-holding. Start with a small, manageable team that can be coached and trained. This will be the start-up group that will work on the initial projects. Once a few successful HPI projects have been completed, the long-term question of who does HPI can be addressed. The advisers will have a keen interest in this topic. Sit down and discuss it with them personally and individually. This is where potential charter issues begin to surface. Be prepared for the request to have members of their organization participate in the early stages.

As you begin to identify candidates for the first people to work in the roles of performance consultant and analyst, consider a number of different sources. Successful HPI requires significant systems-thinking and problem-analysis skills. You can attempt to build those skills into your performance consultants, or you can use people who already have them. Employees from engineering (research and development) and quality normally have superior systems-thinking and problem-solving skills. They are taught these skills early on, and they use them daily in their work. Just having one or two of these folks in the organization can bring important capabilities to the team.

The fourth backroom activity is highly dependent upon your situation. Without making the big presentation to management, you need to identify a couple of people who can start to get skilled up in HPI. The resources do not need to drop everything they are doing and attend weeks of training, but they should start now on their development path. If you are currently the manager of a training department, your task is easier, as you can identify a couple of people within the organization. Detailed information on the development of performance technologists is covered in section four of this book.

Position HPI Into the Organization

The last backroom activity falls to you, the proponent of performance improvement. You need to be able to read the needs of the organization, and suggest HPI as a possible solution. You need to be able to position HPI as a valuable approach to resolving serious problems. In short, you need to be able to sell. Selling is about helping the customer see the value in the product you are offering and how it meets their needs. It is not about cajoling them into buying something they do not want or need. Find someone in sales who can help you with your sales skills and act as your mentor. If your presentation skills are weak, start working on them as well.

With the backroom work done, you are ready to begin the next phase of your work. This next phase is not the big presentation to management. That rarely works at this point because the value of HPI to the organization is unproved. You would be asking the management team to accept on faith that HPI works, and that it will have a positive impact on the business. Rather than selling a promise, sell results.

DEMONSTRATING RESULTS WITH HUMAN PERFORMANCE IMPROVEMENT

Nothing speaks like results. When you choose a solution or a product, doesn't your selection process include looking at the demonstrated effectiveness of the solution? Selling HPI as the solution for improving performance within an organization is much easier when you have established a track record of success. This does pose the chicken-and-egg problem, however. It is difficult to get permission without results, but you can't get results without permission. Or so it may seem.

By now, you and your small team should be ready to take on your first HPI project. You will want to start with just one project that is small in scale and can achieve results in a short time period. Do not go out looking for a problem to solve. Trying to sell a sponsor on an unproved approach to solving an unperceived problem is a formula for frustration. If you are in the training organization, you probably receive a number of requests for training solutions. Every one of these requests represents a potential HPI project. It is simply a matter of selecting a promising request. There are two ways of proceeding with the request: the head-on approach, or the end run.

The head-on approach is the most direct method. When clients ask for the training course, explain the HPI method and ask if they would allow you to take this new approach to working on the training request. Do not be surprised if clients reject the suggestion. They may not have the patience for a new methodology; they may be convinced that training is the right answer; or they may simply not understand the HPI process. Do not get into an argument with them; simply provide what was requested, and try again on the next person who asks for a training course. Some people will be more receptive than others. The head-on approach seems to work well with engineering or research and development managers. Their appreciation of a systems approach to problem solving makes them more open to using the HPI method.

The end run is a different approach to gaining permission to analyze what interventions are needed. Rather than attempting to explain the HPI system and convince the client of its value, simply seek permission to analyze the training need. When permission is given, just take the HPI approach in the analysis and report the results back to the client. On the surface, this may seem rather deceptive, but it is really not. In the past when clients came to you with a request for training, did you sit them down and carefully explain the instructional design model so that they were fully aware of the process that you were using to create the class requested?

Typically not. You probably took the request and used good training design to create the course. The clients were probably not very interested in the process that you used to create the solution. The method is typically a behind-the-scenes issue. Why should HPI be different?

Obtaining permission to proceed with the analysis requires some practice. New performance consultants should practice the dialogue with one another until they can easily engage with a client. A short example of how to work toward permission is found in table 2.

After you have completed a couple of small projects, you are almost ready to move on to the next stage of implementing HPI within the organization.

T A B L E 2 Obtaining Permission to Proceed with an HPI Approach	
Objective	**Dialogue**
Agree to help	Sarah: Jim, I'd like you folks to find or build a two-day training course on customer satisfaction for my salespeople.
	Jim: Sarah, we would be glad to help you with your problem.
Determine the business problem	Jim: You obviously have some driving issue that is causing you to ask for a training course. Would you mind sharing what the problem is? It would help us identify the best solution for you.
	Sarah: Sure. I am disappointed with the way in which. . . .
Seek permission to proceed	Jim: Sarah, I'd like to spend a couple of days talking to the sales folks. I won't take much of their time, but it would really help to ensure that we get the right solution in place for them. I'd like to identify what training they do and do not need. We don't want to waste time and money on training content they already know, and we don't want to leave any important training out. We don't want to do this twice.
	Sarah: I guess that's OK.

With demonstrated results, you now have a credible way of presenting and selling the HPI approach. Take the completed projects and build them into short case studies. Start with the original training request; then show the results of the analysis and the implemented solutions. Finally, show the operational (Level 4) results of the project implementation. If you do not have the Level 4 results yet, consider using cost-avoidance measures. They usually are sufficient in the early stages of selling HPI. For example, one project started as a training request that would have required $230,000 and 14 months to implement. The HPI solution cost about $15,000 and was fully implemented in a month. With results like this in hand, it is time for the next stage.

Building Organizational Awareness

After your HPI team has successfully completed a few projects, it will begin to attract some attention. The clients of the projects will talk to their colleagues about the results they are getting in their organization. Curiosity will generate requests to explain what you did and how you did it. You need to be prepared for these requests. Create a compelling HPI presentation that everybody will want to see. Practice it until you can do it under any circumstance to any audience. When you are ready, show the presentation to everybody who will listen, even if the audience seems inconsequential.

Lacking a speaker for a lunchtime seminar, a manager invited me to address a large group of manufacturing employees. I initially thought that the hour was not a very good time investment, but the people were interested and listened well. A few weeks later, there was an organization-wide assembly where I made the presentation. The human resources manager presented the new training catalog and discussed the organization's training plan. One of the manufacturing employees stood up and asked if this was going to be more of the same time-wasting training, or if they had used the new HPI approach to identify solutions that were going to make a difference in their performance and career prospects. He indicated that he was not interested in ineffective training that did not make a difference back on the job. A significant portion of the crowd agreed with him. Not surprisingly, I was asked to present the HPI method to the human resources manager within the next week.

Familiarity with HPI and the results within the organization accelerates acceptance and enthusiasm. Look for opportunities to spread the word about your successes. There are typically a number of opportunities available in almost every organization:

- Get in the company newspaper—try to get a success story in every issue.

- Create flashy case studies on successful projects and place them in literature racks around the organization.

- Put the case studies on the organization's Web site.

- Send e-mail versions of the case studies to strategic managers within the organization.

- Present at senior manager's staff meetings or off-site meetings.

- Put your entire presentation with commentary on the Web site.

Increased awareness results in an increase in requests to implement HPI projects. The operational results of HPI projects can produce some extraordinary figures. For example, return-on-investment results of more than 10 to 1 cause a lot of excitement from business managers. Some of our results at Hewlett-Packard were far better. Managers will begin to look at performance improvement as a measurable business investment, rather than as a cost. It won't be long until the requests for assistance outstrip the capacity of your team. It rapidly becomes obvious that the time has come for a shift in implementation strategy. This new success brings a new set of issues that need to be addressed.

Dealing with Implementation Barriers

As the implementation of HPI grows within the organization, new problems will begin to occur. Anticipating these problems and working to develop alternatives before they arise will preserve the momentum. Some of the problems will come from within the HPI team that you have developed and grown. Other problems will come from other parts of the organization. These problems can occur at any time, in any order. Several of them are described here.

Resistance from Line Training Managers

In large organizations, there are likely to be other training managers associated with business units, geographic regions, or functional alignment. Hopefully you selected some of the more strategic and influential ones to serve as advisers, and you have generated some level of buy-in. From the other training managers, you can expect a fair level of resistance. For one thing, the implementation of HPI was not led by them, and there is some "not invented here" response. More important, their personal performance metrics may not support HPI activities. Most training managers are measured according to the following criteria:

- participant reaction evaluation results (Level 1)

- number of employee training days, or hours of training per employee

- number and diversity of courses in the training catalog

- cost of training declining over time.

Imagine the case of the training managers who are evaluated as top performers in the organization. Their high evaluation marks are driven by their ability to achieve against the performance areas listed above. What is their motivation to move to HPI? All it will do is introduce risk and the possibility of being evaluated at a lower level. In these cases, it is generally best to sell around the training manager. For example, I attempted to pitch HPI to a training manager in the organization. He was simply not interested in what I had to say. He was too busy running his training enterprise. I happened to bump into his boss one day, and he asked me about what my team was doing. I gave him my 30-second "elevator speech," and he invited me to present at his next staff meeting. Naturally, the training manager was at the meeting. After I finished the presentation, the business manager stated that HPI was truly revolutionary and would change how his organization managed people. He turned to his training manager and asked if there was anything that prevented implementation within the business. The training manager replied that he had already been talking with me, and that he was on top of it. The training manager was in my office the next day to get as much information as possible on deploying HPI.

Implication for Trainers and the Training Department
The move toward an HPI approach can cause panic among professional trainers in the organization. They want to know if their job is changing or going away. A message that you should be incorporating into your HPI pitch is that training will not go away as a result of HPI. Training is a perfectly good solution for closing skill gaps in the organization, and the organization will continue to need high-quality training professionals. HPI simply ensures that when training is done, it is really needed. HPI also ensures that other barriers that can prevent training from being effective are removed. Most training professionals are quite satisfied with this positioning. Some will want to consider becoming performance consultants or performance analysts, and others will want to stay as training professionals. Get the message to the training community before any panic reaction has the opportunity to settle in.

Lack of Knowledge and Skills in Implementing HPI
This turns out to be a serious barrier to deploying HPI within the organization. Most organizations find that there is not a pool of performance consultants and analysts available to be hired into positions. Most organizations must grow their own. This is the same situation that was experienced when starting the first small group, but now it is a much larger issue. Knowledge gaps regarding human performance technology and the HPI process can be dealt with easily. The skill gaps are another issue. Really

good performance consultants and analysts have well-refined systems-thinking, problem-solving, and analysis skills. These skills are not developed overnight, and they tend to represent the largest hurdle for many. One solution is to hire candidates who already have the basic skills. You can then have them work with your experienced performance consultants as mentors, guiding their development and proficiency.

Staffing Issues and Turf Wars

As you consider broader implementation of HPI in the organization, the issue of who "owns" HPI is certain to come up. Because of the relationship of working directly with senior-level managers and performing an analyst role, many organizations will want to have HPI in their charter, and under their control. The decision will likely be made by the management team, based upon best fit within the organization. It is advisable to place HPI in either the training organization or the HRD department, as that is where most managers turn for help in improving performance.

Lack of Familiarity with Noninstructional Solutions

When implementing HPI, a common concern is finding performance consultants who can design and develop the wide variety of solutions necessary to improve performance. This comes from the old organizational model in which managers attempted to own responsibility for all the activities within their process. Performance consultants cannot be expected to be experts in job descriptions, job aids, training, compensation systems, feedback systems, process design, ergonomics, and information systems. But there are performance consultants who know experts in all of these areas, and who can call upon them to participate in their performance improvement projects. This approach also overcomes some of the potential turf problems. If the use of the compensation system is determined to be a performance barrier, performance consultants are not going to attempt to reengineer the system. Rather, they are going to call upon the compensation department to participate on the project, as they are the experts and own the compensation system.

Funding the Transition to Performance Improvement

At the present time, organizations are continually seeking to reduce costs. Funding the creation of the performance improvement group needs to be carefully managed. If you are a training manager, you may have the ability to identify some resources within your organization that can spend some time on small HPI projects. This typically works well in the early stages but becomes difficult as the projects grow in size and number. You will eventually need to identify dedicated performance consultants and analysts;

their funding can be problematic. There are typically two funding models that are used when creating a performance improvement group within an organization: centrally funded or self-funded. Each has its advantages and difficulties.

Centrally funded groups are given an operating budget to fund their activities over the course of a year. Other parts of the organization receive HPI services for free, but must compete with one another to secure the HPI resources to work on their projects. Typically, the manager of the performance consultants and analysts must sell the management team on the value of the HPI group only once per year, during the budgeting process. This offers the advantage of freeing considerable time for the manager. There are less positive aspects to having a fixed budget, however. If the need for performance consultants grows beyond initial funding levels, the manager must go back and secure more funds, or he must allow a large backlog of HPI projects to sit idle.

Self-funded HPI groups are given a very small budget, or none at all. Other parts of the organization must pay for the HPI services they receive, but the HPI team is allowed to grow, based upon the internal revenue that they can generate. This keeps the HPI manager from having to go to war each year to justify or attempt to grow the budget. It does, however, require the manager to spend a considerable amount of time ensuring that the schedule of HPI projects is well balanced. Too few projects during a month means going over budget. Too many projects means asking clients to wait after you have sold them on the value of funding a project. If you manage your initial HPI projects well, you will likely experience the problem of being overbooked. If the organization typically uses central funding, some clients may balk at the idea of paying for HPI projects from their own budgets. One solution is to offer them a guarantee: If they implement the suggested performance solutions and they do not experience at least a 2 to 1 ROI, they will not be charged for the project. If your HPI projects are successful, you will never have project sponsors ask for their funds to be returned.

Dealing with Success

Many leaders of HPI departments have prepared for the barriers associated with implementing their HPI initiatives. Few have been well prepared to deal with success. As the program moves from a small team of practitioners to an organization-wide program, roles will change. You will move from performing HPI to managing a small internal consulting team, and then to managing the development of performance consultants within the organization. The practitioners will move from managing their own HPI projects to mentoring new performance consultants. Be prepared for the changes. Create a position plan for the manager of HPI and keep it handy for when the management team is ready to move. Amidst all the excitement of implementing performance improvement projects, have your experienced performance consultants and analysts start looking at mentoring skills and strategies. Be prepared for success—it is just a matter of time.

The Author

Jim Fuller is the principal consultant for Redwood Mountain Consulting (RMC). He is responsible for assisting client organizations with the strategic implementation of performance consulting, for mentoring new performance consultants, and for workshops to develop performance improvement professionals. Before joining RMC, he was the director of learning and performance technology at the Hewlett-Packard Company (HP), where he worked for 18 years. His organization represented HP's research and development (R&D) efforts in the area of learning and performance, with specific responsibility for performance improvement processes, instructional design methods, education evaluation systems, and the application of technology to accelerate learning. He created HP's performance consulting group, led the development of performance technology practices, and developed HP's performance improvement consultants. He has held management positions in R&D, manufacturing, marketing, sales, support, and education.

Fuller holds an M.S. in instructional and performance technology from Boise State University. He is currently pursuing an Ed.D. in performance technology from the University of Southern California. Fuller is the author of *Managing Performance Improvement Projects* and is a contributing author of *Work Based Education*. He is a frequent speaker at conferences such as the International Society for Performance Improvement, where he was an advocate representative, and the American Society for Training & Development. He has spoken on implementing performance technology, evaluation strategies, use of technology in training delivery, metacognition in learning, and gender-based communications in the workplace. He has also been an invited guest lecturer at several universities.

12

A Look into the Future

by Dana Gaines Robinson and James C. Robinson

QUICK READ

● The authors make the following predictions regarding the future:

—HR, training, and organization development functions will utilize a shared process and form an integrated structure.

—The work process will be centralized while those who operate in support of the process will be decentralized.

—The position of performance consultant will become a normative one in organizations.

—Performance language will be known and used by line managers as they become full performance partners.

In writing this chapter we are reminded of the wisdom expressed by that old sage Yogi Berra when he said:

> "Making forecasts is always difficult, especially when they concern the future."

This is one of the most exhilarating and challenging times to be involved in the human resource development (HRD) field. So much change is happening. What worked before is no longer effective, so new processes and roles are being formed. The services provided before are no longer sufficient, so new services and jobs are being developed. The need to move ahead was certainly articulated in an emphatic manner by William Miller of Steelcase, Inc., when he was interviewed recently. Read his prediction:

> It's the corporate model of training and development that needs to change. Twenty years from now, I don't think there will be much left of the old corporate training model that is even recognizable. ("Learning Ecologies." *Training*, January 1998, p. 38.)

As the many contributing authors to this book attest, one of the changes that will be in evidence is that of focusing on performance improvement—a transition that is already in process. As with any significant change, however, there will be other reciprocating shifts that will occur. In this final chapter of the book, we would like to offer you our perspective on what those other changes may be. We will all need to gather together in about five years' time to determine to what degree these predictions proved accurate, but the seeds for each of the following changes are already in place.

Integrated Structure

In the future, the human resource (HR), training, and organization development functions will utilize a shared process and form an integrated structure. Current organizational structures of the HR and training functions are based on the concept that the work done by each requires different work processes and yields different results. Therefore, we can observe organizational structures such as the following:

● The HR department is a centralized group with various tactical functions reporting into it such as training and development, recruitment, employee relations, and compensation. This structure is illustrated in figure 1.

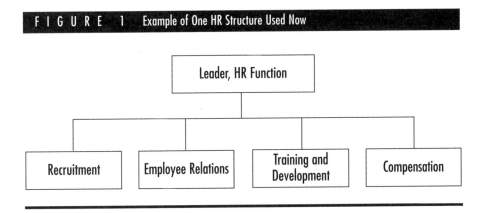

F I G U R E 1   Example of One HR Structure Used Now

- A splintered structure will emerge in which there is a group, called "human resources," under one leader; a second group frequently labeled "organization development" or "organization effectiveness" under another leader; and the training or HRD function under yet a third individual. Frequently these three leaders have no reporting relationship to one another.

Regardless of the structure that is actually used, the work of all those who focus on the people side of business becomes siloed, with all elements operating as a separate entity. Because each of these entities requires information from clients, members of each department call upon management to discuss their specific specialty. For example, people in the training function call upon management to discuss training needs, people in the recruitment function call upon the same management to discuss their recruitment and selection needs, and so on. These are discussions that are biased to solution. Two questions arise: (1) Who is calling upon clients to discuss their business and performance needs, independent of any solution? (2) Who is accountable for ensuring that the appropriate mix of solutions is used?

A shift to a focus on performance improvement makes a siloed structure obsolete. This is because the mission of the function shifts so that there is one, shared goal: to enhance performance in support of business requirements. A shared goal requires a shared process. What also becomes apparent is that while training and other HR functions are unique at the tactical level, there is no difference in the work that is required at the strategic level. The entire department requires knowledge of the client's business needs from which performance implications are determined and performance solutions designed and implemented.

Figure 2 illustrates the type of structure that results when there is a shared focus on performance improvement. In this function, all groups in the organization that focus on enhancing performance of employees and managers are linked. While the labels of "strategic" and "tactical" units as displayed in figure 2 may not be utilized, the differences between the two units are evident. The performance consultants and performance analysts within the strategic unit are accountable for growing and maintaining partnerships with key clients in their respective business units. They are also the individuals who will identify opportunities for performance improvement initiatives providing the necessary assessment to identify performance gaps and their causes. In essence, these are the relationship managers who become the entry point for accessing services of the function, remaining bias-free of using any specific service.

Once causes are identified, it becomes possible to select the interventions required to close the gaps. Many of these interventions will require the expertise of professionals who reside in the tactical side of the department. So the performance consultant will dip into this resource group and utilize these individuals and their expertise during the implementation phase of the performance initiative. In this way, the performance consultant remains strategic, operating at the business needs level. In addition, the performance consultants can remain bias-free of solution because they are not expected to design or deliver any specific intervention; that is the responsibility of those who specialize in the tactical side of the department's services.

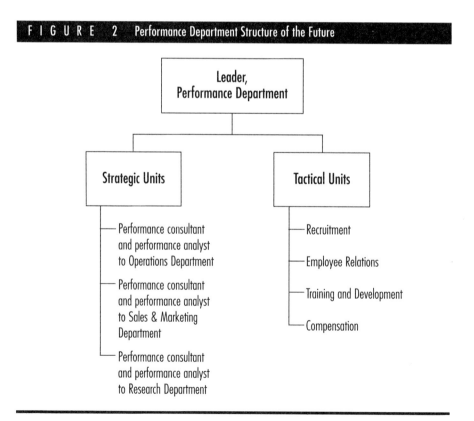

FIGURE 2   Performance Department Structure of the Future

Centralized Work Process with Decentralized Operations

There continues to be a debate over whether the training and HR functions should be centralized or decentralized. With a focus on performance, the answer is obvious. The human performance improvement process must be centralized, with some systems in place to ensure that it is being utilized in a quality manner and as intended by all those working within it. Many of the people who complete the actual work, however, will be dispersed both functionally and geographically. It is highly probable that the performance consultants and performance analysts, who are responsible for the strategic side of the business, will be located at the site of their client groups. These individuals will make one-stop shopping a reality for their clients, as all requests to shape human performance in support of business goals will flow through these consultants and analysts.

The tactical specialists, however, can form a shared services group, which is housed in a central location. For example, instructional designers and compensation specialists can be based in a corporate location. The trend to outsource will continue, and it is the tactical specialists who present the greatest opportunity for brokering services to external suppliers. It is virtually impossible to outsource the relationship with an internal client. Therefore, performance consultants will remain as employees, while those who specialize in the design and implementation of any specific intervention will potentially be drawn from a pool of external suppliers.

Position of Performance Consultant

We, at Partners in Change, continue to conduct research on the position of performance consultant. We have learned that while the job is not always referred to by this title, the demand for people to fill this type of position is escalating tremendously. As described in chapter 9, the people in the job of performance consultant produce three primary outputs:

- establish partnerships with clients

- conduct performance assessments

- implement interventions and manage performance change projects.

These are the people on the front line, helping clients to translate their business goals into human performance requirements. Once clients begin to realize the benefits of such a position, the demand grows for more of these individuals. Therefore, it is safe to say that performance consulting is a growth industry!

Our research also affirms that this position is valued in the marketplace. Time and again, when discussing compensation for the position, we have learned that a performance consultant is the highest-paid individual contributor within the function. Frequently individuals in this position are eligible for bonuses, linked to the performance of the business units they support, while other individual contributors within the department are not provided this benefit. Not only does this bonus enhance the compensation possibilities for the performance consultant but it also clearly indicates that the consultant is viewed as a partner in achieving business success.

Line Managers as Full Performance Partners

Too often, clients request support in solution language such as a request to conduct a project management course for engineers or a team-building session for an intact team. This requires that the individual receiving the request display a high degree of skill in asking the right questions so the client's need is reframed into performance language. Once the need is defined in terms of the results that are needed, rather than the activity to be provided, a performance improvement discussion can begin. It can be challenging, however, to ask questions of a client who has a preconceived idea as to what the solution is. Some clients resist the questioning approach, as they are either highly vested in their solution (making them less willing to consider alternatives) or have limited time to consider other options (everyone is already booked to be here in two weeks). In essence, they see limited value in gathering more data about the performance requirements, performance gaps, or the work environment supports.

It would be far more productive if clients would think and talk performance. Specifically that means that clients need to do the following:

- describe a need for service in performance, not solution, language

- expect and want some level of assessment to occur prior to a solution being implemented

- value determining how the work environment will support, or obstruct, desired performance

- acknowledge the probability that multiple interventions, not a single intervention, will be required in order to change performance.

This performance change will be one of the primary benefits derived from the strong relationships forged between performance consultants and their clients. Through that relationship, learning and development will occur in two directions: The performance consultant will learn about the business of the business, and the client will learn about human performance technology and how to enhance performance in support of business goals. In essence, the technology will be transferred so that each client becomes a performance partner for his or her own performance and area of responsibility.

Closing Thoughts

Hopefully this book has provided you, the reader, with many concepts, techniques, aids, and the motivation to continue your personal journey on the path toward performance improvement. Our profession is immersed in a major transformation; we who work in it must transform as well. While the challenges are many, and there will be disappointments and even some failures, the rewards are multiple and satisfying for those who choose to get on board. Good luck!

Glossary of Terms

Best Practice: An on-the-job behavior that has been affirmed as desired and as one that contributes to performance and operational results.

Business Needs: The operational goals for a unit, department, or the entire organization. These are typically measured numerically. Business needs are related to but different from business strategy, which is a plan or approach for achieving one or more business goals.

Cause Analysis: Identification of the factors that are inhibiting current or future on-the-job performance (inclusive of learning and work environment needs).

Client: The person accountable for achieving one or more business and performance needs and the individual with whom the performance consultant must partner for purposes of enhancing human performance. Frequently a team of people rather than one individual.

Current Practice: On-the-job behavior currently demonstrated by performers, which may or may not be a best practice. (Note: May also be referred to as actual performance.)

Gap Analysis: Identification of current or actual performance as compared to the model or desired performance.

Human Performance Improvement Process: The process used to work with clients in a systematic manner for purposes of analyzing, improving, and managing performance in the workplace through the use of appropriate and varied interventions.

Human Performance Technology: The science of improving human performance through analysis and the design, selection, and implementation of appropriate interventions.

Intervention: A solution or solution component specifically designed to bridge the gap between actual and desired state.

Learning Needs: The skill or knowledge required to perform as needed.

Level 1 Evaluation: Measures the degree of satisfaction that participants had with the learning experience. Frequently referred to as reaction evaluation.

Level 2 Evaluation: Measures the degree of knowledge or skill acquisition that occurred during the learning experience. Frequently referred to as learning evaluation.

Level 3 Evaluation: Measures the degree of performance change that has occurred following the learning and nonlearning actions taken in a performance change initiative. Frequently referred to as performance change evaluation.

Level 4 Evaluation: Measures the degree to which the operational results of a business unit, department, or enterprise have been changed following actions taken in a performance change initiative. Frequently referred to as results evaluation.

Models: Identification of performance requirements for a specific job or role as it must be performed if the business needs are to be realized. Models can be defined in performance language (for example, performance models) or competency language (for example, competency models).

Output: The tangible result or accomplishment that is produced from human performance.

Performance Analysis: The process of identifying performance requirements (for example, models), current performance, and causes for performance gaps.

Performance Analyst Role: Using systemic data gathering method(s) to identify performance requirements, performance gaps, and causes of gaps. The outputs from this role are the formation of performance models, competency models, and gap and cause analyses.

Performance Consultant Role: Partnering with clients for purposes of enhancing human performance in support of business needs and goals. The outputs from this role are strong relationships with clients, identification of potential opportunities for working together, and achievement of human performance improvement.

Performance Department: A function or organizational unit that has as its mission the enhancing of human performance in support of business goals.

Performance Needs: On-the-job requirements for what people must do if the business needs and goals are to be achieved. Typically described and measured behaviorally.

Performer(s): The individual(s) whose job performance is required to change as a result of a performance initiative.

Stakeholder: A person or group that has a vested interest in the results of the performance assessment or the performance change initiative.

Work Environment Needs: Systems or processes that surround performers in their work environment. *Enhancers* are systems or processes in the work environment that encourage desired performance; *barriers* are systems or processes that discourage and even prevent desired performance.

Resources

On the following pages are books identified as resources to learn more about the following areas:

- Assessments

- Measurement

- Consulting

- Performance technology

- Implementation of performance change.

The list that follows is not complete since books are constantly being published in the area of performance improvement. This is, however, a good sampling of the resources that are available. Some of these books are available through the publishers of this book, The American Society for Training & Development and Berrett-Koehler. Other titles can be found at many bookstores or on the World Wide Web. A visit to www.Amazon.com will provide at least a synopsis of most of these books.

We are not endorsing these as the best or only resources available; rather, our intent is to provide you with a list that can get you started in your research on where, and from whom, to obtain additional information. To best use this list we suggest that you do the following: (1) Determine which of the five categories noted above is most relevant to you and your development; (2) review the list of books to determine those that may be appropriate; and (3) use your own network of colleagues to assist you in identifying good resources for additional development in any of the areas noted above.

ASSESSMENT

ASTD Trainer's Toolkit: More Needs Assessment Instruments. Alexandria, VA: American Society for Training & Development, 1993.

Austin, Mary. *Needs Assessment by Focus Group*. (*Info-line* No. 9401). Alexandria, VA: American Society for Training & Development, 1998.

Camp, Robert C. *Business Process Benchmarking*. Milwaukee: American Society for Quality Press, 1995.

Costa, Arthur L., et al. (editors). *Assessment in the Learning Organization: Shifting the Paradigm*. Alexandria, VA: Association for Supervision and Curriculum Development, 1995.

Craig, R.L. (editor). *Training and Development Handbook*. 3d edition. Alexandria, VA: American Society for Training & Development, 1987.

Dubois, D.D. *Competency-Based Performance Improvement: A Strategy for Organizational Change*. Amherst, MA: HRD Press, 1993.

Edwards, Mark R., and Ann J. Ewen. *360 Degrees Feedback: The Powerful New Model for Employee Assessment & Performance Improvement*. New York: AMACOM, 1996.

Fletcher, Jerry L. *Patterns of High Performance: Discovering the Ways People Work Best*. San Francisco: Berrett-Koehler, 1993.

Goldstein, Irwin L. *Training in Organizations: Needs Assessment, Development, and Evaluation*. Pacific Grove, CA: Brooks/Cole Publishing, 1992.

Gupta, Kavita. *Conducting a Mini Needs Assessment*. (*Info-line* No. 9611). Alexandria, VA: American Society for Training & Development, 1996.

Kane, Michael B., and Ruth Mitchell (editors). *Implementing Performance Assessment: Promises, Problems, and Challenges*. Mahwah, NJ: Lawrence Erlbaum Association, 1996.

Kirrane, Diane. *The Role of the Performance Needs Analyst*. (*Info-line* No. 9713). Alexandria, VA: American Society for Training & Development, 1997.

Lesgold, Alan (editor). *Transitions in Work and Learning: Implications for Assessment*. Washington, D.C.: National Academy Press, 1997.

McClelland, Samuel B. *Organizational Needs Assessments: Design, Facilitation, and Analysis*. Westport, CT: Quorum Books, 1995.

Robinson, Dana Gaines, and James C. Robinson. *Training for Impact: How to Link Training to Business Needs and Measure the Results*. San Francisco: Jossey-Bass, 1989.

Rossett, A. *Training Needs Assessment*. Englewood Cliffs, NJ: Educational Technology Publications, 1987.

Spencer, Lyle M., et al. *Competence at Work: Models for Superior Performance*. New York: John Wiley and Sons, 1993.

Swanson, R.A. *Analysis for Improving Performance: Tools for Diagnosing Organizations and Documenting Workplace Expertise*. San Francisco: Berrett-Koehler, 1994.

Swanson, Richard, and Deane B. Gradous. *Forecasting Financial Benefits of Human Resource Development*. San Francisco: Jossey-Bass, 1988.

Watson, Gregory H. *The Benchmarking Workbook: Adapting Best Practices for Performance Improvement*. Portland, OR: Productivity Press, 1993.

Wilcox, John. *ASTD Trainers Toolkit: More Needs Assessment Instruments*. Alexandria, VA: American Society for Training & Development, 1993.

Wolf, Alison. *Competence-Based Assessment*. Buckingham, UK: Open University Press, 1995.

MEASUREMENT

ASTD Trainer's Toolkit: Evaluating Results of Training. Alexandria, VA: American Society for Training & Development, 1992.

Austin, Robert D. *Measuring and Managing Performance in Organizations*. New York: Dorset House, 1996.

Bader, Gloria E. *Measuring Team Performance: A Practical Guide to Tracking Team Success*. Irvine, CA: Chang Associates, 1994.

Baird, George, et al. (editors). *Building Evaluation Techniques*. New York: McGraw-Hill, 1995.

Beyer, Barry K. *How to Conduct a Formative Evaluation*. Alexandria, VA: Association for Supervision & Curriculum Development, 1995.

Bramley, Peter. *Evaluating Training Effectiveness: Translating Theory into Practice*. New York: McGraw-Hill, 1991.

————. *Evaluating Training Effectiveness: Benchmarking Your Training Activity Against Best Practice*. New York: McGraw-Hill, 1996.

Brinkerhoff, Robert, and Dennis Dressler. *Productivity Measurement: A Guide for Managers and Evaluators*. Thousand Oaks, CA: Sage Publications, 1991.

Brown, Stephen M., and Constance J. Seidner (editors). *Evaluating Corporate Training: Models and Issues*. Dordrecht, Netherlands: Kluwer Academic Publishers, 1997.

Chang, Richard Y., and Paul De Young. *Measuring Organizational Improvement Impact: A Practical Guide to Successfully Linking Organizational Improvement Measures*. Irvine, CA: Richard Chang Associates, 1996.

Easterby-Smith, Mark. *Evaluating Management Development, Training and Education*. Brookfield, VT: Ashgate, 1993.

Goldstein, Irwin L. *Training in Organizations: Needs Assessment, Development, and Evaluation*. Pacific Grove, CA: Brooks/Cole Publishing, 1992.

Gordon, J., et al. (editors). *Designing and Delivering Cost-Effective Training and Measuring the Results*. 3rd edition. Minneapolis: Lakewood Publications, 1993.

Harbour, Jerry L. *The Basics of Performance Measurement*. White Plains, NY: Quality Resources, 1997.

Holcomb, J. *Make Training Worth Every Penny: On-Target Evaluation*. San Francisco: Pfeiffer, 1994.

Holloway, Jacky (editor). *Performance Measurement and Evaluation*. Thousand Oaks, CA: Sage Publications, 1995.

Kirkpatrick, Donald L. *Evaluating Training Programs: The Four Levels*. San Francisco: Berrett-Koehler, 1996.

Kaydos, Will. *Measuring, Managing, and Maximizing Performance: What Every Manager Needs to Know About Quality and Productivity to Make Real Improvements in Performance*. Portland, OR: Productivity Press, 1991.

Merwin, S. *Evaluation: 10 Significant Ways for Measuring and Improving Training Impact*. Minneapolis: Resources for Organizations, 1992.

Parry, Scott. *Evaluating the Impact of Training*. Alexandria, VA: American Society for Training & Development, 1997.

Phillips, Jack J. *Accountability in Human Resource Management*. Houston: Gulf Publishing, 1996.

————. *In Action: Measuring Return on Investment*. Vol. 2. Alexandria, VA: American Society for Training & Development, 1997.

————. *Return on Investment in Training and Performance Improvement Programs*. Alexandria, VA: American Society for Training & Development, 1997.

————. *ROI: Level V Evaluation*. (*Info-line* No. 9805). Alexandria, VA: American Society for Training & Development, 1998.

Phillips, Jack J. (editor). *Handbook of Training Evaluation and Measurement Methods*. Alexandria, VA: American Society for Training & Development, 1997.

———— *Measuring Return On Investment*. Alexandria, VA: American Society for Training & Development, 1994.

Robinson, Dana Gaines, and James C. Robinson. *Measuring Affective and Behavioral Change*. (*Info-line* No. 9110). Alexandria, VA: American Society for Training & Development, 1997.

————. *Training for Impact: How to Link Training to Business Needs and Measure the Results*. San Francisco: Jossey-Bass, 1989.

Robinson, Dana Gaines, and James C. Robinson. *Performance Consulting: Moving Beyond Training*. San Francisco: Berrett-Koehler, 1995.

Shapiro, Lester T. *Training Effectiveness Handbook: A High-Results System for Design, Delivery, and Evaluation*. New York: McGraw-Hill, 1995.

Waagen, Alice. *Essentials for Evaluation*. (*Info-line* No. 9705). Alexandria, VA: American Society for Training & Development, 1997.

Zigon, Jack. *How to Measure the Results of Work Teams*. Wallingford, PA: Zigon Performance Group, 1995.

————. *Sample Employee Performance Measures*. Vol. 3. Wallingford, PA: Zigon Performance Group, 1992.

CONSULTING

Bellman, G.M. *The Consultant's Calling: Bringing Who You Are to What You Do*. San Francisco: Jossey-Bass, 1990.

Block, P. *Flawless Consulting: A Guide to Getting Your Expertise Used*. San Diego: Pfeiffer, 1981.

Corrigan, Marilyn. *How to Find Your Consulting Niche*. (*Info-line* No. 9516). Alexandria, VA: American Society for Training & Development, 1995.

Corrigan, Marilyn, and Sally Sparhawk. *Becoming an Outside Consultant*. (*Info-line* No. 9403). Alexandria, VA: American Society for Training & Development, 1994.

Gilley, J.W., and A.J. Goffern. *The Role of the Internal Consultant*. Burr Ridge, IL: Irwin Professional Publishing, 1993.

Holdaway, K., and M. Saunders. *The In-House Trainer as Consultant*. San Diego: Pfeiffer, 1992.

Shaffer, Robert H. *High-Impact Consulting: How Clients and Consultants Can Leverage Rapid Results into Long-Term Gains*. San Francisco: Jossey-Bass, 1997.

IMPLEMENTATION OF PERFORMANCE CHANGE

Argyis, C. *Knowledge for Action: A Guide to Overcoming Barriers to Organizational Change*. San Francisco: Jossey-Bass, 1993.

Conner, D.R. *Managing at the Speed of Change*. San Francisco: Berrett-Koehler, 1993.

Emmons, Shirlee, and Alma Thomas. *Transcending Performance Barriers*. Oxford, UK: Oxford University Press, 1998.

Fuller, Jim. *Managing Performance Improvement Projects: Preparing, Planning, and Implementing*. San Francisco: Pfeiffer, 1997.

Gelinas, Mary, and Roger James. *Developing the Foundation for Change*. Washington, D.C.: International Society for Performance Improvement, 1997.

Jacobs, R.W. *Real Time Strategic Change*. San Francisco: Berrett-Koehler, 1997.

Koehle, Deborah. *The Role of the Performance Change Manager*. (*Info-line* No. 9715). Alexandria, VA: American Society for Training & Development, 1997.

Mohrman, A.M. Jr. *Large-Scale Organizational Change*. San Francisco: Jossey-Bass, 1989.

Schuster, Ray R., and Patricia K. Zingheim. *The New Pay: Linking Employee and Organizational Performance*. San Francisco: Jossey-Bass, 1992.

Smith, Douglas K. *Taking Charge of Change: 10 Principles for Managing People and Performance*. New York: Addison-Wesley, 1996.

Weiss, Tracey B., and Frank Hartle. *Reengineering Performance Management*. Boca Raton, FL: St. Lucie Press, 1997.

PERFORMANCE TECHNOLOGY

Brethower, Dale M., et al. *Performance-Based Instruction: Linking Training to Business Results*. San Francisco: Pfeiffer, 1998.

Bricker, Beverly. *Basics of Performance Technology*. (*Info-line* No. 9211). Alexandria, VA: American Society for Training & Development, 1992.

Brinkerhoff, Robert, and Stephen Gill. *The Learning Alliance*. San Francisco: Jossey-Bass, 1994.

Dean, Peter J., and David E. Ripley. *Performance Improvement Pathfinders: Models for Organizational Learning Systems*. Washington, D.C.: International Society for Performance Improvement, 1997.

Deterline, W.A., and M.J. Rosenberg (editors). *Workplace Productivity: Performance Technology Success Stories*. Alexandria, VA and Washington, D.C.: American Society for Training & Development and National Society for Performance and Instruction, 1992.

Fournies, F.F. *Why Employees Don't Do What They're Supposed to Do . . . and What To Do About It*. New York: McGraw-Hill, 1988.

Gilbert, T.F. *Human Competence: Engineering Worthy Performance*. New York: McGraw-Hill, 1978.

Gill, Stephen J. *Linking Training to Performance Goals.* (*Info-line* No. 9606). Alexandria, VA: American Society for Training & Development, 1996.

Hale, Judith A. *The Performance Consultant's Fieldbook: Tools and Techniques for Improving Organizations and People.* San Francisco: Pfeiffer, 1998.

Kaufman, Roger (editor). *Guidebook for Performance Improvement: Working With Individuals & Organizations.* San Francisco: Jossey-Bass, 1996.

Madelyn, Callahan. *From Training to Performance Consulting.* (*Info-line* No. 9702) Alexandria, VA: American Society for Training & Development, 1997.

————. *The Role of the Performance Evaluator.* (*Info-line* No. 9803). Alexandria, VA: American Society for Training & Development, 1998.

————. *The Role of the Performance Intervention Specialist.* (*Info-line* No. 9714). Alexandria, VA: American Society for Training & Development, 1997.

Mager, R.F. *Making Instruction Work: Or Skillbloomers.* Atlanta: Center for Effective Performance, 1997.

————. *What Every Manager Should Know About Training.* Belmont, CA: Lake Publishing, 1992.

Mager, R.F., and Peter Pipe. *Analyzing Performance Problems: Or You Really Oughta Wanna.* Atlanta: Center for Effective Performance, 1997.

Mink, Oscar G., et al. *Developing High Performance People: The Art of Coaching.* New York: Addison-Wesley, 1993.

Pepitone, James S. *Future Training: A Roadmap for Restructuring the Training Function.* Dallas: AddVantage Learning Press, 1995.

————. *Humaneering.* Dallas: AddVantage Learning Press, in press.

Phillips, Jack J., and Mary L. Broad (editors). *In Action: Transferring Learning to the Workplace.* Alexandria, VA: American Society for Training & Development, 1997.

Robinson, Dana Gaines, and James C. Robinson. *Performance Consulting: Moving Beyond Training.* San Francisco: Berrett-Koehler, 1995.

Rothwell, William J. *ASTD Models for Human Performance Improvement: Roles, Competencies, and Outputs.* Alexandria, VA: American Society for Training & Development, 1996.

————. *Beyond Training and Development: State-of-the-Art Strategies for Enhancing Human Performance.* New York: AMACOM, 1996.

Rummler, Geary A., and Alan P. Brache. *Improving Performance: How to Manage the White Space on the Organizational Chart.* San Francisco: Jossey-Bass, 1995.

Stolovitch, Harold D., and Erica Keeps (editors). *Handbook of Human Performance Technology: A Comprehensive Guide for Analyzing and Solving Performance Problems in Organizations.* San Francisco: Jossey-Bass, 1992.

Stolovitch, Harold D., et al. *Handbook of Human Performance Technology.* San Francisco: Jossey-Bass, Publishers, 1992.

ASSOCIATIONS

American Society for Training & Development (ASTD)
1640 King Street, Box 1443
Alexandria, VA 22313-2043
Phone: 800.628.2783 or 703.683.8100; Web site: www.astd.org

Human Resource Planning Society (HRPS)
41 East 42nd Street, Suite 1509
New York, NY 10017
Phone: 212.490.6387; Web site: www.hrps.org

International Society for Performance Improvement (ISPI)
1300 L Street, NW., Suite 1250
Washington, D.C. 20005
Phone: 202.408.7969; Web site: www.ispi.org

Society of Human Resource Management (SHRM)
1800 Duke Street
Alexandria, VA, 22314
Phone: 703.548.3400; Web site: www.shrm.org

The Editors

Dana Gaines Robinson and **James C. Robinson** are, respectively, president and chairman of Partners in Change, Inc., a consulting company they founded in 1981. Each is a recognized leader in the areas of human resource development (HRD) and performance consulting.

Dana is a frequent speaker at national conferences including the following: the International Conference & Exposition, sponsored by the American Society for Training & Development (ASTD); the TRAINING Conference & Expo and the Training Directors' Forum Conference, sponsored by Lakewood Publications; and the Assessment, Measurement, and Evaluation (AME) Conference, sponsored by Linkage. Dana has developed and utilized a process to measure the impact of a substantial number of performance interventions. Her clients include Steelcase, Royal Bank Financial Group and the Department of Veterans Affairs. Dana has a bachelor's degree in sociology from the University of California, Berkeley, and a master's degree in psychoeducational processes from Temple University, Philadelphia.

James is also a frequent speaker at major conferences, including those of ASTD and the International Society for Performance Improvement (ISPI). He began his career as a line manager with Agway, Inc. For several years he was vice president of DDI and is the primary architect of its successful training program, Interaction Management. Jim's clients include PNC Bank, Hutchinson Technology, Inc., and Petro-Canada. His undergraduate degree is from the University of Massachusetts. Jim has a master's degree in adult education from Syracuse University and a second master's degree from the University of Wisconsin.

Currently, the consulting practice of the Robinsons focuses on assisting HR and HRD departments in transitioning to a focus on performance improvement. Together they have written two books: *Training for Impact*, published by Jossey-Bass in 1989, and *Performance Consulting: Moving Beyond Training*, published by Berrett-Koehler in 1995. Widely acclaimed, this second book has sold more than 35,000 copies and was selected for the 1996 Society for Human Resource Management (SHRM) Book Award.